The Nation.

A Biography

(The First 150 Years)

The Nation.
A Biography
(The First 150 Years)

– – – – – – –

D.D. Guttenplan

Nation.

Published by The Nation Company, L LC.
Visit our website at www.thenation.com/ebooks

First printing 2015

ISBN 978-1-940489-21-6 paperback
ISBN 978-1-940489-20-9 e-book

Book design by Omar Rubio
Printed by BookMobile in the United States and
CPi Books Ltd. in the United Kingdom

Table of Contents

THE Nation.

APRIL 2015

150TH ANNIVERSARY

James Agee
Eqbal Ahmad
Ai Weiwei
Hannah Arendt
James Baldwin
Amiri Baraka
Mongstafa Bayoumi
Wendell Berry
Kai Bird
Margaret Bourke-White
Steve Brodner
Noam Chomsky
Alexander Cockburn
Sue Coe
Stephen F. Cohen
Arthur C. Danto
Bill de Blasio
E.L. Doctorow
Ariel Dorfman
Eric Drooker
W.E.B. Du Bois
Barbara Ehrenreich
Albert Einstein
Frances FitzGerald
Eric Foner
Mark Gevisser
Paula J. Giddings

Allen Ginsberg
Milton Glaser
Emma Goldman
Vivian Gornick
Clement Greenberg
William Gropper
Robert Grossman
D.D. Guttenplan
Melissa Harris-Perry
Christopher Hayes
Christopher Hitchens
Langston Hughes
Molly Ivins
Henry James

Martin Luther King Jr.
Freda Kirchwey
Stuart Klawans
Naomi Klein
Andrew Kopkind
Tony Kushner
John Leonard
Penny Lernoux
David Levine
Maria Margaronis
Michael Massing
Carey McWilliams
H.L. Mencken
Edward Miliband

Arthur Miller
Jessica Mitford
Marianne Moore
Michael Moore
Toni Morrison
Ralph Nader
Victor Navasky
Katha Pollitt
Adolph Reed Jr.
Marilynne Robinson
Edward W. Said

Kshama Sawant
Jeremy Scahill
Jonathan Schell
Ben Shahn
Daniel Singer
Mychal Denzel Smith
Rebecca Solnit
Edward Sorel
Art Spiegelman
John Steinbeck
I.F. Stone
Hunter S. Thompson
Tom Tomorrow
Touré
Calvin Trillin
Dalton Trumbo
Katrina vanden Heuvel
Gore Vidal
Alice Walker
Carrie Mae Weems
Edmund White
Amy Wilentz
Patricia J. Williams
William Appleman Williams
Ellen Willis
JoAnn Wypijewski
Howard Zinn

Introduction

Eric Foner

The *Nation*, the oldest continuously published weekly magazine in the United States, began life a century and a half ago in the wake of the Civil War, a momentous event that preserved the American Union and destroyed the institution of slavery. In this book, D.D. Guttenplan expertly traces the magazine's career since 1865. The account is lively, readable and insightful. Guttenplan introduces the reader to a remarkable cast of characters—the editors, writers, financial backers, admirers and critics who shaped *The Nation*'s evolution—and to the complex political debates in which the magazine became enmeshed. The book sheds light not only on *The Nation*'s history but also on the times in which it has lived. Guttenplan even manages to make the magazine's financial ups and downs interesting and important.

As the pages that follow make clear, through the history of *The Nation* one can track the evolution of that elusive idea, American liberalism (defined here to encompass many radicals as well). The founding editor, the Anglo-Irish journalist E.L. Godkin, adhered steadfastly to the principles of nineteenth-century classical liberalism, with all its strengths and weaknesses. These principles included hostility to slavery and belief in equality before the law—articles of faith among the Northern reformers who founded the magazine—but also free trade, free public education, civil service reform, and an absence of government restraints on individual liberty and economic enterprise. Increasingly, however, as American society changed, these views made Godkin and *The Nation* more and more conservative. Nineteenth-century liberalism had no way of addressing the advent of concentrated corporate power and the advance of economic inequality, especially since it viewed organized action by farmers and laborers to improve their lives as violations of individual liberty.

A new kind of liberalism emerged on both sides of the Atlantic in the early twentieth century, associated in this country with the Progressive movement, which insisted that government should intervene in society to promote greater economic security and to curb corporate power. *The Nation* was late to adhere to these ideas but when it did, under the editor Oswald Garrison Villard, it became what it has remained ever since—a voice demanding far-reaching social change in the name of greater equality and greater freedom. Moreover, in the 1920s *The Nation* embraced two stances neglected by most Progressive reformers that would become central to liberalism later in the twentieth century. One was racial equality, a return to a concern central to the magazine's founding but eventually abandoned by Godkin. The second preoccupation was civil liberties. Most Progressives, entranced by the ways the democratic state could promote the public good, had evinced little interest in the rights of dissenters. But the massive repression during World War I gave birth to a new recognition of the importance of civil liberties. From that time to the present, *The Nation* has identified freedom of expression as an essential hallmark of a free society, and has highlighted and condemned violations of this principle. This was reflected in the vehement opposition to McCarthyism under editor Carey McWilliams and the identification of corporate control of the media as a threat to the free flow of ideas under Victor Navasky, a self-proclaimed First Amendment "absolutist." In addition, thanks to Freda Kirchwey, who joined the staff in 1918 and remained for half a century, eventually becoming editor, the magazine enthusiastically embraced the new feminism, anticipating the more recent absorption into liberalism of issues relating to family life, social and sexual relations, and gender roles. In the 1930s, Kirchwey would make *The Nation* one of the country's strongest voices identifying the rise of fascism as the major threat to world peace and calling for collective action to combat it.

To these hallmarks of modern liberalism, *The Nation*, as Guttenplan shows, added a commitment that went back to Godkin's days—opposition to American military interventions and occupations overseas and to imperialism more broadly. Godkin had opposed the annexation of the Philippines; Villard, American involvement in World War I. Subsequently, *The Nation* became a major critic of Cold War foreign policy. More recently, *The Nation* has courageously stood as the major journalistic voice opposing the 2003 invasion of Iraq and the ongoing, never-ending worldwide "war on terror."

Guttenplan takes note of the amazing roster of important writers who have contributed to *The Nation* over the years, from Emily Dickinson and Henry James to Emma Goldman, I.F. Stone, Hannah Arendt, Arthur Miller, Ralph Nader and Eric Hobsbawm, to name only a few. *The Nation*'s record of publishing black writers is striking, including Claude McKay and Langston Hughes during the Harlem Renaissance and subsequently W.E.B. Du Bois, E. Franklin Frazier, James Baldwin, Martin Luther King Jr. and Toni Morrison. Holding the record for most pieces (if not the most words) published in *The Nation*'s history, is Calvin Trillin, the master of the poem of four or fewer lines.

Of course, *The Nation* has never been simply a big happy family. Guttenplan details some of the internal divisions inevitable when a group of self-assured, politically minded and intrinsically contrarian writers come together to produce a magazine. In the 1930s, the editorial pages displayed sympathy for Stalin's rule in the Soviet Union, while many book reviews were written by followers of Stalin's archenemy Leon Trotsky. On occasion it has seemed that *Nation* writers spent as much effort lambasting one another as critiquing the powers that be. But the house divided managed to stand. Intellectual and political debate has always been one of the magazine's strengths, and after Godkin, who did impose his viewpoint, the pages of *The Nation* have never reflected a single party line.

Today, under editor Katrina vanden Heuvel, *The Nation* holds aloft the banner of twentieth-century liberalism against the floodtide of neoliberal economic policy, continued military adventurism and ongoing efforts from the right to chip away at the gains in racial justice and sexual freedom spawned by the 1960s. But it has also attracted a younger constituency and embraced its social movements, from Occupy Wall Street to the battle to curtail climate change. Vanden Heuvel has moved *The Nation* into the media world of the twenty-first century. The magazine's website now attracts far more readers than the weekly print issue and has become a point of reference for activists throughout the country. Vanden Heuvel, through blogs, tweets and frequent appearances on political talk shows, has helped to make *The Nation* more than ever a part of the country's ongoing political dialogue. And *Nation* writers like Katha Pollitt enjoy a following that reaches far beyond the magazine's subscription list.

So here's to *The Nation* on its 150th birthday. This book makes clear why we should hope that the country's oldest weekly magazine survives for at least another century and a half. ✱

The Nation.

THURSDAY, JULY 6, 1865.

$3 PER ANNUM.

VOL. I.—NO. 1.

JOSEPH H. RICHARDS, PUBLISHER, 130 NASSAU STREET, N. Y.

The Week.

THE WEEK has been singularly barren of exciting events. It is curious to see, however, what a stimulus the return of peace has given to political agitation. As nothing is now dependent on the fortune of war, orators and writers are entering with a confidence which they never displayed as long as their arguments and predictions were liable to reversion or falsification at the hands of Lee or Grant.

THE negro's success in assuming a prominent position in the political arena, seems to be in the inverse ratio of the earnestness with which it is sought to suppress him and put him out of sight. Everybody is heartily tired of discussing his condition and his rights, and yet little else is talked about, and none talk about him so much as those who are most convinced of his insignificance.

THE news from Europe is unimportant, unless we except the doubt which rest upon Napoleon's course in regard to Mexico. The *Moniteur* asserts that the present force in that country will not be increased, but will be kept at its maximum. The English papers borrow their chief topic of discussion from this country, and decision on the proper treatment of the subjugated rebels. Lord Brougham, whose advice we notice in another column, lifts up his voice for clemency, and finds an echo, we are told, in the Paris press. Lord Brougham's impertinence is imitated by "Historicus," the law-writer for the *Times*, who did us good service in the piratical season. He undertakes to define for this country the relation of the Government to its late enemies in arms, but manifestly travels beyond his sphere. The question is one of American Constitutional law, to be decided here, and, we apprehend, with as little respect to the authority of "Historicus" as if he were merely a crier in court, instead of the able barrister that he is. He has an undeniable right to his opinion, but to force it upon the Government of the United States is to insult its capacity for determining the laws by which it exists. "Historicus" had at an earlier stage of the rebellion, when he ventured to inform Mr. Seward of the British Attorney-General's opinion that this Government had no right to suspend the *habeas corpus*. Our Secretary rightly applied a snub direct to such gratuitous instruction. The argument drawn from expediency or humanity may fairly be offered to affect our disposal of Jeff. Davis and his compeers,—for nothing that concerns man anywhere is foreign to the rest of mankind, and international law is simply the product of a free exchange of opinion among nations, which is neither to be deprecated nor avoided,—but every government must be presumed the best, and of course the ultimate, judge of its own powers in dealing with its subjects.

"IT is a marvel," said Cato, "that a couple of soothsayers can look at each other without a grin;" and President Johnson quotes this expression to a South Carolina delegation, in order to disclaim any con-

spiracy with them to deceive the public. He avows more distinctly than heretofore his motive in hastening reconstruction,—that "the loyal men, who were compelled to bow and submit to the rebellion, may, now that the rebellion is ended, stand equal to loyal men everywhere." The war has effected a twofold emancipation of blacks and whites. It is absolutely necessary for South Carolina, before she can hope to return into the Union, to abolish slavery within her territory by legislature or convention, which abolishes and prohibits slavery everywhere. His reluctance to establish or favor—for, on this point, his language is not unmistakable—the enfranchisement of the blacks, arises from a fear lest the landed aristocracy control their votes to the prejudice of the poor whites, whose freedom the President is anxious to confirm. He therefore leaves it to the States, or to that loyal minority in each which he assumes to have constituted the State without intermission, to determine the qualifications for suffrage. At the same time, as a democrat, he is "opposed to class legislation." Such, substantially, is the position now occupied by our Chief Magistrate, though not, we may trust, unchangeably, except in respect of the doom of the slave system. The delegation, in reply, could naturally but assent to the latter condition of restoration, however unwelcome it might be. Their spokesman, Judge Frost, admitted that he and his associates, present and at home, had been cured of three delusions by the war: first, "that slavery is an element of political strength and moral power;" second, that the States' Rights doctrine is a sound one; and, third, that cotton is king. The people of South Carolina, having been defeated and conquered, will acknowledge "the painful fact: already they have submitted to great sacrifices "from their fidelity to honor." "And," continued the Judge, "the same good faith which animated them in the contest will not be found wanting in their pledge of loyal support to the Government." If this assurance were not enough, the delegate was willing to add: "I suppose the oath of allegiance will be taken with as much unanimity in South Carolina as anywhere else." As this cannot possibly be doubted, we suppose the Palmetto gentry will not long be in lack of the Governor for whom they applied.

PRESIDENT JOHNSON has given the finishing touch to the war by abolishing all restrictions on trade East and West. But if some means are not devised of protecting him from "personal interviews" with office-seekers, pardon-seekers, delegations, and busybodies of both sexes, they will make an end of him. It is lamentable that some way cannot be hit on of sifting the President's business before it comes before him. This is done to a certain extent with his letters, but the men and women who want to see him reach him, chaff and all. The easiest way of doing it would be to render access to him more difficult. Whether this could be arranged without raising doubts of his "democracy," we must leave it to others to determine. The present system, under which everybody can reach him who takes the trouble to go to Washington, if not suspected of designs on his life, is anything but democratic. For his time belongs to the whole nation. As matters stand, it is largely consumed in attending to the affairs or listening to the bad speeches of a few hundreds.

FROM an Augusta newspaper we have what purports to be an account of the peace conference at Fortress Monroe in January, by Alexander H. Stephens, one of the Southern commissioners on that occasion. Except certain strictures upon Jefferson Davis for his conduct before and after the colloquy, and certain professions of a genuine desire for peace on the part of Mr. Stephens, there is little that is new in his narrative. He tells, however, a capital story of President Lincoln, who, having at the outset declared that he could not consent to treat with the rebel authori-

Prologue

In the fall of 1960, the United States government's determination to overthrow the Cuban leader Fidel Castro was one of the worst kept secrets in the world. The Cubans knew. Richard Nixon knew—but he couldn't say. All summer long John F. Kennedy, the Democratic candidate for president, had taunted his opponent: "If you can't stand up to Castro, how can you be expected to stand up to Khrushchev?" Two weeks before Kennedy's inauguration the Eisenhower administration broke off relations with Castro in a move described by *Time* magazine as a response to Havana's "propaganda offensive" charging the Americans with "plotting an 'imminent invasion' of Cuba."

Nation readers knew it, too. In October the magazine ran an editorial, "Not Guatemala Again," warning that deposing Castro would not be as easy as the 1954 CIA-led coup that had removed President Jacobo Arbenz Guzmán from power. And on November 19, 1960, editor Carey McWilliams wrote an editorial,[1] "Are We

Training Cuban Guerrillas?", reporting claims that the CIA had acquired a large tract of land in Guatemala as a base for "counter-revolutionaries who are preparing for an eventual landing in Cuba" and calling for further investigation. "If the reports are true," said *The Nation*, "public pressure should be brought on the administration to abandon this dangerous and hare-brained project."

The Nation sent Don Dwiggins, aviation editor for the *Los Angeles Herald*, to Guatemala in January. His detailed account was followed up by *The New York Times*, which confirmed in a front-page article on January 10, 1961, that commandos were being "drilled in guerrilla warfare" by US trainers, but also quoted "Guatemalan authorities" insisting the base was intended to repel a Cuban invasion. When a *Miami Herald* reporter turned in a story saying the Cuban exiles also had a training camp in Florida, his editors were summoned to a meeting with CIA director Allen Dulles and the story was spiked. A similar fate befell "Our Men in Miami," a scoop warning that "US troops may be needed to back up the invasion" which *Washington Post* reporter Karl Meyer wrote for *The New Republic*. After editor Gilbert Harrison messengered the article to Arthur Schlesinger Jr. at the White House for comment it, too, was withdrawn.

Tad Szulc's April 7, 1961, story[2] in *The New York Times* did alert the paper's readers to the Florida camp—and to the exiles' plan to gain a "substantial beachhead" in Cuba. But after interventions from publisher Orville Dryfoos and columnist James Reston, Szulc's editor, Turner Catledge, removed references to the CIA—and to the invasion's planned date. In his memoir Catledge says that in late April, after the invasion had failed, President Kennedy took him aside and told him "Maybe if you had printed more about the operation you would have saved us from a colossal mistake."

If only it were that simple. It takes more than an alert press to save a president determined on regime change from his own folly. If we didn't know that in 1961, we certainly know it now. John Kennedy wouldn't be the last president tempted to intervention by the prospect of a quick victory—or the last to refuse to heed *The Nation*'s warnings about foreign entanglements. But then he wasn't the first either. Nearly a century earlier another president, cheered into the White House by *The Nation*, found his pet scheme to annex the Dominican Republic vigorously opposed by the magazine: "A nation which contains a problem like New York City is morally bound to solve it before taking up another in some respects far more serious."[3] Though in no doubt about "our ability to make money out of" annexation, the editors worried that seizing Santo Domingo in the name of extending "the area of freedom" would corrupt the United States without helping the Dominicans. President Ulysses Grant didn't listen, either. But the country did.

In 150 years *The Nation*—and the country—have changed almost beyond recognition. Though the magazine has generally remained skeptical about military adventures, its views on everything from racial equality to women's suffrage to the sanctity of the First Amendment have varied in ways that might surprise, or even shock, today's readers. The one constant, throughout that history, has been a faith—not in political parties or programs, but in what might happen if you tell the people the truth. ✳

Frederick Law Olmsted

CHAPTER ONE

'No. 1 Is Afloat.'

T*he Nation* has many fathers. On June 25, 1863, while Confederate forces under Robert E. Lee were still fighting their way north toward Gettysburg, a group of wealthy New Yorkers gathered at the Union League Club to hear a pitch. The speaker, Frederick Law Olmsted, was one of the club's founding members. Prevented by illness from attending college, Olmsted instead worked as a journalist, traveling through the cotton South for *The New York Times*, and though he had no formal training as an architect, in 1858 he and his friend Calvert Vaux won the competition to design Central Park. With the outbreak of the Civil War, Olmstead became executive secretary of the United States Sanitary Commission, a precursor of the Red Cross.

That evening Olmsted laid out his "dream of an honest weekly paper." The idea was to aim not for a large circulation but for a select, influential readership—the kind of people who would happily pay fifteen or twenty cents a copy (when the *Times* cost three). Although Olmsted promised the paper should, eventually, pay its way, he told the men he was seeking a year's capital—some $40,000—not as an investment, but in pledges or donations. By the end of the evening Olmsted had his first thousand dollars. By the end of the week he had trustees, a fundraising committee, and an editor, his friend E.L. Godkin. "The thing starts so favorably," he wrote to his wife, Mary, "I shall go into it strong, meaning to succeed."

They had everything but a name. Olmsted considered "The Loyalist" and, in a nod to his sense of the importance of agriculture—his first book was titled *Walks and Talks of an American Farmer*—the "Yeoman's Weekly." In all he rejected forty-five names for his new venture, including Godkin's suggestion of "The Week." Part of the problem was that Olmsted had too many demands on his time. Gettysburg, though a great Union victory, left more than 14,000 wounded Union soldiers who needed medical care, and Olmsted had to race off to tour the battlefield with General Meade. Meanwhile his own position at the Sanitary Commission, where he was in constant conflict with his executive committee, had become unbearable. The Draft Riots in July, which raged right up to the doors of the Union League's clubhouse on 17th Street, made further fundraising difficult.

But Olmsted was also impulsive, and when an offer came that August to manage the Mariposa Estate, an enormous gold mine in California, he booked passage to San Francisco aboard the *Champion* and turned "The Paper," as they still called it, over to Godkin, along with the $3,000 he'd managed to raise, and a letter of introduction to Charles Eliot Norton. In September 1863, Godkin arrived in Boston.

At 36, Norton was only four years older than his visitor, yet possessed everything the younger man wanted for himself—not just money and social position, but real literary authority. And most of all, a sense of being deeply rooted in American soil. The son of a Harvard professor known as the "Unitarian Pope," and the grandson, on his mother's side, of the Boston banker Samuel Eliot (who was himself descended from the Eliot who served on the jury in the Salem witch trials), Charles Eliot Norton was precisely what his friend Oliver Wendell Holmes had in mind when he coined the term "Boston Brahmin."

Though he would later become the first professor of art history at Harvard, Norton was chiefly known as a literary impresario. In 1861 he'd helped his friends Henry Wadsworth Longfellow and James Russell Lowell to start the Dante Club, publishing his own translation of the *Divine Comedy* and the *Vita Nuova*. With Lowell, who at the time was editor of *The Atlantic*, he edited *The North American Review*, the country's first literary quarterly; his friendships also included Thomas Carlyle, John Ruskin, Leslie Stephen (father of Virginia Woolf) and John Kipling (father of Rudyard). Norton, it seemed, had a talent for friendship.

And with Olmsted bound for the California gold fields, E.L. Godkin was very much in need of a friend. Born in County Wicklow, Ireland (a fact Godkin judiciously kept to himself), Edwin Lawrence Godkin had acquired, by his early 30s, the appearance, education and habits of an English gentleman. The reality was a bit more complicated. His father, James Godkin, was Dublin cor-

respondent for *The Times* of London, and a former Congrega-
tional minister. But James's own parents had been Catholic farmers; he converted before he married the daughter of a Protestant
landowner. Forced to leave the ministry because of his passionate
devotion to Irish home rule, James joined forces with Charles
Gavan Duffy, a follower of Daniel O'Connell and the founder of
the Irish *Nation*—a weekly newspaper that became the voice of the
"Young Ireland" movement. As editor in chief of the Dublin *Daily
Express*, James Godkin had even been attacked—for printing fab-
ricated stories of sectarian violence—by the political correspondent of the *New-York Tribune*, one Karl Marx.[4]

E.L. Godkin, then, grew up not in the hushed atmosphere of
a New England parsonage but in a house resounding with controversy and debate—and teeming with journalists. After graduating
from Queen's College, Belfast, and training briefly as a lawyer,
at Lincoln's Inn in London, Godkin found the legal life too con-
fining and was taken on as Crimean War correspondent for the
London *Daily News* simply on the basis of a letter to the editor. He
remained in the Crimea until the end of the war, sending back regular dispatches from Omar Pasha's army and witnessing the siege
of Sebastopol. Of his undergraduate days, Godkin later wrote:
"John Stuart Mill was our prophet, but America was our Promised Land." In 1856 Godkin set out for the United States, making
a tour of the South on horseback—inspired by Olmsted, whose
acquaintance he'd made directly on landing in New York—and
sending his impressions back to the *Daily News*.

Still unsure—not of his abilities but of his financial future as
a journalist—he joined the New York bar. In July 1859 he married

Frances Foote, of New Haven. Fanny, as she was known, was a cousin of Harriet Beecher Stowe and Henry Ward Beecher, a well-known Brooklyn minister and abolitionist. Somewhat more to the point Fanny's father, Samuel Foote, had retired as the president of the Ohio Life Insurance and Trust Company. The newlyweds set sail for Europe, remaining abroad until 1862 when Godkin, whose journalistic output in the interim had been confined to a few letters to the *Daily News* in support of the new Lincoln administration, resumed work as a foreign correspondent for the *Daily News* and a freelance contributor to *The Atlantic*, *The New York Times*, and, after his meeting with Norton, *The North American Review*.

He now had financial security, and social connections. But he wanted more, turning down the offer of regular employment from Henry Raymond, founder of *The New York Times*, partly because he feared a clash between Raymond's political ambitions and the paper's independence. (A member of the New York State Assembly before he started the *Times*, Raymond served a term in Congress and was chairman of the Republican National Committee.) Also he felt his constitution, which had broken down soon after his arrival in Europe, wouldn't withstand the strain of night work, and none of the evening dailies had room for him. "The Paper" project he'd inherited from Olmsted had been his last hope, but when his meeting with Norton produced only encouragement, not investment, he gave up.

"My prospects," he wrote to Olmsted, "are by no means so brilliant as they seemed when I first determined to settle in this country." His career, he worried, had been derailed by his collapse, and "if I were not now sincerely attached to the country… married, and so forth, I would go back to England." The news that another weekly, *The Round Table*, would soon begin publication in New York was the final blow. "The very thing," he complained to Olmsted, "I had in my mind." Instead he accepted an offer to edit the *Sanitary Commission Bulletin*. The work was boring but undemanding, and the salary of $100 a month made him less resentful of the $2 a page he got from *The North American Review*.[5]

Only it turned out Norton wasn't done with him. In April 1865 Godkin wrote to Olmsted to congratulate him on "the great events of the last fortnight." Lee's surrender at Appomattox had left him "dumfoundered" and though he was thrilled by the Union victory, "I confess I should be very anxious about the terms of reconstruction, if Lincoln were not to be president for the next four years."[6] The letter was dated April 12, and long before it reached California, Lincoln was dead. Yet even as the nation was binding up its wounds and mourning the slain emancipator, the prospect of victory was tearing the abolitionist movement apart.

The question was whether the Thirteenth Amendment, in decreeing the end of slavery, meant the abolitionists' work was done. William Lloyd Garrison, editor of *The Liberator*, thought it was. Declaring, "my vocation as an Abolitionist, thank God, is ended," and wanting to devote himself to women's suffrage and other causes, Garrison proposed that the American Anti-Slavery Society, which he had founded, should be dissolved. But Wendell Phillips, who had joined the movement after rescuing Garrison from a Boston lynch mob thirty years earlier, disagreed, and a bitter power struggle ensued.

It was in the midst of this battle—for control not just of the American Anti-Slavery Society but for the future, and legacy, of the abolitionist movement—that James Miller McKim, a Philadelphia activist with friends in both camps, determined to start a national weekly to carry on the work of *The Liberator* "on a broader ground." In 1849, McKim, a Princeton graduate and editor of *The Pennsylvania Freeman*, had been the addressee to which Henry "Box" Brown[7], a slave in Richmond Virginia, had mailed himself to freedom. In 1859 McKim and his wife had escorted Mary Brown to Harper's Ferry to claim the body of her executed husband John Brown.

Turning first to Philadelphia's Quaker community, and to his friends in the Freedman's Aid Society, a group that sent teachers to educate the newly freed slaves, McKim set about raising funds. New York, a bastion of "Copperhead" antiwar sentiment during the war and with many commercial links to the South, proved stony ground. But networks in Baltimore and Boston soon put McKim in reach of his goal of $50,000—at which point he contacted George Stearns. A prosperous manufacturer and ship chandler from Medford, Massachusetts, Stearns was one of the "Secret Six" who funded the raid on Harper's Ferry. In fact Stearns was the legal owner of the 200 Sharps rifles used by Brown and his men. Commissioned a major during the Civil War, Stearns helped recruit the famed 54th and 55th Massachusetts African-American infantry regiments.

By April 1865 McKim had his funding. He also had a name for his new magazine: *The Nation*. Office space had become available at the former headquarters of the American Freedman's Aid Union at 130 Nassau Street in New York. But he needed a staff— McKim thought his daughter Lucy's fiancé, Wendell Phillips Garrison, the son of one abolitionist and namesake of another, might make a suitable literary editor. Garrison, three years out of Har-

vard, had been gaining editorial experience on *The Independent*, a
Brooklyn anti-slavery weekly edited by Henry Ward Beecher and,
later, by his assistant, Theodore Tilton. Tilton's brother-in-law,
Joseph Richards, also at the *Independent*, agreed to serve as publisher of the new venture—under certain conditions. Concerned
not to hoist his name "at the masthead of a sinking ship," Richards
demanded—and got—written assurances that the paper would be
adequately staffed, and that it would get "substantial help" from
the freedmen's organizations, which would recognize it as the heir
to *The Liberator*.[8] But with McKim hoping to start publishing in
July, finding an editor was proving more difficult.

On the recommendation of Norton and Stearns, McKim first
approached George W. Curtis. A former resident of the utopian Brook
Farm commune, and a friend of Olmsted's—whom he'd worked with
on *Putnam's* magazine—Curtis was earning $10,000 a year as editor
of *Harper's Weekly*. Not surprisingly, he turned them down. As did
Whitelaw Reid, an Ohio journalist who had helped Stearns in his
recruiting efforts but was busy speculating on the cotton market.

Norton, of course, knew all about Godkin's interest in starting his own weekly. At that very moment he had Godkin's latest
submission to *The North American Review* on his desk—and that
was the problem. In his article, Godkin considered the argument
that in a country claiming to be a democracy, blacks are entitled
to the vote—and rejected it. Writing to explain his position to
Norton in April 1865, Godkin says "it is not enough to prove the
negro's age, sex and humanity in order to establish his right to the
franchise." Rather, he says, any black who would claim the vote
must overcome "the presumption of his unfitness...his ancestors

having all been either African savages, or as nearly beasts of the field as men can be made." Those who would give the black man the vote "merely *because* it would be an act of justice," are guilty, wrote Godkin, of "a mistake." Instead he proposed testing all prospective voters—white and black—on their ability to read a newspaper. Blacks alone, however, would also be required to prove that they had earned a living for ten years "as a test of that moral fitness against which…having been bred in slavery raises a presumption."

This was hardly the theme to appeal to *The Nation*'s backers. Indeed, as Norton pointed out, it was out of line even with the *Review*'s editorial policy, which strongly supported the radical reconstruction of the South urged by congressional Republicans. Godkin took the hint: "I shall recast all that I have said about the negroes, and put it in a shape which will not clash with your own opinions, and those of the *Review*," he promised Norton. [9] Norton in turn put in a word on his behalf with Stearns and McKim, the latter being convinced immediately. Stearns, however, subjected Godkin to a four-hour grilling, by himself and Wendell Phillips, probing the candidate's views on reconstruction, negro suffrage and aid for the freedmen before pronouncing himself satisfied. For the moment.

§

"No. I is afloat," Godkin wrote to Norton on July 5, 1865, "and the tranquility which still reigns in this city, under the circumstances, I confess amazes me. I hope you like it. The verdict here seems favorable." To Olmsted he was a little more confidential: "We have got the first number of the Nation out, after the struggle and agony usual in such cases, and are now fairly afloat…. It is a joint stock company, capital $100,000—shares $1,000 each, and what is most wonderful—we have got the money paid up."

Godkin's salary was $5,000 a year—about $77,000 today—with 12 percent of the profits. If there ever were any profits. Produced on good quality paper using 9-point ("bourgeois," in the typographer's parlance) type, *The Nation* asked its initial subscribers to pay $3 a year—half what Godkin and Richards estimated the magazine cost to produce. The idea, Godkin said, was "to get an audience at the outset." Within three weeks the magazine had attracted 5,000 subscribers. In October, after burning through capital at the rate of $4,000 a month, they raised the subscription to $6. A single issue cost a reassuringly expensive fifteen cents. (In today's money that would be $93 a year, or $2.30 a copy—making today's *Nation* introductory print subscription rate of $32 a year something of a bargain.)

In his prospectus[10] for subscribers and potential investors, Godkin promised a magazine whose "main objects" would be the discussion of legal, economical and constitutional questions "with greater accuracy and moderation than are now to be found in the daily press" and which would campaign for "a more equal distribution of the fruits of progress and civilization." Regarding the freed slaves, *The Nation* favored "the removal of all artificial distinctions between them and the rest of the population" in order to allow them "an equal chance in the race of life." This was a matter of urgency, since "there can be no real stability for the Republic so long as they are left in ignorance and degradation." The "political importance of popular education"—at a time when the South had no public schools to speak of—was also stressed. Finally, due attention would be given to "sound and impartial criticism of books and works of art."

The Nation, it pledged, "will not be the organ of any party, sect or body. It will, on the contrary, make an earnest effort to bring to the discussions of political and social questions a really critical spirit, and to wage war upon the vices of violence, exaggeration and misrepresentation by which so much of the political writing of the day is marred."

"It has been a week singularly barren of exciting events."

So begins Volume 1, Number 1, page 1, of the first issue of *The Nation*, dated July 6, 1865. The opening of each issue, a section Godkin called "The Week" after his old favorite name for the magazine, was a digest covering recent events. His model here was the London *Spectator*; the section, Godkin said, would contain "not news, but comments on anything and everything of interest." Prospective contributors were told to submit items written with "force or brilliancy or both" for which they would be paid $10 a page.

Godkin himself proved a clear, vigorous writer—and a deadly effective polemicist. Addressing "The Essence of the Reconstruction Question"[11] in the first issue his private ambivalence has vanished: "Nobody whose opinion is of any consequence" he now insists, rejects the freedmen's "claim for political equality." Challenging those who argue (as he had) that the former slaves' lack of education renders them unfit, he asks "what worse consequences to the State could possibly result from the voting of one-half million of benighted Africans than already resulted from the voting of a million of benighted Caucasians? If greater calamities can come on a State than the 'superior race' recently brought on the South, we do not know what they are."

"The political complexion of *The Nation* is not at all doubtful," sniffed *The New York Times* in a mildly facetious review of the first issue. Radical on all questions regarding the freed slaves, the magazine viewed the Civil War's end as a triumph[12] not just for the Union, but for "democratic principles everywhere," a counter to the wave of reaction that swept Europe after the revolutions of 1848: "The tide is turning in favor of liberalism with resistless force. The French democrats already begin to show signs of life and activity, and the English Tories are retiring to their inner line of defense.... We utter no idle boast when we say that if the conflict of ages, the great strife between the few and the many, between privilege and equality, between law and power, between opinion and the sword, was not closed on the day on which Lee threw down his arms, the issue was placed beyond doubt."

Such confident optimism was easy to mock—though perhaps not as easy as *The Nation*'s report from the front lines of New York club land, where "the erudition of the members" may not "bristle out like that of Bostonians," but where a visitor might still "find a lion of the trotting turf who is an authority on medieval Latin, and a crack billiard player who is great at annotating Virgil." Yet Godkin's prophecies proved sound enough: the Second Empire had just five years left to run, and the first of William Gladstone's three Liberal governments would come to power even sooner.

The struggle between the few and the many still rages. But the Civil War did mark a revolution in economic as well as racial relations. The Union war effort forged a modern industrial nation-state; during the last two years of the war alone the federal government gave 75 million acres of public land to the railroads, eventually binding the West Coast to the East in a national market while providing for the immediate movement of goods, passengers—and troops. Though enacted to raise the funds to fight the war, the Morrill Tariff gave America's manufacturers respite from European competition; likewise Lincoln's "greenbacks"—the first national paper currency, issued as a temporary measure to pay Union soldiers—allowed the government to finance the war and, when used to pay for goods, spurred a boom in domestic consumption. (The new national banking system also solidified Wall Street's dominance over the country's finances, condemning the South to decades of inadequate credit.)

But the biggest economic consequence of the war was also the least digested: the federal government's expropriation and liquidation of the South's largest asset class, the slaves themselves. Americans might argue forever about whether Washington *should* take this or that step to intervene in the private sector, but given what Lincoln had done with the Emancipation Proclamation, and what the whole Congress accomplished in the Thirteenth Amendment (already ratified by twenty-three states in July 1865 and incorporated into the Constitution that December), there was no doubt about what the government *could* do. In 1860 the 4 million African-Americans in slavery were worth about $3 billion[*] (between $65 billion and $11 *trillion* today[13]) to their owners—representing in many cases the bulk of their wealth.[14] Before the war even most abolitionists balked at the cost of "buying out" slavery; when the English abolished slavery in the colonies in 1833 the government

---

[*]   The total federal budget in 1860 was only $78 million.

paid slave owners £20 million in compensation[*]—an enormous sum, accounting for fully 40 percent of the Treasury's annual budget, or the equivalent in today's money of at least $26 billion.[15] (Viewed in those terms, as Christopher Hayes recently observed in *The Nation*,[16] the most radical demands of the climate justice movement are truly modest proposals.)

That the same man—and the same magazine—should glory in such an expansive assertion of state power, yet view the call for an eight-hour[17] workday as "tyrannical interference of the Government with the freedom of industry and the sanctity of contracts" gives one indication of the distance between Godkin's liberalism and our own. Educated in Britain, his was the Manchester Liberalism of Richard Cobden and John Bright—opposed to feudalism (and slavery), denouncing high tariffs as a tax on the working man, and equally committed, as I.F. Stone once observed,[18] to free trade and free speech.

On free trade Godkin's hands were tied. As he explained in a letter to Edward Atkinson, one of the magazine's Boston backers, "a large amount of stock was subscribed in Philadelphia...in the understanding that *The Nation* was not to be a free trade paper." This left him, he said "rather awkwardly situated" but it was "better than no paper at all."[19] And the crisis over Reconstruction afforded Godkin's pen an abundant supply of other outlets. In Washington, Andrew Johnson, who had been targeted along with President Lincoln—the

---

[*]   According to a recent study of British government records, those claiming compensation included George Orwell's great-grandfather, Charles Blair, who received £4,442 for the 218 slaves he owned; William Gladstone's father, John, who collected £106,769 for his 2,508 slaves; and a distant forebear of Prime Minister David Cameron.

vice president's attacker got drunk and spent the night walking the streets of the capital—faced three urgent questions: Under what conditions should the former Confederate states be allowed to return to the Union? What obligation did the federal government have to the freed slaves? How should those who took an active part in the rebellion be punished? A Southerner himself, a slave owner, and a war-Democrat picked by Lincoln to be his running mate on the National Union ticket, Johnson, his motives—and his actions—were always going to be suspect in the eyes of Radical Republicans. But with Congress in recess until December, he was free to act.

On July 7, with the first issue of *The Nation* still on the newsstands, the four surviving members of the conspiracy to assassinate the president—including George Atzerodt, who was supposed to have killed Johnson, and Mary Suratt, the Confederate sympathizer who owned the tavern where John Wilkes Booth and his fellow plotters met—were hanged. Nor had Johnson's tenure as military governor of Tennessee earned him a reputation for leniency. But as president, Johnson decided it was in the country's interest to proceed as if the rebel states had never left the Union. The speedy installation of loyal governments was all that was needed, the president argued, for peace to be established and the Union restored. (It may well have occurred to Johnson that a low bar for readmission to the Union would also improve his prospects for election in 1868.) In May, Johnson issued an amnesty to all former rebels except those possessing property worth more than $20,000. He also appointed new governors in the ex-Confederate states.

As an experiment, the new president's conciliatory approach might at least claim to be following Lincoln's wish. But by the time Congress returned, it was clear the experiment had failed. In Virginia, as in the other re-admitted Southern states, elections held without the participation of black voters returned former Confederate officials to office. Far from being able to exercise their rights, freed slaves throughout the South found themselves subject to "Black Codes"—rushed into law by the newly elected legislatures—which were designed to keep them on the land, and in continued subjugation to their former owners.

From the first, *The Nation* took the Radical Republican view that in seceding, the Confederate states had terminated their membership in the United States and that Congress could set whatever conditions it chose for readmission. But to Johnson himself the magazine was initially sympathetic. When Senator Charles Sumner accused Johnson of "Whitewashing" conditions in the South, Godkin defended the president. (Sumner, Godkin once wrote, "works his adjectives so hard that if they ever catch him alone they will murder him.") But when Johnson claimed the constitution prevented him from imposing negro suffrage on the Southern states, Godkin pointed out[20] he hadn't hesitated to disenfranchise the prewar upper class in those states. Nor should he have. "However much opposed we may be to political vengeance," Godkin wrote,[21] "there is nobody who will deny that men who have made themselves conspicuous in instigating an appeal from the ballot to the sword ought to be compelled, after defeat in the field, to hold their tongues for the remainder of their days."

Accusing[22] the president of running "a pardoning machine, which works night and day," turning the "vilest traitor" into a "a clean, white-robed citizen," Godkin warned[23] that Johnson's laxity had led the South "into a revelation of its real feelings and inten-tions" shown clearly by the passage of the Black Codes. "Unless Congress does its duty, we shall witness at the South, during the next few years, one of the most tremendous and revolting crimes ever perpetrated by a community laying claims to civilization." The freedman, said *The Nation*,[24] was entitled to nothing less than "absolute political justice.... That justice he will have, though an armed occupation...be necessary during the existing generation."

Congress did its duty, passing the Civil Rights Act in 1866 to guarantee all citizens equality before the law—but President Johnson vetoed it, inspiring in Godkin a "feeling of impatient con-tempt." There are, he wrote,[25] "few public men whose opinion upon a point of Constitutional law would have attracted less atten-tion a year ago than Mr. Johnson and we are inclined to believe that there are few whose judgment will carry less weight after his official term has expired."

But Godkin's pen wasn't always so well aimed. When Wendell Phillips took exception to *The Nation*'s treatment of Sumner, Godkin dismissed[26] the abolitionist as one who "from a great height in the air [behaves] as a kind of vulture to scare the more mindless, coward-ly, and laggard Radicals into a show of eagerness and activity." The weaker among them "make the more frantic and pitiable efforts to get to the extreme as the only place in which they are sure of safe-ty from his claws and beak." Wendell Phillips Garrison joined the attack, sneering[27] at the man whose name he bore: "One of the pen-alties of the successful cultivation of his style of oratory is, that the orator comes at last to lose all sense of the exact force of language."

Godkin's evident contempt for Phillips, and his only partly

concealed wobbling on the question of negro suffrage—ideally, he suggested[28] in the second issue, the government should "exclude everybody from the polls who can neither read nor write"—upset the magazine's Radical backers. "I am afraid to visit Boston this winter, lest the stockholders of the Nation should lynch me," Godkin said to a friend in 1866. Nor were his enemies confined to Boston. A Philadelphia backer complained that the magazine was rude about Jay Cooke, the financier who was also a *Nation* advertiser. A Richmond newspaper detected the hidden hand of Wendell Phillips, and behind that the likelihood that the whole venture was funded by "British Gold" as a means of sapping American might.[29]

But it was "Friend Stearns," as Godkin referred to him, who made the most trouble. Piqued by an editorial in the first issue suggesting "everybody is heartily tired" of discussing the freed slaves' "condition" or their "rights," Stearns wrote to Godkin and Norton reminding them that those were precisely the topics for which he'd funded the magazine. Godkin ignored the letter, which only enraged Stearns further. Accusing Godkin of misleading him and the other Boston stockholders—who had put $16,000 into *The Nation* left over from the Massachusetts "Recruiting Committee" for African-American soldiers—Stearns wrote an open letter, addressed to Norton, complaining that if Godkin had been as honest "as I was with him, I would have saved $10,000," and demanding that either the editor be fired or his money refunded. He also accused Godkin of trimming his sails on free trade. Both charges were not without merit, but Stearns's alliance with Wendell Phillips pushed Garrisonites into defending Godkin, who also benefited when Stearns accused him of lying about his origins: "Common report…says he is an Irishman."[30] Meanwhile the Baltimore stockholders also wanted *The Nation* to be more outspoken on behalf of civil rights for blacks, while another backer, George Dodge—described by Godkin as "very rich, *good*, a rigid blue Presbyterian, wife ditto"—said he found the magazine "sensational" while his wife objected to its "vulgarity" and "slanginess." All of which, Godkin wrote to Norton, who remained a staunch friend, "proves more clearly than ever the necessity of getting out of reach of the Stockholders."[31]

Matters came to a head in May 1866. Stearns and his Boston allies went to court to force Godkin and Norton to buy back their shares. When that suit failed, Stearns departed, though his $10,000 did not. Olmsted, back East after the collapse of his mining scheme, signed on as associate editor. They were joined briefly by the young William Dean Howells, whose wife boasted: "Mr. Howells has got an engagement on one of the best literary papers in the country—*The Nation*." From the first, however, readers conflated the magazine's personality with that of its founding editor, remarking "Godkin says" rather than "*The Nation* says" when citing a particularly pungent editorial, regardless of who wrote it. Howells soon left for *The Atlantic*, which offered him considerably more than the $40 a week he'd been getting—and a clear line to the top job. Meanwhile *The Nation*, which had largely exhausted its initial capital, fired Richards and whittled down its backers from forty "Nation Associates" to just three: Godkin now held half the stock, McKim kept a third, while Olmsted took the remaining sixth. Though Garrison took over the publisher's duties in addition to editing the literary pages, the name of the reorganized firm left no doubt as to who was in charge: E.L. Godkin and Company. ✳

E.L. Godkin

CHAPTER TWO

'Radical' and 'Liberal'

T hose were different times. If we are to have any hope of understanding the passions of the late nineteenth century, or of rescuing Godkin's *Nation* from what E.P. Thompson (a frequent *Nation* contributor in the twentieth century) called "the enormous condescension of posterity," we must first resist the temptation to see the past only as prologue to the present. Godkin and his readers knew the Civil War had been won, and slavery destroyed; the Great Experiment endured. But what kind of country would the newly re-United States become? What role would the former slaves—and their former masters—play? How would a federal government armed and mobilized for war face challenges that could not be overcome with powder and steel? The only thing of which the new magazine and its readers could be certain was that there would be no going back to the old certainties.

Perhaps the most vivid register of the gulf between their time and our own is the fierce battle, fought partly in the pages of *The Nation*, over the right to the banners "Radical" and "Liberal"—labels that in the 1860s were considered marks of prestige. Though it might not have satisfied George Stearns, *The Nation* remained a radical organ. Whether the topic was female suffrage—a movement Godkin wished "all possible success," arguing[1] both that women deserved the vote "if they desire it," and that "we think they ought to desire it"—or the possibility of using solar energy[2] as a replacement for coal, *The Nation* did not shy away from radical solutions. Especially in the South, where Godkin had little patience with President Johnson's scruples over constitutional niceties.

America, Godkin held, was bound "by higher considerations than…can be made of this or that clause of the Federal Constitution" to repay the debt incurred "to a people who furnished us 150,000 fighting men, and who are entitled to share in that which has been, in part at least, preserved by their valor and their labors." The president, said[3] Godkin, must "take care that the new society at the South shall not be reorganized in such fashion that a man may be excluded from civil rights for the ridiculous reason that his skin is of a particular hue," lest "we make ourselves a laughing-stock every time we undertake to preach democratic principles to the rest of mankind."

Pronouncing itself in favor of "strict adherence to the Constitution, but not strict construction of it" the *Nation* urged[4] the president to defer to the people's representatives—and warned the Supreme Court not to interfere: "All devices for protection against the will of a decided majority of the governing class are certain to fail, and nothing is more unwise than to thrust a few judges across the path which such a majority has resolved to pursue." Frankly majoritarian, it was also confident in the ability of democracy—at least at the federal level—to solve its problems.

Were the separate states too weak to force the great railroad barons to provide safe transportation at a reasonable price? (About the ability of corporations to buy off state legislatures *The Nation* had no illusions: "What power commands at Trenton? Is it not the Camden and Amboy? What at Harrisburg? Is it not the Pennsylvania Central? What at Albany? Is it not the New York Central?") The solution[5] was clear: "The highways of the nation should be regulated by the national Government." Did the Southern states persist in defying the will of Congress? Then they must be brought into line—at the point of federal bayonets if necessary: "If this can only be done by force, force we must have." It was precisely this cheerful embrace of federal power, and their serene acknowledgment that Reconstruction represented, in Eric Foner's phrase, "less a fulfillment of the Revolution's principles than a radical repudiation of the nation's actual practice" that distinguished the Radicals[6].

As for Liberalism, in nineteenth-century America, the word had only the meanings given to it by John Locke, Adam Smith and John Stuart Mill: noninterference in the religious, commercial and political lives of individuals. In Godkin's hands, Liberalism would eventually boil down to a belief that "nature had created a perfectly balanced economic order, governed by immutable laws."[7] But at the close of the Civil War, Godkin, like most Republicans, believed[8] he had reached the end of history: "Sovereignty without centralization, consolidation without despotism, nationality under democratic forms, this is a fact now for the first time established in the history of government." All that was required for the nation—and *The Nation*—to prosper was for those in power to heed his message of renewal and reform.

The president, however, wasn't listening. But when Wendell Phillips and Ben Butler—both allies of Stearns, and perhaps the only two men in the country Godkin detested more than Johnson—first agitated for impeachment, *The Nation* was opposed. The charges, wrote[9] Godkin, were "vague, indefinite, difficult of proof, and rest, in many instances, on doubtful points of constitutional law." He also worried that impeaching the president was a "party measure" that could just as easily be used by Democrats if they were in the majority. The country, he wrote,[10] should be spared "the paltry and degrading spectacle of a whole nation trying [Johnson] judicially for having been presumptuous, obstinate, uneducated, and for having passed the flower of his years as a little village politician in a slave State."

However when Johnson fired Secretary of War Edwin Stanton, in direct defiance of the Tenure of Office Act, which forbade the dismissal of cabinet members without the Senate's approval, Godkin found[11] that the president "with truly wonderful fatuity, furnished…[his opponents] with a good case against him." Once the trial began in the Senate, in March 1868, the magazine's enthusiasm again began to waver, though the editor admitted[12] that in advising Southern legislatures to refuse to ratify the Fourteenth Amendment, Johnson was guilty of "a bold plain violation of his official duty." And when the Senate came one vote short of removing Johnson, *The Nation* responded mainly with relief—turning its ire instead on those who attacked the seven Republicans who voted for acquittal.

§

By then *The Nation* was what is called in publishing circles a "critical success." This may have been due, in part, to the dearth of competition. The dreaded *Round Table* came out a few months after *The Nation* only to expire from the ill effects of a libel suit. *Harper's Weekly* and *Frank Leslie's Illustrated Weekly* had the same frequency, and under George W. Curtis the former took a similar view of Reconstruction. But both were more miscellaneous than *The Nation*, and both, crowded with photographs and cartoons, aimed at a mass audience. James Russell Lowell, first at *The Atlantic* and later, with Charles Eliot Norton at *The North American Review*, shared an outlook with Godkin; the three men were close friends. And all three magazines used many of the same writers. But *The Atlantic* was a monthly and *The North American Review* a quarterly, so Godkin used them more often and, on topical matters, to greater effect.

In its very first issue *The Nation* published reviews by Henry James Sr. and his 22-year-old son. Henry Jr., who called his friendship with Godkin "one of the longest and happiest…in my life," would go on to write more than 200 articles for *The Nation*, whose frequent assignments formed the basis of the novelist's financial independence.[13] Henry's older brother William, who also wrote for the magazine, credited *The Nation* with his "whole political education," calling Godkin "to my generation...the towering influence in all thought concerning public affairs." Historians Charles Bancroft and Francis Parkman were devotees—Parkman, a sometime contributor, even donated funds to the magazine. In Britain, Matthew Arnold pronounced *The Nation* the best weekly in the United States, and possibly the world. His countryman James Bryce, the distinguished jurist, became the magazine's first London correspondent, while Jessie White Mario, comrade to Mazzini and Garibaldi, wrote from Italy. Her articles, like all contributions to the magazine, were unsigned*, or signed only with her initials, which meant that her role as a pioneering female foreign correspondent (second only to Margaret Fuller of the *Tribune* in importance) went largely unrecognized.

In Washington, when Henry Adams—son of Lincoln's ambassador to Britain; grandson and great-grandson to two presidents—decided he could no longer act as *The Nation*'s secret Washington correspondent, he was replaced by Carl Schurz. A former brigadier general in the Union Army, when Godkin recruited him Schurz had recently been elected to the Senate from Missouri. Had *The Nation* run a masthead, however, Schurz would have been outranked by Jacob Dolson Cox, a Union major general who between serving as governor of Ohio and secretary of the interior wrote regularly on military affairs. On academic mat-

---

* "The publication of names," Godkin assured one disgruntled author, only makes an editor careless of quality, "converting his paper into a dumping ground where 'celebrities' shuck their rubbish." (Godkin to Moses Coit Tyler, May 25, 1867.)

ters the magazine called on Theodore Woolsey, the president of Yale—Godkin had first met his wife at Woolsey's home—and on Harvard's new president Charles W. Eliot. Godkin was partial to Harvard, at one point advising William Whitney, the Yale Sanskrit scholar, that "the *University* atmosphere" was better in Cambridge than New Haven. And Harvard returned the favor, with undergraduate devotion to the magazine's *dictats* slavish enough to be lampooned by the class of 1880 Hasty Pudding revue: "May the Puddings leave their *Nation*s, and neglect their recitations."[14]

If that sounds cozy, it's because it was cozy. Godkin might not have known each of his 5,000 subscribers personally, but then again he might have—and if he didn't, he certainly knew men like them. Not many people read *The Nation*—but those who did included most of the country's editorial writers, and a fair sampling of its leading academics. The writer Charles Dudley Warner, an editor at *Harper's* and the first president of the National Institute of Arts and Letters, called it "the weekly Day of Judgment."

It has been said that Godkin's *Nation* not only spoke for its readers, it spoke *to* them. Consider, for example, the magazine's persistent attention to the "Servant Question." [15] Too hard to come by in the first place, Godkin lamented, no sooner is a girl "fairly trained and is really useful," than "she has become initiated in the ways of the class, and, hearing of a better situation, coolly gives notice and leaves, or decamps without notice." That this was offered partly tongue in cheek—and in the service of an argument for higher wages—signifies no more than the plea,[16] in the same issue, to recognize that "degradation of one part is the degradation of all, and…that every man has both a selfish and a fraternal interest in the elevation of every other man."

What comes through clearly is the voice of a certain class: "They…married one another's sisters and cousins," wrote Nancy Cohen in her pitiless dissection of the group, "and summered together in Saratoga, the Berkshires, or Newport; they spent evenings in all-male clubs with politicians and businessmen, dining, smoking and conversing as gentlemen…."[17] In the 1860s this class was still high-minded. But they thought, and acted, as a class. And when they moved, *The Nation* moved with them.

The transformation was gradual. *The Nation*'s earliest, and most significant, contribution to the national debate about the fate of the conquered Confederacy was to supply not rhetoric, but facts. John Richard Dennett had been Harvard's class poet in 1862, making his way immediately after graduation to the Sea Islands off the coast of South Carolina, whose white residents had fled, leaving some 10,000 slaves in the care of Union troops. Developing the islands as a naval base, federal officials and abolitionist volunteers also set up the "Port Royal Experiment" as a demonstration of the former slaves' ability to farm the land and live free of white control, forming all-black communities such as Mitchelville on Hilton Head island. Dennett had joined the experiment as superintendent of plantations and spent a year at Harvard Law School when Godkin commissioned him to make a nine-month, seven-state tour, reporting on "The South As It Is."

Clear-eyed and written in unadorned prose, Dennett's dispatches show a white South that, far from vanquished, regards its military defeat as no reason to abandon its way of life, and where white supremacy is merely waiting for the departure of Union troops to reassert its authority. In Louisiana Dennett meets an Ohio man, opposed to Lincoln and abolition but pro-Union, who tells him: "I came out with the kindest feelings for these people down here; I wanted to see it made easy; we had whipped them, and I wanted it to end there. I thought the South wanted it to end there. But I was tremendously mistaken. They hate us and despise us and all belonging to us…. The only people I find that a Northern man can make a friend of, the only ones that like the government and believe in it, are the Negroes."[18] Returning North, Dennett joined Godkin's staff as assistant editor.

Throughout the 1860s *The Nation* maintained a benevolent, if increasingly theoretical, commitment to the welfare of the former slaves. The new Florida constitution, drafted by a convention whose delegates were nearly one-third black, was pronounced[19] "clearly superior to the current or newly proposed constitution by the cream of the white population in New York." In 1867 Lucy McKim Garrison (daughter of James McKim and wife of W.P. Garrison) was one of three editors of *Slave Songs of the United States*,[20] the first, and most influential, anthology of African-American spirituals, many of which had been collected during her travels in the Sea Islands. Three years later *Nation* readers could still buy *Slave Songs* "c/o The Publisher of 'The Nation.'" By then, however, the magazine had already begun to change its tune.

§

At first, *The Nation* greeted the election of Ulysses S. Grant with confidence that the victor at Shiloh and Vicksburg would be just the man to cure the country of its ills. "Grant is not a regular politician," Godkin assured *Nation* readers in

October 1868. "He will be the first President the country has had in many a long day on whom the old party doctrines as to 'spoils' and 'claims' will have no influence...." Getting rid of the "spoils" system, in place since Andrew Jackson, under which each administration displaced the employees of the previous one, was Godkin's new political passion. In Britain Gladstone's government, spurred by the administrative disasters of the Crimean War, had put in place a civil service, inspired by the Prussian model, with competitive examinations replacing party loyalty as the criterion for government employment. *The Nation*, having witnessed at close quarters the iron grip maintained by William Tweed and his Tammany Hall machine over New York City, wanted Washington to do the same.

Grant, "by education and temperament the foe of jobbers, intriguers and blatterers," would, Godkin predicted,[21] "undoubtedly apply to the civil service, in so far as he can, the rules of selection and promotion by the aid of which he has given such splendid illustration to American military annals." But when the Republican bosses who had chosen Grant as their champion proved as attached to patronage as any Tammany hack, the president turned his attention elsewhere. Godkin, however, did not, with *The Nation* becoming increasingly disillusioned as the Credit Mobilier and Whiskey Ring scandals revealed the extent of Republican corruption.

At the same time *The Nation*, along with the rest of the country, gradually wearied of Reconstruction—ironically just at the point when Grant, exasperated by Southern resistance, finally sent federal troops to protect the former slaves against the violent depredations of the Ku Klux Klan. And it wasn't only Reconstruction.

Clinging to the two masts of civil service reform in politics and free trade and hard money in economics, *The Nation* unceremoniously threw overboard its enthusiasm for any more far-reaching social change. From encouraging women's suffrage, it now worried[22] about what might happen when "every female politician knows that she holds her male colleagues or opponents at her mercy, either by offering temptations which the best men do not always withstand, or making charges which...however false, are never made against any man without leaving behind a stain which he and his children are sure to rue as long as they live." In the luridly titled "Sex in Politics,"[23] Godkin asked readers to imagine how the press, already quick to sniff out scandal, would report "the probable influence of Mr. Smith's liaison with Miss Brown on their both voting against the San Domingo annexation."

Where it had once urged federal regulation of the railroads—and even contemplated nationalization of the "public highways" with equanimity—*The Nation* now rejoiced[24] that "this great, indeed we might almost say wonderful work" of running the railroads "has come, by a sort of process of natural selection, to be committed to the hands of what is perhaps the ablest body of men in the United States." In 1868 Godkin denounced the opponents of regulation as "driven to the position that the Constitution was only framed for the state of things, physical as well as political, which existed at the time of its adoption."[25] Six years later, despite worrying that "the expanding power and influence of these great railway corporations appears to know no limit,"[26] the magazine, faced with the prospect that Congress might act, suddenly adopted[27] the originalist doctrine of constitutional interpretation: "To 'regulate commerce' is such a vague general term that it is absolutely necessary to go back to the time of its introduction to know what its design was, and if there is anything clear in the world it is that in the year 1787 no one in the world supposed it to have anything to do with the freight rates charged by the Chicago, Burlington and Quincy or the New York Central."

But it is *The Nation*'s abandonment of the freed slaves that makes the most painful reading. When in 1866 the Supreme Court, in *ex parte Milligan* and two other cases, restricted the government's ability to enforce Reconstruction, *The Nation* was unconvinced even though David Dudley Field, in whose office Godkin had studied for the New York bar exam, argued for the winning side. "No people," protested[28] Godkin, "ever will...permit the perpetuation in its government of principles which it deems immoral or unsound because nine judges think it ought to do so. It may be legally proper that it should, but it would be logically and morally absurd." On the eve of Grant's election, *The Nation* urged[29] no let-up: "To govern the South militarily so long is the best thing the Republican party has done next to emancipation, and if it could...which we admit it cannot, keep it under military rule for four years more, it would be rendering the South the highest service it can receive through any human agency."

Yet when, in response to violence by the Klan and other racist groups aimed at driving blacks out of political life, the Grant administration passed three "Force Bills" to enable federal troops to enforce the law, Godkin balked. The first hint came in February

1870. Reporting the ratification of the Fifteenth Amendment[*] *The Nation* declared[30]: "The reconstruction process may be considered closed for all practical purposes...." That March the magazine suggested[31] that reports of white violence were probably exaggerated and should be looked at "in a skeptical and not a credulous spirit." In April *The Nation* came down in favor of ending racial discrimination in hotels, theaters and public conveyances—but with the proviso[32] that having passed such a law Congress should return "the South to its normal condition; or, in other words, to the government of the majority of its inhabitants.... The Government of the United States has something to think of besides either punishing the whites for their treason or rewarding the blacks for their fidelity." The South, wrote[33] Godkin, "ought now to be dropped by Congress."

The shift in tone soon showed itself in the magazine's increasingly frequent references to "carpet baggers" and "scalawags," the former defined[34] as "men who having failed to succeed elsewhere in ordinary industry have been attracted to the negro as the dead ox attracts the buzzard." Without making any attempt at independent investigation, *The Nation* simply repeated accounts of widespread corruption in Reconstruction state legislatures, remarking[35]: "Surely it is not a wonder that the respectable portion of Southern society, seeing what rogues and thieves their lawmakers are, should not be very earnest in putting down the bands of lawless young men who, if they do disgrace themselves...do also whip a greedy tax-collector, shoot a bribed law-maker, and compel a dis-

[*] "The right of citizens of the United States to vote shall not be denied or abridged by the United States or by any State on account of race, color, or previous condition of servitude."

reputable office-holder to run the country." In March 1871, when the respectable portion of Meridian, Mississippi, went on a three-day rampage, with the Klan killing some thirty blacks while local law enforcement did nothing, an enraged Congress passed the Ku Klux Klan Act allowing the president to intervene, and to suppress habeas corpus in the case of civil disorder. Godkin responded with the longest editorial[36] *The Nation* ever ran dealing with Reconstruction, condemning the law as "a monstrous perversion of legal language" that violates the entire spirit of the Constitution.

Two years later, when the Klan murdered 100 freedmen in Colfax, Louisiana, *The Nation* depicted[37] the massacre as a battle between a government "composed not of civilized men, but of, in large part, ignorant negroes and white rogues" and the more able citizens "who find their civilized and complex society...suddenly taken possession of by a large body of people sunk in barbarism and managed by the dregs of northern society." Claiming that in Georgia, Virginia and other states "which the whites...hold the State government beyond all peradventure, there is as much order and security for blacks as for whites," the magazine suggested blacks should cease agitating for political parity. "To those who say the negroes cannot trust the whites to govern them," *The Nation* replied: "Where they are forced to trust them, all goes well."

South Carolina, where a Radical Reconstruction government remained in power, brought out the worst[38] in Godkin: "The average intelligence...is very low—so low that they are but slightly above the level of animals." At present "a queer aristocracy of color is set up, with the rich Congo thief on top and the degraded Anglo-Saxon at the bottom." Such an inversion of the natural order, concluded *The Nation*, could have only one cause: "This is what socialism has done for South Carolina."

Nor did *The Nation* simply turn its back on the freedmen—the group on whose behalf the magazine had been founded. Though it certainly did that, making the Pilate-like pronouncement[39] that while "the race still suffers keenly from injustice," the country, happily, "no longer has a negro problem to settle." When W.P. Garrison wrote his brother in 1874 that negroes would be well advised to "drop back" and stay out of politics, he was simply parroting the *Nation* line. But the magazine's role was not merely one of passive resignation; working in tandem with James S. Pike, a reporter for the *New-York Tribune* who, without having set foot in the South since the war[*], launched a propaganda campaign attacking the administration of South Carolina as one of "ignorance and barbarism," *The Nation* was a crucial voice in persuading "enlightened" Northern opinion to abandon Reconstruction.[40]

If "a great mistake was committed in conferring the suffrage on the negro," Godkin wrote[41] in 1877, the remedy was to stop enforcing the law: "The laws may still stand…but they will only have the efficiency and vitality of a very perfect and muscular corpse. Indeed, situated as the negro is, it would not be at all surprising if he himself should be the first to reach an adverse conclusion by seeing for himself that he had not exercised his rights in such a way as to conduce to his own advantage."

The Baltimore Sun, which celebrated the return to power of

----

[*] Pike did journey to South Carolina a year later, where he found his prejudices sufficiently confirmed to publish *The Prostrate State: South Carolina Under Negro Government.*

white-supremacist "Redeemer" governments across the South, credited Godkin "more than any other one man, through *The Nation* and otherwise," for alerting "the conscience of the North to a feeling of the wrong done the South by the scalawag and carpet-bag regime. The scandals of the period from 1865 to 1876 were mercilessly exposed by him, and with such ability that they at length became unbearable and the South was freed from the violent interferences of federal troops and office-holders."[42] Time and again those historians most responsible for spreading what W.E.B. Du Bois calls the myths of negro rule* support their accounts by appeal to *The Nation*, which by 1872 condemned[43] the whole effort as "simply a cover for robbery."

§

Beyond excuse, beyond extenuation, *The Nation*'s betrayal of African-Americans also defies simple explanation. What can be said is that from 1870 onward Godkin and *The Nation* became increasingly the voice not merely of the Eastern establishment, but of the most reactionary elements within that establishment. Bound by his "liberal" principles to oppose any attempt to interfere with the "freedom of contract," Godkin had always resisted calls for an eight-hour workday, and worried that a government able to prohibit children from working in factories—a goal, he allowed,[44] for which "there is a great deal to be said"—might end by telling "us what to eat, drink, avoid, hope, fear, and believe."

Reading through *The Nation* in the 1870s and 1880s, one sees

---

*   William A. Dunning's notorious *Reconstruction, Political and Economic:1865-1877*, for example, repeatedly cites The Nation.

clearly the rising sense of paranoia: "Godkin and his disciples," observed John Sproat, whose book *The Best Men* is a vivid portrait of the Liberal reformers as a class, "were morbidly preoccupied with violence, with the threat of anarchy and communism they saw hanging over the nation during this period. They seem always to sense revolution breathing down their necks, to smell the blood of martyrs, indeed, to anticipate the sharp edge of the guillotine."[45]

To today's reader, *The Nation*'s bloodthirsty response to the Haymarket riot is nearly as shocking as its callousness toward the former slaves. When a peaceful demonstration on May 4, 1886, at Haymarket Square in Chicago demanding the enforcement of the Illinois Eight Hour law* was disrupted by a bomb, seven police officers and at least four civilians were killed in the ensuing exchange of gunfire. No one was ever charged with throwing the bomb, but many of the speakers at the rally were anarchists, making the movement the target of America's first Red Scare. "There are no good anarchists except dead anarchists," proclaimed the St. Louis *Globe-Democrat*. The front page of *The New York Times*, declaring the bombing the work of "Anarchy's Red Hand," prescribed strong medicine: "In the early stages of an acute outbreak of anarchy a Gatling gun, or if the case be severe, two, is the sovereign remedy. Later on hemp, in judicious doses, has an admirable effect in preventing the spread of the disease."[46]

Eight anarchists were eventually put on trial, and though the defense had no trouble establishing that six of them weren't even

---

* Despite *The Nation*'s opposition, Illinois was one of many states that passed Eight Hour laws immediately after the Union victory. Marx called such measures "the first fruit of the Civil War."

present when the bomb was thrown, all eight were convicted. Seven were sentenced to death. Godkin's friend William Dean Howells called the trial "an atrocious piece of frenzy and cruelty, for which we must stand ashamed forever before history."[47] But *The Nation* was satisfied: "The courts of the law are on the side of both the poor and the rich so long as they obey the laws."

What worried[48] Godkin was not the total absence of evidence tying any of the men to the bomb but the possibility that the effort by "a good many people—some of them clergymen, some philanthropists, and some simply soft-headed who sign all papers presented to them"—to get the sentences commuted might succeed. "It is a great pity," he wrote, "that we cannot shut up the mouths of the Anarchists by love. But as we cannot shut them up by love, we must do it by fear, that is, by inflicting on them the penalties which they most dread: and the one most appropriate to their case when they kill people, is death."

Four of the defendants were hanged; one committed suicide; two had their sentences commuted. Where a distraught Howells wrote "this free Republic has killed five men for their opinions," Godkin complained[49] that in allowing any of the Haymarket martyrs to escape the hangman's noose, the trial's salutary message had been diluted: "There is not a city in the country in which a little circle of malcontents…may not be found—that is, of men who think there is a fund belonging to the public in general which the owners of property have got hold of, and refuse to divide with the poor, and who are gradually learning to hate every man who saves, and wears good clothes…. Into the hands of these social pests, clergymen among us in their pulpits, and professors in their lecture-rooms, are every day playing, either by vague intimations that there is shortly going to be a great 'social revolution,' in which we shall all lie on our backs and make machinery do our work for us, or that the present distribution of property is in the main the result of cheating."

Godkin's disgust had been building for some time. Horrified by the Paris Commune, he condemned[50] "the doctrine that the end justifies the means" as "detestable…in the hands of the democrat as of the priest or king." And when the first great railroad strikes convulsed the country in July 1877 Godkin was appalled: No government, he wrote,[51] could tolerate conditions in which a few thousand "day-laborers of the lowest class can suspend, even for a whole day, the traffic and industry of a great nation, merely as a means of extorting ten or twenty cents a day more in wages…." Blaming the unrest on foreign agitators, *The Nation* called[52] for a show of force: "The kindest thing which can be done for the great multitudes of untaught men who have been received on these shores, and are daily arriving…is to show them promptly that society as here organized, on individual freedom of thought and action, is impregnable, and can be no more shaken than the order of nature."

But there may also have been personal factors at work. The opposite of "critical success" is "commercial success," not critical failure. By November 1869 *The Nation* had exhausted its capital. After three years of working for half his salary "nothing is left," Godkin wrote to James McKim. Circulation had fallen below 5,000 and "I cannot go on at this pace." Though McKim agreed to keep making good the magazine's losses, the pressure on Godkin was intense. He wrote to George Jones, publisher of *The*

New York Times, proposing to write two pieces a week if the paper could "make it worth my while" and the arrangement was "*kept private.*"[53] Yet when Charles W. Eliot, the incoming president of Harvard, offered Godkin a chair as professor of history in 1870, he turned him down. Not immediately—he wrote to Olmsted that "I am inclined, if I could combine it with *The Nation*, to take it." The Harvard Corporation, however, demanded "absolute cessation of all control or direction of the paper on my part."

For Godkin, control meant independence. "Journalism, unless you can have a paper, and own it, is not a profession," he wrote to Olmsted, who, preoccupied with building Prospect Park, now persuaded the magazine's other backers to donate their shares to E.L. Godkin and Co. Not that financial difficulties—or political considerations—alone account for Godkin's growing discomfort with democracy. In April 1873 his beloved daughter Elizabeth died—a blow from which Fanny, who herself died two years later, never recovered. Nor were the family permitted to grieve in peace. In 1874 Fanny's cousin, Henry Ward Beecher, was accused of "criminal conversation"—a legal euphemism for adultery—by Theodore Tilton, editor of the Brooklyn *Independent* and, along with his patron Wendell Phillips, a frequent figure of abuse in *The Nation*. Given Beecher's fame as a preacher of "the Gospel of Love," and Mrs. Tilton's confession of the affair, the public trial and resultant scandal was a national sensation.

Disgusted by the way the whole affair played out in the press, Godkin denounced what he called "Chromo-Civilization"[54]: "A large body of persons has arisen, under the influence of the common-schools, magazines, newspapers, and the rapid acquisition of wealth, who are not only engaged in enjoying themselves after their fashion, but who firmly believe that they have reached, in the matter of social, mental, and moral culture, all that is attainable or desirable by anybody...." The result, said Godkin, is "a kind of mental and moral chaos, in which many of the fundamental rules of living, which have been worked out painfully by thousands of years of bitter human experience, seem in imminent risk of disappearing."

Buffeted by the popular press—especially the New York *Sun*, a paper whose commercial success was built on crime and scandal and whose editor, Charles A. Dana, liked to torment Godkin by referring to him as "Larry"—and alarmed by the rise of the labor movement, *The Nation* retreated hastily from Radicalism to Liberal Republicanism. Begun in 1872 as an abortive attempt to deny Grant a second term, the Liberal Republican revolt, in which Godkin and Carl Schurz played leading roles, brought the two men into closer contact with Henry Villard. A German immigrant who, like Schurz, wrote for both the German- and English-language press, Villard covered the Civil War for the *New-York Daily Tribune*. He also married Helen Frances Garrison, the sister of *Nation* publisher W.P. Garrison. Returning briefly to Germany for health reasons, he was asked by a group of German investors to manage their interests in American railroads, eventually taking control of the Northern Pacific.

Godkin and Schurz had been close collaborators since 1876, when *The Nation* was persuaded, against Godkin's better judgment, to back Republican Rutherford B. Hayes for the presidency. ("I suppose we must support him...I confess I do it with great misgivings," Godkin confided to Charles Eliot Norton.) Schurz became secretary of the interior in the new administration—a

position that made him especially useful to Villard and his associate, Horace White, a former editor of the *Chicago Tribune* who
had covered the Lincoln-Douglass debates with Villard. During
the 1870s Godkin tried several times to sell *The Nation* to White;
according to Godkin biographer William Armstrong both men
also joined a number of "Villard's speculative schemes."[55]

In 1881 Godkin found a way to unload *The Nation*—and to
maintain control. Flush with the proceeds of his proxy fight for the
Northern Pacific, Villard wanted to buy the *New-York Evening Post*
as a vehicle for his interests. But he also wanted to keep his involvement a secret, and proposed announcing that Schurz, Godkin and
White were the purchasers. Schurz, eager to return to journalism,
agreed, and White was already Villard's employee. Both men were
given shares in the *Post*. Godkin, however, came at a higher price:
in addition to being named one of the *Post*'s new "editorship of all
the talents," Godkin demanded that Villard also buy *The Nation*,
leaving Villard's brother-in-law, W.P. Garrison, in nominal charge
(Godkin, who had been bossing Garrison around for fifteen years,
had little to fear in the way of editorial independence). The purchase price of $40,000 was less than the magazine's capitalization, so
the long-suffering backers, who included Republican Congressman
Henry Cabot Lodge and Thomas Wentworth Higginson, Emily
Dickinson's friend and mentor, lost a third of their investment.[56]

Godkin, however, had finally made his fortune. And though
Schurz, the former diplomat, general, senator and cabinet minister,
was nominally editor in chief, within two years Godkin had forced
him out, gaining control of both the daily *Post* and the weekly *Nation*,
which often now ran editorials recycled from the *Post*. With Garrison

treasurer of the whole enterprise and their *Nation* colleague Arthur Sedgwick now assistant editor of the *Post*, Godkin also made sure the new paper's backers were loyal to him. "I want to have as much of the stock as possible held by my friends," he wrote to Lodge.

It was a labor dispute that caused the final rupture. In 1883, when the telegraphers went out on strike, Schurz thought the paper should remain neutral, like the *Times* and the *Herald*. Godkin, who was seldom neutral, wrote an editorial attacking the strikers and had it printed without consulting his colleague, who in response wrote his own editorial. Godkin then had his editorial—but not Schurz's—reprinted in *The Nation*. For months Godkin had been complaining about his editor in chief to anyone who would listen—including Villard. Now the conflict, which had previously been waged behind Schurz's back, came out into the open. When Godkin ran another editorial arguing that workers "employed in telegraphic and railroad services are an army, and should be governed on the same principles as an army," Schurz exploded. "No man has to be 'governed' on army principles," he wrote to Godkin, "except those who enlist in the army."[57] By the end of the year, Schurz was gone, leaving Godkin in control of the *Post* and *The Nation*. ✳

Wendell Phillips Garrison

CHAPTER THREE

Those Pesky Anti-Imperialists

Like its Roman originals, *The Nation*'s editorial triumvirate proved unstable. With Horace White preoccupied managing the business side, Godkin now had a daily newspaper at his disposal—and in Gilded Age New York the editor of a daily, no matter how feeble its circulation, outranked the editor of any mere magazine. Though in many ways an appendage of the *Post*, *The Nation*'s editorials were still Warner's "weekly Day of Judgment." But as Mark Twain, the author (with Warner) of *The Gilded Age*, is supposed to have said, "Never pick a fight with a man who buys ink by the barrel." Godkin now bought ink by the ton. He soon used it to pick two fights that would do much to secure his lasting political influence—and to salvage what remained of *The Nation*'s reputation. And oddly enough, in both of them Schurz and White were key allies.

The first fight was with the Republican Party. Although *The Nation* had often praised the theoretical importance of independence—deploring the Democratic Tweed Ring's depredations in New York City and condemning upstate Republican Roscoe Conkling, whose control of New York's Custom House was probably the most lucrative patronage plum in the country, with nearly equal vigor—when it came to national elections Godkin held his nose and voted Republican. In 1876, as editor of *The Nation*, he'd felt obliged to back Rutherford B. Hayes even though, as he admitted to Charles Eliot Norton, "it runs against all my convictions."[1] Hayes's opponent, Samuel Tilden, may have, as Godkin wrote[2], shown "courage and determination" and given an "excellent example in the governorship of New York," but he was also a Democrat—the party of corruption, immigrants, ignorance and the defense of slavery, and that was enough to rule him out.

Four years later Godkin was still denouncing[3] Democrats—this time as a party full of "Communists." By "Communist" he meant simply critics of the gold standard—those "sworn enemies of public and private credit. They like high taxes, to be paid by the industrious people who save. They like also to have money made plenty without labor, by the free use of the printing-press. They hate colleges and all institutions of learning as producing persons with marks of mental superiority to the simple Democrat who carries the hod up to the bricklayer." Though regretting that James Garfield, the Republican nominee in 1880, betrayed "a want of backbone," there was no question of Godkin—or *The Nation*—endorsing his opponent.

Yet in 1884 it was Godkin, Schurz and White who led Liberal Republicans—men for whom the cause of civil service reform had become an obsession—out of the party in support of Grover Cleveland, a hard-money Democrat who as mayor of Buffalo and then governor had won a reputation as a corruption fighter. None of the three had ever been admirers of James G. Blaine, Speaker of the House of Representatives and a politician who, though perhaps no more corrupt than many others, had been foolish enough to leave behind a set of incriminating correspondence which terminated with the phrase "Kindly burn this letter." Godkin loathed Blaine, going all in for Cleveland. No candidate, he wrote[4], "except Lincoln in his second term, has offered reformers such solid guarantees that as President he will do his own thinking, and be his own master." And where Godkin went the *Post* and *Nation* followed—as did Schurz (now editorial writer for *Harper's Weekly*), White, Villard and most of the Eastern intellectual class. The spectacle of so many Republican chiefs bolting the Grand Old Party prompted Charles A. Dana to lampoon them as "mugwumps"—from the Algonquin word for a "war leader."

Since the two parties differed very little on matters of principle, the campaign—one of the least edifying in American history—centered on issues of character. Here Blaine was at a distinct disadvantage, until July, when a Buffalo newspaper revealed that the unmarried Cleveland had fathered a child, giving rise to the Republican chant of "Ma, Ma, Where's my Pa?" Godkin held firm, however, no doubt influenced by his own family's unhappy brush with scandal—and by the determination of such friends and backers as Villard and J.P. Morgan, who had secretly loaned the editor $23,000.[5]

The exodus of the grandees was not universal. Henry Cabot

Lodge, whose hopes of a political career rested on the Massachusetts Republican Party, felt constrained to remain loyal. So, for similar reasons, did Lodge's close friend, the young assemblyman from New York's Upper East Side, Theodore Roosevelt. When Roosevelt, having fought alongside the Mugwumps at the Republican convention, declined to join their revolt he made a lifelong enemy of Godkin, who wrote[6] that so far as the Blaine supporters were concerned the New Yorker "is simply a crank and a nuisance, whose influence is an absurdity."

For once Godkin had met his match as a master of invective. In a letter to Lodge, Roosevelt declared that *The Nation* editor must be ill—certainly his language showed symptoms of "a species of moral myopia, complicated with intellectual strabismus."[7] And though Roosevelt may have had the last laugh, Godkin had the first one. In New York, the state whose thirty-six electoral votes put Grover Cleveland in the White House, ending his party's twenty-eight-year losing streak, the Democrat's margin of victory was just 1,149 votes. The magazine might never wield such influence again, but in 1884 Godkin could claim with some justification that he, and *The Nation*, had swung the election.

§

The Nation's second fight was with the whole country—indeed the whole trend of contemporary American foreign policy. And if that battle didn't end so well—some might argue it hasn't ended at all—it certainly began gloriously enough.

During his first term Grover Cleveland had given Godkin ample cause for satisfaction. From his early announcement that qualified and competent Republican appointees would be allowed to remain in office, to his persistent campaign to reduce the tariff—described by the president in his third State of the Union address as "indefensible extortion...a hoarding place for money needlessly withdrawn from trade and the people's use"—to his abandonment of his predecessor's scheme to build a canal across Nicaragua, the Democrat's policies met with cheers from *The Nation* and the *Post*, whose editors' views were frequently sought (if not always followed) on personnel* and policy matters.

Although a bachelor when elected, Cleveland soon married 21-year-old Frances Folsom, the daughter of his late friend Oscar Folsom (the child whose birth figured in the 1884 campaign was named Oscar Folsom Cleveland; his mother apparently had relationships with both men). Godkin, too, had a new bride, Katharine Sands, whose family was socially prominent in New York and London. The Clevelands entertained the Godkins at the White House, and at their summer cottage at Saranac Lake, New York. *The Nation* warmly supported Cleveland both in 1888, when he won the popular vote but lost the election to Benjamin Harrison, and in 1892, when he returned to the White House. It was during this period that David Hill, a Democratic Party regular who followed Cleveland to the governor's mansion and was his rival for the nomination, complained of Godkin's *Post*: "The trouble with that damned sheet is that every editor in New York State reads it."[8]

---

* One occasion when Cleveland presumably did heed Godkin's advice he later regretted. In 1886 Arthur Sedgwick, a member of *The Nation*'s editorial board and editor at the *Post*, was sent to Mexico on a diplomatic mission only to become himself the cause of an international incident after he was found dead drunk in a Mexican whorehouse. (Armstrong, *E.L. Godkin*, p. 163.)

After the election Godkin and the publications he edited stood beside Cleveland in his fight to repeal the Sherman Silver Coinage Act (thus putting the country back on the gold standard), endorsed his response to the Panic of 1893, and spurred on his efforts to roll back Harrison's high tariffs.

So it must have come as something of a shock to the president in December 1895 to see[9] himself "morally impeached of high crimes and misdemeanors" by *The Nation*, which went on to denounce him as "an anarchist" whose latest initiative was nothing less than "a mad appeal to the basest passions of the mob." Spread over seven pages of the magazine, Godkin's rant reached its climax by asking "Was there ever such another case of a civilized man throwing away his clothes and joining the howling savages?" Then, just in case the magazine's contempt was insufficiently clear, it likened Cleveland to *The Nation*'s—and the country's—greatest hate figure, the leader of the previous summer's massive strike against the Pullman railway car company, Eugene V. Debs!

During that strike *The Nation* had compared[10] the threat posed by Debs and the railway unions to "the assault of slavery upon the national life." What had Grover Cleveland, the man who, heartily approved by Godkin, had used federal troops to break the Pullman strike, done to provoke such rancor? He had endorsed a note by his secretary of state, Richard Olney, inserting the United States into a boundary dispute between Great Britain and Venezuela. It was not the terms of the dispute that concerned Godkin, but the belligerent tone of what came to be aptly labeled "Olney's 20 inch gun." Reiterating the Monroe Doctrine, which said that America would no longer permit European powers to meddle in the

Western Hemisphere (but which also promised noninterference with existing colonies), Olney demanded that Britain submit to US arbitration—which was precisely what Venezuela's Washington lobbyist, William Scruggs, wanted.

Britain might be the world's greatest military power, but Olney's language seemed calculated to produced offense: "Today the United States is practically sovereign on this continent, and its fiat is law upon the subjects to which it confines its interposition." The American public, understandably perceiving the letter as a threat of war and whipped into a frenzy by the jingo press, abandoned itself to patriotic fervor. Cleveland announced, and Congress duly authorized the funds for, a boundary commission that would investigate—with or without Britain's permission. Though Britain's eventual compliance averted war, and the ensuing arbitration did much to strengthen US-British relations, the episode had other long-lasting effects.

For Roosevelt, who had rushed to support the American ultimatum, it confirmed his abhorrence of "papers like the *Post* and *The Nation*."[11] In a letter[12] to the Harvard *Crimson* Roosevelt derided "the stock-jobbing timidity, the Baboo kind of statesmanship" by "men who put monetary gain before national honor, or who are still intellectually in a state of colonial dependence on England." Roosevelt's jibes did not go unanswered; two days later William James called on Harvard students—and all those opposed to a policy "bound to alter all the national ideals"—to stay in the fight. Those who heeded his words found *The Nation* waiting for them.

The roots of the magazine's opposition to America becoming a global empire are as tangled as the history of US anti-imperialism. "America goes not abroad in search of monsters to

destroy," President John Quincy Adams boasted in 1821—the
same Adams who as secretary of state had crafted the Monroe
Doctrine, acquired Florida and pushed the country's western bor-
der to the Pacific. And though many of those who, like Adams,
Lincoln and Emerson, opposed America's war with Mexico did so
for the reasons cited by Henry David Thoreau in "Civil Disobedience," there had also always been a less high-minded reluctance
to get entangled in the affairs of darker, non-European peoples—
especially if they might then become American citizens. Nothing
but trouble, warned *The Nation*, would come from "dependencies
inhabited by ignorant and inferior races" with whom Americans
had no business other than "carpet-baggery."

There was also the argument that more territory meant more
government—and more opportunities for corruption. *The Nation*
had criticized[13] William Seward's purchase of Alaska not on isolationist or racial grounds—though it did note the vast territory
had a "white population…hardly big enough to furnish juries in
criminal cases"—but because it meant "adding a large number of
functionaries to the present list, and entrusting them with a large
amount of discretionary power." Though authorized by the president and endorsed by Congress, "Who was not paid," *The Nation*
wondered, "who ever opened his mouth upon the subject?"

The magazine's opposition to Hawaiian annexation united all
of these strands. When a group of British and American adventur-
ers deposed Queen Lili'uokalani in 1893 and petitioned President
Benjamin Harrison to make the islands an American protectorate,
The Nation demanded[14]: "On what theory of democracy, self-government, or home rule has the tender of the Hawaiian Islands been made

to this country?" At the same time, in the *Post*, Godkin warned that in gaining Hawaii the United States would also be acquiring a body of "ignorant, superstitious, and foreign tongued" future voters.[15]

Yet *The Nation* also saw the grab for Hawaii as motivated by the same greed and grandiosity behind various American filibusters (a term that at the time meant "privateer" or military freebooter) like William Walker's abortive attempt to seize Nicaragua in the 1850s. Taking aim at those who "propose to change the government of a distant country without asking the consent of the governed in any way whatever," a scathing editorial[16] noted the prominence of Alabama Senator John Morgan among the annexationists: "He is an ex-slaveholder. He belongs to a class who are in office by virtue of suppressing the votes of the black men and also of such whites as do not vote their ticket." Such men "began with cheating the negro. They have ended by cheating each other."

If *The Nation* opposed such ventures partly under the laissez-faire doctrine that free trade, not conquest, was the means to spread American influence—and out of a recognition that an empire can't be run on the cheap—the magazine had also consistently ridiculed the views of Alfred T. Mahan, whose book *The Influence of Sea Power Upon History* furnished the intellectual underpinnings of American imperialism. "We believe," Godkin wrote[17] in 1892, "the theory on which...Captain Mahan's advocacy of a great navy is based, that the world contains a great many thrones, principalities and powers only too ready to insult, revile, trample on and annoy the United States...is the hallucination of an able man who has devoted himself too long and too deeply to a single topic."[18] Accusing Mahan and his friends of "deliberately misleading the public," *The Nation* warned[19]: "Behind every navy of any size there lurks a secret determination to bully some weaker power." Mahan's greatest disciple, Theodore Roosevelt, sent him a note of commiseration: "What fearful mental degeneracy results from reading…*The Nation* as a steady thing."[20]

The increasingly popular view that "trade follows the flag," and the bellicose assumption, common to both Joseph Pulitzer's *New York World* and William Randolph Hearst's *Journal*, that international commerce was merely a polite form of war—and that an overseas empire was a prerequisite for American prosperity—struck Godkin as a grotesque parody of his most deeply held Liberal beliefs.[21] So when the cruiser *Maine* sank in Havana Harbor on February 15, 1898, *The Nation* was ready. "The need of opposing and exposing the diabolical newspapers which are trying to lie the country into war must be obvious," the magazine declared.[22] A *Post* editorial in April 1898 found Americans living under a "regime in which a blackguard boy [Hearst] with several million dollars at his disposal has more influence on the use a great nation may make of its credit, its army and navy, its name and traditions, than all the statesmen and philosophers and professors in the country."[23]

Though *The Nation* had endorsed William McKinley in 1896—branding Democrat William Jennings Bryan's populist attacks on the gold standard as "The Platform of Revolution,"[24]—the magazine's relentless opposition to the Spanish-American War reportedly led the president to consider charging Godkin or his younger protégé, Rollo Ogden, who penned many of the more stinging editorials in both *The Nation* and the *Post*, with treason. Sold as a crusade to liberate the Cuban people from the Spanish yoke—and supported on those grounds by Mark Twain and Bryan, who had himself commissioned as a colonel in the Third Nebraska Volunteers—the war's effects soon surpassed all of Godkin's worst fears. While direct annexation of Cuba would have been awkward, military victory was followed by years of occupation and decades of political domination. Puerto Rico, having been made no promise of self-government, was simply seized as a trophy of victory. And though the war proved a short one, it was long enough to allow Roosevelt, McKinley's secretary of the navy, to finally steer through the annexation of Hawaii under the pretext of giving the United States a coaling station in the Pacific.[25]

Why did the United States need a Pacific naval base? Because while the war had made Washington the heir to Spanish power in the Caribbean, it left open the destiny of the Philippines, where for decades *Katipunan* rebels had been fighting for independence from Spain. Though Adm. George Dewey's destruction of the Spanish fleet in Manila Bay on May 1, 1898, made headlines in New York, by the end of the month the rebels, led by Emilio Aguinaldo, had effective control of the archipelago. The Philippine Republic declared its independence on June 12, but America, which had been allied with Aguinaldo in his struggle against the Spanish, refused to recognize his government.

"We must on no account let the islands go," wrote Henry Cabot Lodge. "The American flag is up and it must stay." *The Nation*[26] was equally clear: "When one nation engages in an avowed crusade against another in the interest of good government, it must itself bear some of the burden, and it must see that in enlarging the 'area of freedom' in one direction it does not sow the earth with salt in another...."[*] As the temptations of empire seemed, in the historian Barbara Tuchman's phrase, "to glow with the fatal evil of the apple in the Garden of Eden,"[27] the question, Godkin wrote[28] presciently, "is not, 'What are we going to do with the Philippines?' but 'What the Philippines is going to do to us?'" Inflamed by visions of "the new career of commercial activity upon which I trust we are about to enter"—the speaker was Peter Grosscup, the judge who issued the injunction that broke the Pullman strike—Americans heeded Rudyard Kipling's invitation to "Take up the White Man's burden, The savage wars of peace."[29]

The result was more than just a bloodbath. On February 4, 1899, US forces opened fire on Filipino troops in Manila. On February 6 the Senate approved the Treaty of Paris, making the Philippines an American colony. Taking the lives of at least 20,000 Filipino combatants—and as many as 200,000 civilians—the "insurrection" also marked the debut of "the water cure" (a variant of the torture now better known as waterboarding) as an American tactic. As the war dragged on, the conflict became increasingly racialized, with officers like Gen. Adna Chaffee, a veteran of the Indian Wars in Texas and Arizona, adopting a similar approach to the native population. Though Gen. Jacob Smith's notorious order to kill every Filipino "capable of bearing arms"—which he defined as anyone over the age of 10—was too much even for Hearst's *Journal*, America's eventual victory on July 4, 1902, was celebrated as a triumph of civilization.

---

[*] This extraordinary editorial, which sadly could have run with very little revision several times in the twenty-first century, was written by Arthur Sedgwick after his return from Mexico.

Not by E.L. Godkin, who had returned to England in disgust, and died there on May 12, 1902. And not by his successors at *The Nation*. Rollo Ogden, who took over chief editorial writing duties at both *The Nation* and the *Post*, wrote[30]: "What the lonely and ridiculous Anti-Imperialist was whispering in the closet, a year ago, thousands are now shouting from the housetops." He may have been overly optimistic. Certainly Ogden's claim that "Anti-Imperialism is only another name for old-fashioned Americanism" would seem contrary to the main current of the newborn American century. But of all the causes in *The Nation*'s history, anti-imperialism is the one on which the magazine has never wavered.

The war against the Philippines brought Godkin, Schurz, and White together for the last time—backed to the hilt by Henry Villard, whose son, Oswald Garrison Villard, had just started out at *The Nation*. Revulsion over the Philippines prompted the younger Villard to join Godkin, Schurz, Grover Cleveland, Mark Twain, union leader Samuel Gompers, industrialist Andrew Carnegie, and Henry and William James to form the Anti-Imperialist League. Twain's caustic satire, "To the Person Sitting in Darkness" followed Godkin's many bitter attacks in *The Nation* on the clergymen who sanctified America's conquests. And though the group didn't succeed in stopping American militarism, the League did force the first accounting of the costs of empire. It also forged bonds of trust among its members that allowed many of them to work together on other causes, especially in the field of civil rights.

Godkin of course would not be with them. But *The Nation* would.

§

The biography of a magazine, like that of a person, is dominated by one brute fact: we know where the story is going even if, in the case of a live subject, we don't know exactly where or how or when it is going to end. Founded as a Radical (with a capital R) Republican organ, *The Nation* today is a journal whose sympathies, though not precise in a doctrinaire sense, clearly lie on that part of the political spectrum that extends from liberalism through radicalism. Yet like many people, *The Nation* did not follow a straight path; rather it arrived at its current trajectory via the high roads of American conservatism and literary culture.

Wendell Phillips Garrison, who did much of the editorial work at the weekly once Godkin took over at the *Post*, had always been a literary man. Not that he was without political opinions; as the son of William Lloyd Garrison, the breath of controversy furnished the atmosphere of his childhood. But where his father famously scorned compromise, declaring "I will not equivocate—I will not excuse—I will not retreat a single inch—AND I WILL BE HEARD," Wendell Garrison's views were neither as fixed nor as fervent, at least on political matters. A red-hot Radical who, before he met Godkin, once tried to organize a meeting of white and black abolitionists to protest Lincoln's moderation, W.P. Garrison followed the older man's lead in abandoning[31] the freedman to his fate as a "somewhat heavily weighted wayfarer on the dusty and rugged highway of competition."

"I have never forgiven the *Harvard Monthly* for its vulgar typography," he wrote in 1892, as *The Nation* geared up for its assault on imperialism. Not merely a born editor but a born copy editor, Garrison shared Emily Dickinson's terror of a misplaced comma—and quoted her remark "When I think of the hearts it has scuttled and sunk, I almost fear to lift my Hand to so much as a punctuation" in his essay undertaking to set out the correct use of the colon, the dash, and the exclamation mark in the *Atlantic Monthly*.[32] A reticent man who wrote relatively little under his own name during his forty-plus years at *The Nation* (one of the exceptions being a thorough review of reforms to the spelling of the French language),[33] Garrison was, in a word, bookish.

Yet this very diffidence made him the ideal founder and steward for *The Nation*'s literary and cultural pages—the whole domain that today is covered by the rubric "the back of the book." W.C. Brownell, who joined *The Nation* after a stint as city editor at the *New York World*, described Garrison's method: "to treat every book as a trust, to be reviewed only by the most competent men in the United States, Canada, or England, without regard to any timeliness." Then, as now, such indifference "was the despair of the business office and a source of deep irritation to publishers [then, but, sadly, not now, a major source of advertising revenue], who were furious when a review appeared three or six months after the publication of the book."[34] Lord Bryce said[35] that Garrison's standards were "as high as that of the best literary journals of Europe"—but then the author of *The American Commonwealth* was also a frequent contributor, so his testimony may have been biased.

Henry Holt, however, was one of those publishers driven to distraction by *The Nation*'s indifference to commercial timing. "I still vividly remember my surprise and enlightenment," he recalled on the occasion of the magazine's fiftieth anniversary,[36] "when [assistant editor John Richard] Dennett happened into my office just as the first volume of [Hippolyte] Taine's *Italy* came in from the binder, and I handed him a copy, and he said: 'Let me see!

To whom shall I send this for review? Who knows Italy?' And after a little reflection he decided to send it to [William Dean] Howells. Now, so far as I know, doing this as a matter of course was something new in American journalism."

Holt may be overstating* when he says *The Nation* "did more than all other influences to raise the standard of our literary criticism." But there is no doubt that the magazine, in contrast not only with *Harper's* and other American weeklies, but also with British political weeklies such as the *Spectator*, delivered on its promise of "competent criticism of art exhibitions and works of art, the drama, etc." In doing so it followed no school, but rather two rules of its own fashioning. Criticism was not to be influenced by personal motives. Though the nineteenth century was no more free of logrolling and score settling than our own, in the first issue *The Nation* declared "any review thus inspired is worth exactly its weight in Confederate paper." The second dictum, equally demanding, was perhaps even more difficult to put into practice: criticism might be sharp, but never dull. Dennett himself set a high standard with his takedown[37] of the Knickerbocker school of American literature as "authors whom we all remember as forgotten."

In addition to the Jameses, *père et fils* (including Henry Jr.'s "deliciously wicked"[38] dispatches from London reporting the American painter J.A.M. Whistler's libel suit against the critic John Ruskin), Garrison's regulars included Schurz, Olmsted, Norton, the English critic Leslie Stephen, the painters William

---

*   Holt also credits Godkin as the inventor of "the use of quotation marks in sarcasm"—what today are called "scare quotes"—though that coinage is generally attributed to one of Godkin's successors, Carey McWilliams.

A. Coffin and Kenyon Cox, and Russell Sturgis, one of the first professional art critics in America. Elizabeth Robins Pennell, who wrote articles on cooking and travel under her own name for a number of ladies' magazines, but who, writing as "N.N" for *The Nation*, may have been the first female American art critic. In 1893 the young Bernard Berenson, who had previously published a couple of testy letters in the magazine, became a regular contributor on Italian art.

Under Garrison *The Nation* quickly became a cultural as well as political force to reckon with. Indeed its cultural reach extended into circles where its politics would have met with scorn—as attested by the lively correspondence P.T. Barnum maintained with the magazine. Garrison's literary judgment was not infallible. His reviewer, Charles Eliot Norton, gave a guarded welcome to the English poet Algernon Charles Swinburne's shockingly pagan *Atalanta in Calydon*, but for decades the magazine greeted Walt Whitman's verse with contempt—including a brutal dismissal of *Drum Taps* by Henry James. Thomas Wentworth Higginson, in his *Nation* obituary for Whitman, denounced the poet as "a bad influence—we speak from personal observation"—on the lives of young men. Yet it was the same Higginson, a regular reviewer, who rescued Emily Dickinson from obscurity.[39]

Garrison's most lasting contribution to *The Nation*'s—and the country's—intellectual life may well have been his, and the magazine's, steadfast support of philosopher Charles Sanders Peirce, the father of pragmatism. Peirce, a tormented polymath who worked variously for the Coastal and Geodetic Survey, the Harvard observatory, as an untenured lecturer at Johns Hopkins and then as a farmer, waged a constant, and losing, battle with poverty. An occasional reviewer for *The Nation*, in 1890 he and Garrison agreed to increase the frequency of his assignments significantly; the 300 articles Peirce went on to write for the magazine were his main source of income for the next sixteen years.[40]

When Garrison retired Peirce wrote a touching acknowledgment of his patron's "graciousness": "Every head of a works, to ensure his success, must have a genuine sympathy for his workmen; but there is no other class so difficult to deal with as those who are skillful with the pen."[41] In a letter to philosopher Josiah Royce, whose book *The World and the Individual* he'd given a mixed review, Peirce revealed more of his own concerns as well as Garrison's methods: "I'm going to try to say what should be said of your second volume. I shall send Garrison something which is too long for anybody to read and too short to express what I try to cram into it; and Garrison will cut it down so as to leave what will strike the afternoon businessman on his way uptown, hanging onto a strap, as smartly said…. So in case it shouldn't get said there…your best years of philosophic reflection are still before you. The time is ripe and you are the very man to accomplish the great achievement… [of joining philosophy to science]. Yet you could not do it with your present views of logic…. My entreaty is that you will study logic."[42]

Garrison, having grown old with *The Nation*, was originally content to see the magazine expire when he retired in 1906, since he could think of nobody "fit to carry it on who would respect it and its traditions." At which point young Villard piped up to suggest Hammond Lamont,[43] a genteel Harvard graduate who

had been professor of rhetoric at Brown, written a textbook on
English composition, and was currently managing editor of the
Post. Under Lamont's tenure *The Nation* continued to sink into
obscurity, rousing itself occasionally to complain about the influx
of foreigners, or to deplore the decline of public morals. Though
this was the golden age of muckraking—Ida Tarbell's *The History
of the Standard Oil Company* was published in 1902; Upton Sinclair's *The Jungle* and David Graham Phillips's *The Treason of the
Senate* in 1906—*The Nation* took no part in the movement. Lincoln Steffens, who worked under Godkin at the *Post*, found the
experience depressing, in part because of his boss's conviction that
"bad men" rather than a corrupt system, were to blame for urban
decay. It was only after he moved to *McClure's*, and worked with
Tarbell and Ray Stannard Baker, that Steffens was able to write
The Shame of the Cities.

Like a sleepwalker, *The Nation* continued to reprint *Post*
editorials denouncing the tariffs and, with nearly as much fervor, the continuing epidemic of lynching,[44] "a crime which is
a national disgrace." But when President Roosevelt responded to *The Jungle*'s revelations by launching a federal investigation of the meatpacking industry in Chicago, *The Nation*
accused him of leaving the Constitution "thousands of miles"
behind. As the muckrakers highlighted the extent to which
corruption, "a disease which we have complacently assumed
to be confined to politicians," was at least as rampant "among
business men," *The Nation* put its hope[45] not in investigation
or legislative action but "in a quickened conscience and a
moral toning up all around."

Lamont's tenure lasted less than three years. After he died*
during a minor operation on his jaw, his successor, Paul Elmer
More, completed *The Nation*'s transformation into an organ of
"wise conservatism." Not that many people noticed, since the
magazine's circulation, in decline from a high of 12,000, continued its downward spiral. A scholar of Latin, Greek and Sanskrit
before taking to journalism, More's preoccupations were religious
and literary. Edmund Wilson, who knew him during the 1920s,
described[46] More as "a man of true spiritual vocation, unable to
remain a simple rationalist but prevented by a Protestant education and an obstinate hard-headed common sense from finding a
basis in the mysticism of Rome, he had devoted long and diligent
years to establishing a historical tradition which would justify his
peculiar point of view."

Worn out from teaching, More had retreated to a hut in
Shelburne, New Hampshire, to compose learned essays. With his
friend and teacher Irving Babbitt, he was a founder of the New
Humanism and, according to Russell Kirk, an important influence
on the "Conservative mind"—though More apparently preferred
the label "reactionary."[47] At *The Nation*, More occupied himself
chiefly with baiting Roosevelt. In 1909, when the former president, in full Bull Moose Progressive mode, announced that "the

---

* This did not, however, end his family's connection with *The
Nation*. Hammond Lamont's younger brother, Thomas, also worked
as a journalist before becoming a partner and eventually chairman
at J.P. Morgan. Thomas Lamont's son, the philosopher and activist
Corliss Lamont, was a longtime benefactor to the magazine. In 2006
The Nation supported Thomas's great-grandson, Ned Lamont, in his
unsuccessful campaign for the US Senate from Connecticut.

betterment which we seek must be accomplished, I believe, mainly through the national government...[and would involve] far more governmental interference with social and economic conditions than we have yet had, but I think we have got to face the fact that such increase is now necessary," *The Nation* attacked this "half-baked Rooseveltian Socialism."[48]

"The great question," proclaimed[49] *The Nation*, "is whether or not the old-time American sturdiness and common sense still have sufficient vitality to throw off this pseudo-socialist virus before it has done immeasurable mischief." The more immediate question, More wrote to a friend, is whether "Villard's influence will cheapen The Nation and deprive it of its unique quality."

Since his father's death in 1900 Oswald Garrison Villard had served a long apprenticeship, only becoming president of the Nation Company—effectively the magazine's publisher—in 1908. Slowly, however, he was beginning to make his influence felt. In 1910 Villard was part of a small group of black and white Americans including W.E.B. Du Bois and Ida Wells who founded[50] the National Association for the Advancement of Colored People (NAACP). Moorfield Storey, the veteran anti-imperialist campaigner (and frequent *Nation* contributor) was elected as the group's first president. Villard also pushed *The Nation* into endorsing Woodrow Wilson after being impressed with the Princeton president's efforts to abolish the elitist "eating clubs" from campus. A chance meeting on a cruise from Bermuda cemented the friendship between the two men.[51]

But in the four-way race among Wilson, the Republican incumbent William Howard Taft, Progressive Theodore Roosevelt and the Socialist candidate Eugene V. Debs, Wilson could also be defended as the conservative choice—which is precisely how *The Nation* explained matters: "Wilson and the Democratic party," the magazine assured its readers, will "preserve the ancient freedom and self-dependence of American citizens. Between this position and that of the Rooseveltians there is a deep gulf fixed. But between the Rooseveltians and a full-fledged socialistic state, taking under its wing all the economic activities of the nation, and leaving no standing ground for individual self-assertion and development, no man can erect any substantial barrier."

When More finally retired in March 1914, he managed to hand off *The Nation* to his friend Harold deWolf Fuller—another former professor, whose most notable accomplishment was the translation of a fourteenth-century Dutch legend. During Fuller's four years, *The Nation*'s persistent vegetative state reached a point where H.L. Mencken, writing in *The Baltimore Sun*, called it "perhaps the dullest publication of any sort ever printed in the world." Help, however, was close at hand. ✻

Oswald Garrison Villard

CHAPTER FOUR

Reluctant Radical

I n many ways, the man in the photograph[1] is exactly what he seems: a middle-aged patrician in a three-piece suit, expensive tie perfectly knotted, bottom button of his beautifully tailored waistcoat undone and, dangling just above to lend a note of intellectual distinction, a Phi Beta Kappa key on a gold chain. It is a portrait that, done in tasteful oils, would not look at all out of place on the walls of the Century Association or the University Club—the subject was a longstanding member of both, along with the Harvard Club and, when work took him to Washington, the Cosmos Club. Or perhaps in the vestibule of the New York Philharmonic, where his level gaze, only partly screened behind a pince-nez, could serve as a memento of his two years as that organization's president. The sense of dignified command conveyed by the bald head and trimmed moustache, the hands thrust firmly into pockets, are entirely what we might expect from the son of a railroad tycoon (as he was) or the owner of an iron mine (as he also was) or even the founder of *Yachting* magazine, as he also was.

Yet this portrait comes not from a club collection, or a newspaper society page, or a financial journal, but from the personal archive of W.E.B. Du Bois, the historian and civil rights activist who, with Oswald Garrison Villard, the man in the photograph, founded the NAACP as an alliance between the African-American-led Niagara Movement and a group of prominent white reformers. And if any members of the University happened to glance out of the club's windows onto Fifth Avenue on the morning of May 6, 1911, they might well have been surprised to see Oswald Garrison Villard, erect amid the jeers and the volleys of rotten eggs, marching with the Men's League for Women's Suffrage in a parade headed by his mother, Helen Frances Garrison Villard. Already president of the New York *Post* and *The Nation*, Villard inherited his wealth, along with his newspapers, from his father. Political courage, however, he had on both sides.

Before he became a tycoon, or an American, Henry Villard had been a "forty-eighter"—a partisan of the revolutionary uprising that swept Europe in 1848, led by students and intellectuals demanding national unity, democratic reforms and freedom of the press. Though only a teenager at the time, Ferdinand Heinrich Gustav Hilgard sided with his uncle, the head of the provisional Bavarian government, rather than with his father, a conservative judge, and when the revolutionary regime collapsed he changed his name and fled to America, arriving in 1853 with twenty dollars in his pocket. Supporting himself by writing for the German-language press that, with the coming of the forty-eighters, spread from New York to the Midwest (ten years later the young Joseph Pulitzer would follow a similar trajectory from Boston to St. Louis), Henry Villard covered the 1860 presidential campaign, the Colorado gold rush, and the Civil War battles of Bull Run, Shiloh and Missionary Ridge before the *New-York Tribune* sent him back to Germany as a correspondent.

His son Oswald was born in Weisbaden on March 13, 1872. During their stay Henry Villard was asked by a group of German investors to act as their American agent—and eventually gained control of the Northern Pacific railroad. As an 11-year-old, Oswald was taken in a chartered train to Gold Creek, Montana, to watch his father and former president Ulysses S. Grant drive in the "golden spike" completing the transcontinental line. Over the next few years Henry Villard waged a fierce battle for the Northern Pacific with Jay Gould, James J. Hill and other robber barons. Owning the *Post* gave him an extra lever, but after his empire unraveled, it didn't save Villard from having to sell the palatial set of six interlocking townhouses he'd just had built for his family. (The commission was the first in New York City for the young firm of McKim, Mead and White*, whose later work includes the Century and the University clubs, as well as the campus and many buildings at Columbia University.) On the other hand, Henry's

---

* Although Villard's family lived there for only a few months, the Villard Houses, as they are still known today, have been preserved and incorporated into the Palace Hotel, on Madison Avenue between Fiftieth and Fifty-first Streets. Their design was chiefly the work of Joe Wells, at the time a junior man in the office, whose senior partner, Charles Follen McKim, was the son of James Miller McKim, *The Nation*'s original benefactor.

early involvement with Thomas Edison, whom he helped to form the Edison General Electric Company—ancestor of today's GE—meant the family was never in danger of losing Thorwood Park, their mansion overlooking the Hudson at Dobbs Ferry, or that there was any question of Oswald going anywhere but Harvard.

Fanny Garrison Villard's influence on her son can be detected not just in his staunch feminism, but in his lifelong adherence to the temperance pledge she extracted from him as a teenager. As the only daughter of William Lloyd Garrison, Fanny inherited her father's disdain for compromise as well as his appetite for a good fight. "To modify any position she took for reasons of expediency was unthinkable," according to her son.[2] Though some contemporaries purported to detect a conflict in values between the editor of *The Liberator* and his buccaneering son-in-law, Oswald Garrison Villard always maintained that the two men "could hardly have been closer together."[3] So when, after a year wrestling with his master's thesis, he wrote to his father to say that teaching felt "like sitting in a club window and watching the world go by on the pavement outside," the elder Villard, while perhaps disappointed, couldn't have been terribly surprised.

Besides, in 1897 the staff at the *Post*, chafing under Godkin's absolute abhorrence at any hint of color, sentiment or interpretation in reporting, staged a mass exit to *The Commercial Advertiser*, a nearly defunct daily where they would be allowed to experiment with more literary forms of journalism. This created several openings—one of which the owner's son, fortified by six months' apprenticeship on the *Philadelphia Press*, soon occupied. Although an enthusiastic member of the Anti-Imperialist League, Villard at first played little role in determining policy either at the *Post* or *The Nation*. But slowly, particularly in *The Nation*, a new tone of respect began to appear in articles discussing civil rights. The claim[4] that "open discrimination against the negro as a voter cannot stop there. It really means discrimination against him as a man" might well have appeared under Godkin. But the magazine's argument that "the true implication of the exhortation to the colored men to give up their 'nonsense' about political right, and to turn to 'useful pursuits'" is the desire for "a subject class of willing or forced workers," though aimed partly at supporters of Booker T. Washington, was also an implicit criticism of *The Nation*'s accommodationist policy. And in the further claim that "wrapped up in the caste spirit which would shut the negro out from his political rights, is the intention to deny him his human rights," an attentive reader could detect a note of militancy that, if not entirely new, certainly had been long absent from the magazine.

W.E.B. Du Bois was one such reader, beginning a correspondence with Villard soon afterward. Both were proud men, and for Villard the shock of encountering a black man who was, like himself, a product of Harvard and of the German education system and who, from the very beginning of their acquaintance, treated him as an equal, must have been considerable. While it would be overstating matters to call them intimate friends, they became, and remained, close comrades. Both men entertained high hopes for the presidency of Woodrow Wilson, who during his campaign had written to black church leaders promising "they may count upon me for absolute fair dealing for everything by which I could assist in advancing the interests of their race."

Though sometimes described as being the president's chief adviser on race, in practice Villard's support for Wilson gained him access, but not influence—at least not on a matter the Virginia-born president judged might cost him the support of Southern Democrats in Congress. Du Bois, too, was optimistic, writing an open letter[5] to Wilson in March 1913 reminding the president "we black men by our votes helped to put you in your high position" and explaining the grounds for his belief that "while a Southerner in birth and tradition, you have escaped the provincial training of the South and you have not had burned into your soul desperate hatred and despising of your darker fellow men."

What did Du Bois want? "We want to be treated as men. We want to vote. We want our children educated. We want lynching stopped. We want no longer to be herded as cattle on street cars and railroads. We want the right to earn a living, to own our own property and to spend our income unhindered and uncursed." Instead Wilson fired black officials, allowed segregation to become the official policy of the Treasury and the Post Office, and held a special screening in the White House of *The Birth of a Nation*, D.W. Griffith's heroic portrayal of the origins of the Ku Klux Klan.

§

Despite his advanced views on race and women's suffrage, Oswald Garrison Villard entered Wilson's first term, and his own fifth decade, as a pillar of society. If he, and the papers he owned, remained dubious about America's overseas adventures, much the same could be said of the Democratic Party, whose platform in 1912 promised independence for the Philippines.

At home *The Nation* eventually reconciled itself to the idea of an income tax, though it argued for flat rather than progressive taxation, worrying[6] that "with the rule of a uniform rate abandoned, there is absolutely no principle that can serve as a guide." Indeed the magazine remained resolutely outside the Progressive ferment championed by Theodore Roosevelt and such reformers as Jane Addams, Walter Lippmann and Upton Sinclair. In part this is because Villard, like his predecessors, was still wary of any call for expanding the role of the state. Even the exploitation of children in sweatshops seemed[7] to *The Nation* less dangerous than establishing "a precedent of almost boundless potency for the assertion, as the occasion may present itself, of Federal authority over one department after another of the life of the people." Or as Villard put it in a 1908 letter to Lillian Wald, the founder of the Henry Street settlement, explaining why he was withdrawing his support from the Child Labor League: "this running to Washington for aid sets back local and state progress immeasurably."[8] *The Nation* had been suspicious of the Grangers, and opposed the Populists. And under More and Fuller the magazine remained actively hostile to any call for radical reform.

But there was also a difference of temperament, and priorities, between Villard and the Progressives, whose bold prescriptions were curiously silent when it came to racial discrimination, and in whose enthusiasm for the extension of state power, at home and abroad, Villard could detect little tolerance for dissent, and no deep commitment to civil liberties. Above all Villard distrusted the Progressives' belligerent confidence, their eagerness to use what Herbert Croly described as "Hamiltonian means" to achieve "Jeffersonian ends."[9]

Finally, though, it was his pacifism that set Villard, and *The*

Nation, on a course that took them far beyond the polite bounds of Progressive reform. "Does any statesman really foresee the chance of our engaging in hostilities with the German Empire, or with Russia, or with France?" the magazine asked[10] in September 1913. "Situated here on the Western Continent, at a remote distance from the age-old rivalries that make of Europe an armed camp, these United States are as unlikely to be the armed enemies of one European country as of any other."

The outbreak of war in Europe in August 1914 caught Villard by surprise. With Lillian Wald, Fanny Villard led 1,200 women in a Peace Parade[11] up Fifth Avenue. For her son, pacifist principle and sentimental and family ties to Germany made American entry into the war unthinkable. He also feared what he saw as the inevitable regimentation of a society mobilized for war. But as a newspaper owner in a city and country where the public was more receptive to the British point of view, Villard had to tread carefully. For a while, he resolved his problem by distinguishing between the German people—and German culture—and their rulers. "The Germany of the Kaiser, the Germany of militarism and the mailed fist is not the Germany the *Post* has sympathy for," he wrote in an editorial titled "The Real Crime Against Germany." Villard denounced Germany's violation of Belgian neutrality, blaming the Kaiser for starting the war. At the same time, he raged against British censorship.[12]

President Wilson, too, was determined to keep America out of the war—a position that brought the two men closer than ever. Editorials in both the *Post* and *The Nation* praising Wilson's "non-partisan attitude toward the belligerent nations" brought a note of thanks from the president for Villard's "generous spirit."

Firmly of the belief that to prepare for war is to prepare for war, Villard, encouraged by Wilson's dismissal of Roosevelt and other advocates of greater military spending as "nervous and excited," helped to found the League to Limit Armaments. The sinking of the passenger liner *Lusitania* by a German U-boat in May 1915 only sharpened the debate. Villard, who labeled the attack "a violation of the fundamental decencies of civilization," nonetheless assured his readers that Wilson would avoid a rash response. When Roosevelt accused "Professor Wilson" of taking his lead from "mollycoddles and flap-doodle pacifists," calling the sinking an act of piracy, Villard replied that he never doubted Roosevelt's credentials as an authority on piracy. And when Wilson, in a speech in Philadelphia, borrowed Villard's phrase in describing the country as "too proud to fight," the rapprochement was complete.[13]

Villard's influence was such that *The New York Times* even named him as a possible replacement for Colonel Edward House, Wilson's chief diplomatic adviser. The German announcement, in September 1915, that they were ending the policy of open submarine warfare against noncombatants seemed to both men like a vindication. Villard celebrated by running Wilson's picture on the front page of the *Post*—breaking a 114-year precedent—with the caption "The man who, without rattling a sword, won for civilization."

This second honeymoon was short-lived. One sour note was the occupation of Haiti by US Marines—ostensibly to restore order, but actually to protect the interests of the National City Bank, the principal American investor in the country. Though the NAACP journal *The Crisis*, edited by Du Bois, was the first American publication to puncture the pretense of benign neighborly assistance, *The Nation* was close behind, with Villard calling the occupation "imperialism of the rankest kind."[14] In October, when Wilson, under intense pressure, changed his mind about preparedness, Villard accused him of trying to scare the country "with veiled hints." By early 1916 Villard, who had been acting as chief Washington correspondent for the *Post*, was back in New York after realizing that White House resentment of his criticism made him a journalistic liability.

One new voice in support of the president was *The New Republic*, a weekly founded by Herbert Croly in 1914. Funded by Willard Straight, a partner at J.P. Morgan, and his wife Dorothy Whitney Straight, after they both read Croly's *The Promise of American Life*, *The New Republic* was from the first a guide and mouthpiece for Progressivism, far friendlier to the cause of organized labor than *The Nation*, and far less abashed about the use of government for progressive ends. Initially opposed to war, Croly and his colleagues Walter Weyl and Walter Lippmann increasingly came to feel that by remaining on the sidelines America was in danger of losing influence. Lippmann in particular began to develop the idea that this was "a new kind of war" which it was America's responsibility to lead. With Straight active in the Mayor's Committee on National Defense—a mainstay of the Preparedness movement—and also acting as US purchasing agent for the French and British governments, Wilson's harder line was warmly welcomed by *The New Republic*. Under a covering barrage of euphemisms like "aggressive pacifism" and "differential neutrality," Lippmann and Croly began to prod the president toward a declaration of war. Their magazine, in turn, acquired a host of new readers, with the circulation rising from 874 copies of the first issue to 15,000 at the end of the first year.[15]

Though Woodrow Wilson campaigned for re-election on the slogan "He kept us out of war," both *The Nation* and *The New Republic* were convinced that war was at hand. Lippmann, who had grown increasingly impatient, engineered his magazine's endorsement for Wilson—and was joined not just by those dubbed "war intellectuals" by his colleague Randolph Bourne, but by Bourne himself, along with Jane Addams, John Dewey, Max Eastman, Lincoln Steffens and Lillian Wald. *The Nation*, like the *Post*, also endorsed Wilson. But Villard couldn't bring himself to vote for the man he had come to despise, instead seeking "refuge with the Prohibitionists."[16]

Villard still didn't see himself as an outsider. Not yet. In March 1917 he phoned Josephus Daniels, a North Carolina newspaperman serving as Wilson's secretary of the navy, to complain that if the administration's new censorship bill passed "he might go to jail." Daniels replied: "In some circles your being put in jail would be a very popular act."[17] After April 6—when in response to Germany's resumption of unrestricted submarine warfare and the disclosure of the Zimmermann telegram proposing a military alliance with Mexico against the United States, Congress finally declared war on Germany—those circles grew to include most of the country. David Lawrence, the *Post*'s new Washington correspondent, told Villard the administration was preparing a special concentration camp just for him.

That was a joke, but when his neighbors started calling him "the Kaiser" and his children heard their "pro-German" father insulted at school—even his dachshund was attacked—Villard stopped laughing. "Cut" at his clubs, Villard was asked to resign his presidency of the Philharmonic. As even such charter members of the League to Limit Armaments as Rabbi Benjamin Wise and Columbia president Nicholas Murray Butler announced their support for the war, and a host of American Socialists followed their European comrades into what they had all condemned as a capitalist war, Villard regrouped, but he never retreated.

Instead he attacked on two fronts. The first was civil liberties. "The right to criticize the Government is never more vital than in war time," he wrote. For nearly a decade members of the Industrial Workers of the World (IWW), or Wobblies, had waged a series of losing, often brutal, battles over the right to free speech with barely a discouraging word from *The Nation*, which whatever its slow-growing tolerance for labor unions had no affection for what it called "the gospel of violence." At the same time, and with even less notice from *The Nation*, Emma Goldman and Margaret Sanger had been repeatedly arrested, and sometimes imprisoned, for distributing information about birth control.[18] Villard now recognized that the 1917 Espionage Act—which gave Albert Burleson, the Texas postmaster general who had made racial segregation the rule in his department, the power to suppress "subversive" publications—put him, and *The Nation*, on the side of the outlaws.

And not just political radicals. In his third message to Congress[19]—before war had even been declared—Wilson identified "the gravest threats to our national peace and safety" as coming from Americans "born under other flags, but welcomed under our generous naturalization laws" who "have poured the poison of disloyalty into the very arteries of our national life." Once American

troops joined the fighting, tempers on the home front grew shorter. In Benton, Illinois, a woman accused of being pro-German was
ridden out of town on a rail; in Montana a member of the IWW
executive committee was lynched by a masked mob.

Despite the dangers, Villard kept pressing for what Wilson
himself had once promised the country, "a peace without victory." Though Villard, and *The Nation*, greeted Wilson's "Fourteen
Points" in January 1918 making free trade, open agreements, and
democracy and self-determination America's official war aims, Villard also praised "those amazing men, Lenin and Trotsky," whose
revolutionary victory brought Russia out of the war. Villard's refusal to join Wilson's crusade set him apart from every other editor
in New York—including many of his own employees. Deciding to
concentrate his efforts, and lift some of the financial burden, he
fired Harold de Wolf Fuller on January 18, 1918, and took over
at *The Nation*. He also decided to sell the *Post*—but before he did
he forced the paper, against the wishes of its editor, to publish in
full the secret treaties detailing the sordid backroom deals made
among France (which claimed Alsace, Lorraine and the other ter-
ritories lost in the Franco-Prussian War), England (which coveted
Germany's African colonies), Italy (Istria and Dalmatia) and Japan
(which had been promised China's Shantung peninsula). Discovered by the Bolsheviks, who released them in an effort to expose
the war as little more than a capitalist looting spree, the treaties,
Villard said, had been given to him by a Russian sailor who smug-
gled them past the censors under his shirt.

Though Villard had the treaties bound into a pamphlet and
distributed to every member of Congress, only nine other papers

picked up his scoop. Walter Weyl tried to persuade *The New Republic* to publish the treaties, and when Lippmann and Croly balked, wrote a critical editorial, "Tired Radicals," which they also refused to publish. *The New York Times* denounced the release—the WikiLeaks of its day—as "beyond the pale," warning that any nation capable of such an "act of dishonor" would "not stop at…confiscating all property of nationals and foreigners alike."[20] In July Villard sold the *Post*—or as the White House had come to view it, the "whipping *Post*"—to Thomas Lamont, a Morgan partner and Wilson ally. Radicalized by the war, Villard, and *The Nation*, were now free.

§

The first item in "The Week" of September 21, 1918,[21] was an apology: "We deeply regret that last week's issue of *The Nation* is detained by the Post Office." The problem was an article by Albert Jay Nock attacking the Wilson administration for sending Samuel Gompers to a conference of Labor and Socialist parties meeting in England. The immigrant cigar worker who had risen from the sweatshops of the Lower East Side to the head of the American Federation of Labor had never been a favorite of *The Nation*. The magazine had opposed his campaign for the eight-hour day, his support for the Chinese Exclusion Act, and his enthusiasm for the Spanish-American War—mostly from a position to the right of Gompers, who did, however, join the Anti-Imperialist League in protest over the war in the Philippines. In 1915 *The Nation* painted a pen-portrait[22] of the labor leader. The result was not pretty: "Note the big head, heavy foreign features, and burly frame. His face is as hard as a mask. His voice has nothing winsome in it. His manner is forbidding."

Now that Villard was turning *The Nation* to the left, Gompers was too tepid, too hostile to socialism, and too bound to Woodrow Wilson to be a satisfactory voice for America's workers. In Nock's depiction[23] Gompers was little more than a traveling salesman sent "to shepherd the erring brethren of alleged pacifist tendency back into the way they should go." Nock, whose two years at *The Nation* were a brief rest stop on his journey to the wilder shores of right-wing libertarianism, was meant to be the nucleus of a team of young writers Villard and his new managing editor, Henry R. Mussey, hired to help drag the magazine, and its brand of liberalism, into the twentieth century. That August Villard and Nock had joined to condemn the American military expedition to Siberia—part of the Allied intervention on the side of the White army in the Russian Civil War: "The President has assured us that it is only to be a little intervention, and we are to forgive it…on the grounds of its littleness."

But if that criticism, like the intervention itself, went largely unnoticed, *The Nation*'s seizure by the Post Office did not. Villard maintained a pretense of outraged innocence but was secretly delighted. Suddenly everyone was talking about this subversive sheet. Nor did they have to wait long for a look, since after personal interventions from Colonel House, Secretary of the Interior Franklin Lane (a friend of Villard) and the president's private secretary Joseph Tumulty, Wilson himself lifted the ban within a few days. In a letter to William Lamar, the Post Office solicitor responsible for the seizure, Villard thanked him for a "splendid advertisement" he reckoned was worth at least $100,000 in free publicity.[24] *The Nation*'s circulation, which had fallen from a high of 12,000 in the Godkin era to an anemic 7,200 in 1918, rocketed to more than 38,000 during the next two years.

Nor were all of Godkin's new hires as eccentric* as Nock. Mussey had been a Barnard economics professor until his opposition to the war cost him his job. Upon hearing that a similar fate had befallen Emily Balch, a former Wellesley professor, Villard hired her to work on the magazine's new International Relations section (IRS). Started in October 1918, the IRS was Villard's response to what he felt was the screen of propaganda and censorship—on issues ranging from German culpability to the nature of the Bolshevik regime—keeping the American media from reporting the truth about overseas developments. Functioning as a paper version of what would today be called an aggregator, it reprinted and digested articles from the foreign press alongside comments by *Nation* staff and other contributors. Tomas Masaryk, the future president of Czechoslovakia, was an early contributor, as was the South African statesman Jan Smuts, who gave Villard an exclusive when the IRS published his draft plan for a League of Nations. In March 1919 the IRS published the manifesto of the Spartacist uprising in Germany, whose signers included Rosa Luxembourg, Karl Leibknecht, Franz

---

* During Nock's employment he refused to let his editors know his home address. Nock's *Nation* salary was actually paid for by Francis Neilson, a former British Liberal MP who was married to the packing heiress Helen Swift. Nock and his patron were both devotees of the "single tax" philosophy of Henry George, whose bestselling book *Progress and Poverty* (1879), which held that a tax on the value of land was the best way to economic justice and prosperity, was long considered an American riposte to Marx's *Capital* (1867). Unable to recruit Villard, in 1920 Neilson took Nock and his $30,000-a-year subvention and started *The Freeman*, a libertarian magazine. Nock's last benefactor was the Texas oil magnate William F. Buckley Sr.; *National Review*, the magazine started by his son, inherited many of *The Freeman*'s contributors.

Mehring, and Clara Zetkin. The editors appended a brief note: "The first two have been murdered. Mehring has died."[25]

Though Balch moved on to found the Women's International League for Peace and Freedom—for which she was awarded the Nobel Peace Prize in 1946—her assistant, a 23-year-old Barnard graduate, who soon took over responsibility for the section, would have a lasting impact on *The Nation*. Freda Kirchwey had been fired from her job clipping "fillers"—small news items—at the *Tribune* as part of a wholesale purge after her boss, Ernest Gruening, had published a photograph of a recent lynching in the South side by side with a photo of African-American soldiers, newly returned from France, parading down Fifth Avenue. A former student of Mussey's, she'd written to him: "If you think I'm the man for the job, will you put in a word for me?" It probably didn't hurt that Villard was a friend of her father's—or that she was a suffragist, a member of the Women's Peace Party, and just the previous spring had been part of a women's delegation demonstrating in front of the Capitol in Washington. Villard offered her $25 a week. Gruening joined *The Nation* soon afterward.

What was it like working in such a hive of activism? The section, Kirchwey recalled, "was housed in the 'barn'—an area covering the entire fourth floor of a small loft building that adjoined the *Post* building in which *The Nation*'s main offices were located. You walked from one into the other through a fire door, permanently latched open. The 'barn' had no divisions except those marked off by desks and rows of filing and book cases. The lighting was poor and the walls grimy."

"I read reports and documents in English from uncounted

countries. I read newspapers in equal numbers. I also clipped and filed in high filing cases everything of possible editorial value from the whole English-language press, and woe to me if a cutting (we called them 'cuttings' for some Anglophilic reason) needed by my boss or by any other editor could not be quickly exhumed." Kirchwey's friend Alma Wertheim, whose husband, the investment banker Maurice Wertheim, was a *Nation* investor, often came in to help—which may make her the first *Nation* intern!

Kirchwey's and Balch's boss was William MacDonald, a former Brown history professor who, stranded in France on sabbatical by the war, became *The Nation*'s special correspondent. Though Villard personally covered the Peace Conference in Paris, it was McDonald who wrote "The Madness at Versailles,"[26] the editorial that launched *The Nation*'s most blistering attack ever on Woodrow Wilson, for his role in negotiating the peace treaty it branded "an international crime." The "world's masses," wrote MacDonald, had made the American president "their idol as well as their friend and guide…. How Mr. Wilson has repaid the confidence which the peoples gave him, all the world now knows. The one-time idol of democracy stands today discredited and condemned…not a friend faithful to the last, but an arrogant autocrat and a compromising politician." Only John Dos Passos's description, in his novel *1919*, of Clemenceau, Lloyd George and Wilson as "three old men shuffling the pack, dealing out the cards" rivals MacDonald for bitter disillusion.

Fighting Senate ratification of the treaty and against the League of Nations was only one of *The Nation*'s battles in the 1920s—but it was the one that made the oddest coalition, with Villard, Senator Robert M. La Follette and, eventually, *The New*

Republic on the left joining hands with Senator Henry Cabot Lodge and his fellow isolationist Republican Philander C. Knox on the right. When friends challenged him on his new bedfellows, Villard responded that the others had come over "to our side." Besides, in the fraught atmosphere of the times Villard needed allies. In 1919, after a series of anarchist bombings, including one targeting the home of Attorney General A. Mitchell Palmer, the Justice Department launched a sweeping crackdown on radicals of all stripes. Directed by the 24-year-old J. Edgar Hoover, the raids devastated the IWW. Hundreds of foreign-born activists, including Emma Goldman, were deported without trial. Five Socialists elected to the New York State Assembly were expelled by the legislature. *The Nation* and the new American Civil Liberties Union—whose founder, Roger Baldwin, was a frequent *Nation* contributor—protested, but *The Washington Post*'s comment, "There is no time to waste on hairsplitting over infringement of liberties," was more typical of the press response.

Villard's *Nation* also pushed against the boundaries of traditional gender roles. "These Modern Women"—a series of seventeen anonymous essays by "women active in professional and public life"—showcased changing attitudes about "men, marriage, children and jobs." An earlier series, "New Morals for Old," included essays by Bertrand Russell, Charlotte Perkins Gilman, H.L. Mencken and Floyd Dell—former editor of the Greenwich Village radical journal *The Masses*, which had been shut down by wartime censorship—who asked,[27] "Can Men And Women Be Friends?" Ludwig Lewisohn, *The Nation*'s drama critic, put theory into practice, living a love life so scandalous that his thinly novelized memoir,

The Case of Mr. Crump, was banned from America despite a blurb from Sigmund Freud himself, who called it "an incomparable masterpiece." (Twenty years later a much-abridged version became a bestseller under the title *The Tyranny of Sex*.)[28] Literary editor Carl Van Doren, who passed the job on to his younger brother, the poet Mark Van Doren*, kept standards high in the back of the book. But Villard sometimes found the younger Van Doren's enthusiasms trying. When he printed a poem by Babette Deutsch that contained the line "as dozing bitches break their dream to bark," Villard objected to "this new poetical license," adding that he found some of the magazine's poetry "execrable."[29]

Nor did *The Nation* neglect events outside America's borders. In 1920 it sent James Weldon Johnson, author of "Lift Ev'ry Voice and Sing" and newly elected executive secretary of the NAACP (the first nonwhite to hold that position) to report on conditions in Haiti. His four-part exposé,[30] "Self-Determining Haiti" described a brutal military occupation "Of, By and For the National City Bank." In 1928 Villard cabled Carleton Beals, who had reported on the Mexican revolution for *The Nation*, to find out what the US Marines were doing in Nicaragua: "CAN YOU PROCEED IMMEDIATELY NICARAGUA FOR NATION SENDING EXCLUSIVE STORIES AMERICAN POLICY MARINE RULE POPULAR FEELING ETCETERA, REACHING SANDINO IF POSSIBLE. TRIP POSSIBLY OCCUPY A MONTH. CAN OFFER A HUNDRED A WEEK

---

* In 1939 Carl's biography *Benjamin Franklin* won the Pulitzer Prize; Mark had to wait till the following year, when he won for his *Collected Poems*.

AND EXPENSES. WIRE COLLECT." Beal's account of his trek through the jungle, and his exclusive interview with Augusto Sandino, made headlines around the world.

And of course there was always Russia. In November 1927, on the tenth anniversary of the Revolution, *The Nation* devoted a whole issue to "The Land of Hope"—but Villard was not listed among the contributors. Though the *World* labeled *The Nation* "distinctly Bolshevistic," the position of the magazine, and its editor, was far more ambivalent. As early as 1920 *The Nation* featured[31] Bertrand Russell's growing disquiet: "I went to Russia believing myself a communist; but contact with those who have no doubts has intensified a thousandfold my own doubts, not only of communism, but of every creed so firmly held that for its sake men are willing to inflict widespread misery." Villard repeatedly called for diplomatic recognition of the Soviet government, and often expressed admiration for the energy of the Russian people and the vitality of the Soviet economy—which to many observers offered a pointed contrast with America's laissez-faire approach to the miseries of the Great Depression—but he also made it clear[32] that for liberals a government that resorted to "the methods of a Caesar, a Cromwell, a Franz Joseph, a Nicholas and a Mussolini" could never be acceptable. After spending a month visiting the country with the American-Soviet Chamber of Commerce, Villard remained[33] unconvinced: "For myself I can see no compromise on this question, no argument which shatters the intensity of my belief that those who take the sword shall perish by the sword." At the same time Villard allowed Louis Fischer, one of Stalin's most energetic apologists, to remain as *The Nation*'s Moscow correspondent.

But then Villard's *Nation*, unlike Godkin's, was a venue for open, spirited debate between radicals and liberals on a whole range of issues. Where there was unanimity—as, for example, on the shared revulsion at the execution of the Italian-American anarchists Nicola Sacco and Bartolomeo Vanzetti—*The Nation* spoke[34] with great power: "Massachusetts has triumphantly killed an Italian fishmonger and an Italian cobbler, but she has blackened the name of the United States across all the seas." Where there was controversy, Villard let it run. Perhaps the best example of his forbearance was when, returning from his annual summer holiday, Villard found that the magazine had published an editorial[35] by MacDonald arguing "no man has a moral right to close the doors of a building which he does not use." With New York facing (not for the last time) an acute shortage of affordable housing, "the municipal government should not hesitate to take possession, fix a fair rental, and let the people in." Though such a policy could have cost him a house, Villard never uttered a word of reproach (in his memoirs he admitted it "bowled me over when I saw it").

§

Separated by a widening gulf of years from the concerns of his young staff, as the roaring twenties gave way to the terrifying thirties, Villard also found himself increasingly out of step at *The Nation*. At a time when many on the left were wondering if even socialism was sufficiently strong medicine for America's flailing economy—or whether, as John Dos Passos said, to support the Socialists in the present crisis was like drinking near beer—Villard remained resolutely liberal. In 1928, despite loathing Herbert Hoover, he'd been unable to choose between Democrat Al Smith, whom he faulted both for his ties to Tammany Hall and his opposition to Prohibition, and the Socialist Party candidate Norman Thomas. And Thomas had been a *Nation* contributing editor at the time! In 1932 the magazine did manage to endorse Thomas—as did *The New Republic*, W.E.B. Du Bois, George Gershwin and a host of *Nation* contributors.

But by 1932 the thunder was on the left. Mussolini—whose rise to power in Italy had been cheered by Paul Elmer More's Harvard mentor, Irving Babbitt, as well as William Randolph Hearst (who gave the *Duce* a column in his newspapers) and even the veteran muckraker Lincoln Steffens—never fooled Villard. *The Nation* was one of the first American publications to sound the alarm against fascism. As for Hitler, Villard wrote an entire book[*] warning that should he come to power "the loss to Germany would be incredible." When Hitler did become Chancellor, Villard wrote "if something should remove him now, some accident, it might mean the saving of millions of lives."[36] But waiting for an accident—or a miracle—was hardly an answer to Nazism. Many *Nation* contributors, including Newton Arvin, Granville Hicks, Sidney Hook and Matthew Josephson joined *New Republic* colleagues Malcolm Cowley and Edmund Wilson in endorsing William Z. Foster and the Communist Party.

Once in office the improvisational daring of Franklin Delano Roosevelt's first hundred days astonished many of his critics on the left, including those at *The Nation*, which soon became one of the New Deal's loudest, and most reliable, cheerleaders. But like Moses,

---

[*] *The German Phoenix: The Story of the Republic* (1933)

who was allowed to glimpse the Promised Land from the mountaintop but not to enter, Oswald Garrison Villard would not really be a part of that. In 1933 the man they called "O.G.V.," or simply "the boss" turned over editorial control of *The Nation* to a "board of editors" made up of Freda Kirchwey, the literary critic Joseph Wood Krutch, the magazine's literary editor Henry Hazlitt and Mauritz Hallgren, who had reported extensively for the magazine on the impact of the Depression. In 1934 Villard, whose response to fascism was to withdraw further into isolationism, put *The Nation* up for sale.

A year earlier Maurice Wertheim, a longtime backer of the magazine, had offered Villard $50,000—but Villard turned him down. In all the years he'd owned it, *The Nation* broke even precisely once: in 1927. The following year it had even turned a small profit.[37] But that was before the Depression, when circulation floated above 40,000 and the magazine was flush with advertising. Villard briefly considered selling to Raymond Moley, a member of Roosevelt's "Brains Trust" who was becoming increasingly critical of the New Deal, but the rumor alone prompted two editors to resign. So when Wertheim repeated his interest—this time offering only $25,000—Villard agreed. The man who "made more acres of public men acutely miserable per unit of circulation than any other editor alive" agreed to stay on as a contributor. For the moment.[38] *

Freda Kirchwey

CHAPTER FIVE

A Practical Utopian

O f the four editors who took charge of *The Nation* on its sale to Maurice Wertheim, it would have been a very rash—or astute—gambler who picked Freda Kirchwey to end up as editor in chief. Not only because she was the sole member of the board to have been voted "best looking" by her college classmates. Mauritz Hallgren, the youngest of the four, had been a reporter for the *Chicago Tribune* and a member of the United Press Berlin bureau before joining *The Nation* in 1930 as an associate editor. Henry Hazlitt, who started out at the *Wall Street Journal* as a teenager, then became financial editor of the *New York Evening Mail*, had also been literary editor of the New York *Sun* before taking a similar post at *The Nation.* By 1934 Joseph Wood Krutch, *The Nation*'s drama critic, had already published three books—one of them the bestselling collection *The Modern*

Temper. Hazlitt and Hallgren were also published authors—and if
H.L. Mencken hadn't picked Hazlitt to succeed him as editor of
The American Mercury, it might well have been *The Nation*'s pages
where, in 1938, he announced the advent of the Austrian economist Ludwig von Mises, calling his work "the most devastating
analysis of socialism yet penned." Instead Hazlitt[*] was replaced by
Ernest Gruening, who left shortly afterward to become editor of
the *New York Post*.

Older by a few months than Krutch, the senior man on
the board, Freda Kirchwey had written no books—though *The
Nation* series she'd edited on "Our Changing Morality" had been
published as a collection. Like Hazlitt and Krutch, and unlike
Godkin or Villard, Kirchwey was interested in current literature
as well as current events. As a student at Barnard—where she'd
also been voted "most popular," "most famous in the future," and
"most militant" in recognition of her fervor as a pacifist and a
suffragette—she'd written poems and short stories. And though
she'd originally been hired to work on *The Nation*'s International
Relations section, in 1927 she replaced Mark Van Doren as literary editor. Krutch, who had come to respect her greatly, wrote to
Villard pledging his "oath of fealty," to his new boss: "the King
has abdicated—long live the Queen!"[1]

---

[*]   After a conflict with Alfred Knopf, the *Mercury*'s publisher, Hazlitt's career
took him to *The New York Times*, where he became a columnist as well as the
paper's chief editorial writer on economics. He continued to promote the work
of von Mises and his fellow émigré Friedrich Hayek, whose *Road to Serfdom*
he reviewed favorably in the *Times*. Along with former *Nation* colleagues
Albert Jay Nock and Suzanne La Follette, Hazlitt edited *The Freeman* before
ending up, from the 1950s onward, as a contributor to *National Review*.

But it wasn't just the simple fact of her sex that set Kirchwey apart from her male peers. For one thing being a woman editor at a national weekly turned out to be far from simple. Even before she arrived at *The Nation* Kirchwey—whose husband, Evans Clark, was at the time employed by the American Fund for Public Service (better known as the Garland Fund after its benefactor, Wall Street heir Charles Garland)—had already given birth to, and buried, her first child. Brewster Clark lived just eight months. In 1918, when she took over at the IRS, she was seven months pregnant with her second child. As the visibly very pregnant Kirchwey carried on "strolling around the office, interviewing foreign authors" a flustered Villard would sometimes introduce her as "Miss Freda Kirchwey, but she is really Mrs. Evans Clark." Despite such occasional awkwardnesses, Villard "let me stay at work right up until my baby was born." However, she wrote, "I think I'd have gotten a lot more satisfaction out of having a baby if I'd taken some time off. It was very hard." [2]

Instead she was back at work within a month, and for the next nine months every day at noon she walked from the *Nation* office across the Brooklyn Bridge to her apartment on Montague Street to nurse her son. In 1922, pregnant again, she was made managing editor, partly at the urging of associate editor Norman Thomas. Though she found her third pregnancy "blankedly uncomfortable" her new job, which required her to act as "planner, editor, contact man, traffic manager" and several other functions left her little time to rest. Indeed she was writing to Villard on magazine business within thirty-six hours of the delivery, promising, "I'm not going to let it hurt the Nation." A nurse-

maid and a daily cleaner allowed Kirchwey again to return speed-
ily to work, where she overcame Villard's objections to the introduction of cartoons into the magazine, and organized a series of
special issues, including one commemorating the sixth anniversary of the Russian Revolution and, in 1926, a *Nation* symposium
on "Wages for Wives." She also joined Heterodoxy, a feminist
discussion group whose founder, Marie Jenney Howe, had been
arrested in the postwar Red Scare. Other members included the
novelist Charlotte Perkins Gilman, dancer Agnes De Mille, journalist Ruth Hale and Rose Pastor Stokes, one of the founders of
the American Communist Party.

But when, in the winter of 1930, her 8-year-old son, Jeffrey,
came home from boarding school with tuberculosis, she took a
leave of absence from *The Nation* to journey, alone with the boy,
to Sarasota, Florida, to try and nurse him back to health. Though
she kept up a correspondence with her husband, who remained
at his job, and with Villard, the sheer exhaustion of three months
of round-the-clock nursing left her completely drained. After Jeffrey failed to improve, she brought him back to New York, where
he died in March. The following January, Kirchwey was still too
grief-stricken to work; Villard, who had kept her on the masthead
as an associate editor, moved her name to the list of contributing
editors. She wrote the odd book review, and entered psychoanal-
ysis. When she finally felt able to return, in 1932, Villard was so
pleased to have her back he initially promised her $100 a week—a
considerable salary at the height of the Depression—later reduced
to $90 because it might "make trouble in the office" if she were
paid more than Krutch or Hazlitt.

In her approach to politics Kirchwey represented something new. For E.L. Godkin the great cause had first been Reconstruction—the fight to gain justice for the freed slaves. Later he, and *The Nation*, gravitated toward free trade and civil service reform. Yet Godkin was neither government employee nor merchant nor former slave. For Oswald Garrison Villard the sense of *noblesse oblige* behind his political commitments was even more pronounced. There may have been a similar element prompting the daughter of George Washington Kirchwey, dean of the Columbia Law School and reforming warden at Sing Sing prison (and himself the child of forty-eighters) toward pacifism. But when Freda Kirchwey marched for votes for women, she marched as a woman; when her cause embraced compromises or resorted to opportunistic methods to gain power, she responded not as an idealist but as a feminist. "A Suffrage campaign," she wrote, "is no place for a moralist."

This dual focus on practical politics and a utopian vision allowed Kirchwey, and *The Nation*, to survive—and thrive—during the most politically turbulent decades in modern American history. It was, she soon realized, a quality she shared with Franklin Roosevelt. It was also a constant cause of friction with some of her contemporaries.

§

From the very beginnings of the New Deal *The Nation* positioned itself firmly on the president's left. During his Hundred Days, Roosevelt moved quickly to stabilize the banking system, instituting a bank holiday, closing failed banks and recapitalizing those that remained. But this bailout—most of which had been drawn up by Herbert Hoover's advisers—was not bold enough for *The Nation*, which ran an article[3] by Norman Thomas outlining "A

Socialist Program for Banking." Interestingly, Thomas does not call for nationalizing all banks. "Given the practical and psychological hold of capitalist finance on our existing order, I have grave doubts" such a measure would be possible, he wrote. Instead he proposed regulating privately owned banks in return for guaranteeing deposits (a measure later instituted by FDR) but also establishing a system of publicly owned state and municipal banks, plus a national Post Office savings system (as had long existed in Britain) that would assume the assets of any banks requiring federal assistance.

Nor was *The Nation* satisfied with what it saw as the president's sluggish efforts on social welfare. Instead of hailing the Social Security Act of 1935 as the landmark it now seems, *The Nation* highlighted[4] the compromises that had occurred between the bold original proposal and the final legislation, pointing out such deficiencies as the exclusion of agricultural and domestic workers from coverage, and arguing that by requiring coverage to be "self-sustaining" the program effectively billed workers twice—once to cover their own contributions, and then again to pay, either in higher prices or lower wages, for the contributions made by their employers. As FDR prepared to campaign for re-election, *The Nation*, in what would become a long tradition of curbing its enthusiasm even for the most politically sympathetic elected officials, summed up[5] his first term as "Roosevelt's Hollow Triumph." In love with planning, like much of the American left at the time, *The Nation* did salute the Tennessee Valley Authority and the president's experiments in public power (rural electrification being almost as important to Roosevelt as it was to Lenin), which it labeled "the best of New Deal measures."

Still, the magazine's failure to endorse Roosevelt's Socialist opponent in 1936 probably owed more to that party being split between the Old Guard, backed by the needle-trade unions in New York, and the Militants, led by the radical pacifist (and former *Nation* editor) Norman Thomas, than to any great enthusiasm for the president. The Socialist split, like all left-wing faction fights, was an over-determined mix of personal motives, political differences and power struggles. Initially *The Nation* had good relations with both sides. In 1932, as the split was beginning, the *Jewish Daily Forward*, the organ and principal weapon of the Old Guard (and a significant source of income for the party) actually loaned *The Nation* $5,000.[6] However, Thomas's positions—and his willingness, at least for a period, to enter into coalitions with Communists, Trotskyists and others on the left—were much more in line with *The Nation*'s view of what the times required. Events abroad would eventually make such collaboration impossible. But with Roosevelt courting business support, *The Nation* worried[7] that the New Deal might be coming to a premature end. Arguing that too much remained to be accomplished at home to back a third party—especially given the Socialists' disarray—*The Nation* tepidly endorsed FDR. Kirchwey, though, voted for Norman Thomas. As did Villard—one of the last times they agreed.

Villard and his successors were in harmony, however, about the danger posed by the rise of fascism—in Europe and at home. Villard retained a column in the magazine, and he used it repeatedly to attack Father Charles Coughlin, a Catholic priest whose broadcasts from Michigan's Shrine of the Little Flower gave him a national audience, and whose magazine, *Social Justice*, took over from

Henry Ford's *Dearborn Independent* as the voice of American anti-Semitism. Pointing out[8] "the fascist technique" behind Coughlin's attack on New Deal labor legislation, and the dictator's fist hidden inside the demagogic glove of Louisiana Senator Huey Long's "Share the Wealth" program, *The Nation* warned[9] that both movements, "for all their glamorous radical sound, are capitalist radicalism."

The Nation was also one of the earliest—and loudest—voices acknowledging that Germany's anti-Semitic Nuremberg Laws, passed in September 1935, which excluded Jews from German citizenship and made marriage, or sexual relations, between Germans and non-Aryans illegal, would have repercussions far beyond that country's borders. Kirchwey and her colleagues—none of them Jewish—were among the few American journalists to recognize that for Europe's Jews the choice was now between emigration and death. One reason the stakes—so glaringly obvious in hindsight—remained so long unacknowledged is indicated by the response to *The Nation*'s suggestion, on the eve of the *Kristallnacht* pogrom[10], that the United States "ought to do more" to take in the refugees. Surely, asked[11] Kirchwey, "a nation of 130 million could absorb" an additional 50,000 to 75,000 immigrants "without economic disaster." To which modest proposal Henry Pratt Fairchild, a professor at New York University and a founder of Planned Parenthood, wrote[*] indignantly: "Do you mean to add a certain number of refugees to the ten or twelve million American residents already unemployed

---

[*]   Perhaps as a kindness to Fairchild, a *Nation* contributor and ally of Margaret Sanger, the magazine did not publish his letter.

or in the relief rolls?"[12] Like Oswald Garrison Villard, who was
certain that Hitler must be stopped—and equally certain that the
United States should stay out of any European conflict—the fate of
European Jewry was deplored in the abstract by statesmen on both
sides of the Atlantic whose compassion for the Jews' suffering was
exceeded only by their determination not to do anything about it.

By 1937 Kirchwey had authority over the magazine's signed
articles, while Max Lerner, a professor at Sarah Lawrence College,
had been hired by Wertheim to write editorials. Margaret Marshall,
the new literary editor, was friendly with a whole group of writers,
soon to be based at *Partisan Review*, who were as devoted to literary
modernism as they were opposed to Stalinism (many of the group,
though not all, remained loyal to Trotsky). With no single person
in charge, it sometimes must have seemed as if *The Nation* was suffering from multiple personality disorder. From week to week its
editorial attitude to the New Deal oscillated between "too little, too
late" and the realization of progressive (and Progressive) hopes for
harnessing the power of government for the general welfare.

The Nation's attitude toward Trotsky and Stalin was even more
confusing. In October 1936 it published an editorial[13] denouncing
the first Soviet purge trial as "conducted in a manner foreign to
democratic ideals of justice" and calling the "conduct of the gov-
ernment-controlled press…particularly shocking." Casting doubt
on the confessions of Trotsky's supposed fellow conspirators, the
editorial said the former head of the Red Army "was entitled to his
day in court." The same issue carried a letter from Trotsky himself
explaining how his recent *Nation* report[14] on the political situation
in France got him in trouble with passport officials in Norway,

where he was then living in exile. The issue also featured a long dispatch[15] from Louis Fischer that made no mention of the trials at all! But then Fischer, writing from Kiev, also managed to produce a paean to Soviet agriculture—in which "tractors and combines are ubiquitous," and "the peasantry never ate so well as it eats now." This from Ukraine, where millions had died from Stalin's induced famine[16] just a few years earlier—also unmentioned by Fischer.

Yet it was another controversy entirely that finally drove Maurice Wertheim to despair. For all its reservations about the New Deal's limited ambition, *The Nation* remained a staunch defender of Roosevelt's "bold, persistent experimentation." As early as the summer of 1933 Paul Y. Anderson, a frequent *Nation* contributor who had won a Pulitzer Prize for his role exposing the Teapot Dome scandal for the *St. Louis Post-Dispatch*, wondered[17] what might happen if the Supreme Court ruled the New Deal unconstitutional. Noting that there were "at least three reactionary old men on that bench who would take profound pleasure in standing by their plutocratic concepts of society," Anderson suggested "Congress could pass an act requiring members of the court to retire on passing the age of retirement." Alternatively "the size of the court could be increased by law to permit the appointment of additional Justices." So when, four years later, Roosevelt proposed to do both, it should have surprised no one that *The Nation* backed him, urging[18] fellow "progressives" to "overcome…the myth of Supreme Court divinity." Not only did the magazine call the president's "attack on government by senility" a "brilliant tour de force"—it printed a list of six judges[*] it hoped might be used to "pack" the court! "What Is *The Nation* Coming To?" asked[19] a horrified Villard, while Wertheim, in a rare, bylined piece[20] by the magazine's owner, wrote "it is unthinkable that a progressive and liberal journal should actually advocate any plan by which new judges are placed on our supreme tribunal who will decide cases on instructions."

Though couched in constitutional terms, the debate was intensely political. Ever since Godkin's day the Supreme Court had functioned as the last bastion protecting the rights of property; employers from the Gilded Age onward relied on court injunctions— backed by state and federal power—as the ultimate strike-breaking weapon. But in 1937 labor had a new tactic: the sit-down strike. The same issue of *The Nation* with the offending editorial also had a report from Flint, Michigan, where the United Auto Workers union had shut down the General Motors assembly line. Despite mounting political and media pressure, Governor Frank Murphy[†] was refusing to call out the militia. "If I send these men against the strikers there will be a massacre," said Murphy. As *The Nation* observed: "One of the significant things about the sit-down is that…it puts the burden of violence on the employers." Yet not only did Maurice Wertheim have to contend with increasing obloquy from his fellow capitalists, he also had to endure the scorn[21] of Heywood Broun—a columnist he had hired in a vain attempt to "stack" *The Nation*.

---

[*]   Two of the six *Nation* nominees, Felix Frankfurter and Robert Jackson, would later sit on the Supreme Court.

[†]   Murphy never did call out the militia. The battle of Flint was a huge victory for the fledgling UAW, and led to the unionization of the American automobile industry. In 1940 Franklin Roosevelt named Murphy to the Supreme Court.

In response to Wertheim's "personal dissent," Broun branded *The Nation*'s owner "a Wall Street progressive," which he defined as "a man who has just left the room when the fight begins." Villard and Wertheim might prefer to change the Court by constitutional amendment rather than, as FDR proposed, through legislation. But "American industrial and agricultural workers are not content to wait," said Broun. Declaring he was "sick of *The Nation*'s policy…of everybody must be heard whether or not he has anything to say," Broun made little attempt to disguise his contempt: "This isn't an amateur tennis match. It's a fight, and the well-being of masses of men and women depends on the result."

Wertheim liked Freda Kirchwey; she and his wife Alma[22] were good friends. And his daughter, Barbara—who later became better known under her married name, Barbara Tuchman—had recently become a *Nation* contributor. But when his second attempt to balance the magazine's politics—by bringing in Max Lerner to write editorials—also failed after Lerner, too, supported *The Nation*'s position on the New Deal, Wertheim decided he'd had enough. In June 1937 he told Kirchwey and Krutch that if Kirchwey, "whom he considered a true liberal," didn't want to buy *The Nation* he'd sell it to "the first person who would take it off his hands—no matter who, or what his views." Kirchwey countered with a request that he give her time to form a syndicate, but Wertheim insisted it was either her alone or sale to the highest bidder. The price was $30,000, of which Kirchwey put up $15,000 "from a small trust fund my husband had inherited from his mother" and was given an interest-free loan for the rest by Wertheim.[23]

Time magazine, recording[24] the sale of the "famed old pinko weekly" headlined the story "Angel Steps Out." In *The Nation*, Kirchwey wrote, "we believe that militant liberalism has come of age and can pay its own way." That last claim may have been wishful thinking, but it was also a dig at the competition. Though Freda Kirchwey wasn't poor, she wasn't in the same league as Dorothy Payne Whitney Straight, who carried on bankrolling *The New Republic* following the death of her husband during the 1918 flu epidemic. At the end of the Great War both journals had been bitterly disillusioned by Versailles. *The New Republic*, with its cool, cerebral, analytical approach, stayed disillusioned—especially during the 1930s, when it remained resolutely pacifist, and skeptical of "collective security." During the same period *The Nation* responded to the rise of fascism with increasing belligerence, arguing—as *The New Republic* had in 1916—that the coming conflict was America's fight.

§

Granville Hicks, editor of the *New Masses* and frequent *Nation* reviewer during his journey toward communism in the 1920s, best caught the magazine's character at the end of the 1930s. Examining[25] *The Nation*'s treatment of the twentieth anniversary of the October Revolution, Hicks finds an article and editorial hailing "Russia as the bulwark of western civilization against the onslaught of fascist barbarism" in the same issue as a book review[26] discussing starvation, torture and slave psychology in the Soviet Union, a country the reviewer, Edmund Wilson, depicts as heading "in the direction of fascism." Describing *The Nation* as "a liberal magazine providing a forum for the various points of view the editors regarded as progressive," Hicks noted it "has published articles for and against the Soviet Union, for and against the people's front in France, for and against the loyalist government in Spain, for and against the Communist Party. From our point of view, it has often been open to criticism, but it has taken the right side on many issues, and it has always tried to be fair."

The problem was the book review section, which "seceded from the rest of the magazine" some years ago and "still exists in a state of rebellion."[*] As evidence for his thesis that literary editor Margaret Marshall "will make the book section of *The Nation* an organ of the Trotskyites," Hicks cites her use of the novelist James T. Farrell, author of the Studs Lonigan trilogy, to review other proletarian novels, subjecting them to "exactly the kind of strong-arm job for which Mr. Farrell is notorious."

But the communists weren't the only ones exasperated by "A 'Nation' Divided" (as Hicks had titled his article). Farrell himself, who since the early 1930s had been writing for *The Nation* on everything from literary criticism to the career of Joe Louis, viewed the magazine the other way around, with an open-minded liberal-to-left literary section corrupted by the front of the book's slavish admiration for Joseph Stalin and all his works. They each had a point: to partisans in the bitter ideological battles of what the poet W.H. Auden would later describe as the "low, dishonest decade" of the 1930s, *The Nation* was bound to seem unsatisfactory. For Farrell

---

[*]   This at least was the view of Hicks in 1937. Three years later, having left the Communist Party, Hicks wrote a *Nation* essay warning of "The Blind Alley of Marxism." An eager witness before the House Committee on Un-American Activities, by the 1950s Hicks was lamenting "The Liberals Who Haven't Learned" in the pages of *Commentary*.

and his comrades the ouster of Trotsky and the perversion of the Russian Revolution by Stalin was the defining issue of the epoch, beside which all other considerations—the rise of fascism in Germany and Italy, the fate of organized labor in the United States, the persecution of European Jews, or the plight of black Americans—receded in significance. Communists meanwhile, whose late conversion to the ecumenical politics of the Popular Front may have been dictated by expediency, but who yielded nothing in fervor to their opponents, viewed any criticism of either the American Communist Party or the Soviet Union—or even the New Deal—as giving aid and comfort to the fascist enemy.

Freda Kirchwey remained a democrat (small-d, though she saw herself loyally pushing the New Deal to the left) in politics, and a socialist in economics. As *The Nation*'s owner and editor, she tolerated a range of views—and shrugged off catalogues of abuse—in a heroic effort to remain, not impartial, but *engaged* with all potential allies in the coming fight against fascism. In 1937, reflecting on yet another round of purges, she wrote[27] "the recent executions…provided a field day for the enemies of Moscow at a time when Soviet policy in Europe needs all the friends it can find." If that seems like an instrumental, rather than a moral, approach to Soviet communism perhaps that's because Kirchwey, unlike Hicks or Sidney Hook or Dwight Macdonald or Clement Greenberg or Irving Howe—*Nation* contributors all—never mistook either Stalin or Trotsky for democrats.

On domestic issues Kirchwey and *The Nation* remained closer to Norman Thomas's Socialists than Earl Browder's Communists—even after the CPUSA renounced any attempt to "subvert, undermine, weaken, or overthrow any or all institutions of American democracy." Ridiculing[28] the party's 1938 makeover, with "Browder and William Z. Foster as spiritual descendants of Jefferson and Lincoln, communism as the flowering spirit of '76, and Yankee Doodle about to supplant the Internationale," *The Nation* highlighted "the danger of [the CP] infecting the labor and progressive groups, to which it appeals in the name of democracy, with its doctrinaire vendettas." But then Thomas's Socialists, who retained at least an aspiration to socialism, were if anything more radical than the Communists domestically.

Abroad was another matter—and not only because Thomas and his party stayed committed to pacifism long past the point when Kirchwey, and *The Nation*, were calling for a boycott of Nazi Germany, an embargo against Fascist Italy, military aid to Britain, diplomatic recognition of the Soviet Union and any other measure that might strengthen potential allies in a war that she had come to view as both inevitable and welcome. For Kirchwey, as for so many of her generation, the crucible was Spain. From the moment in July 1936 when a group of generals, soon led by Francisco Franco, launched a coup against that country's elected Popular Front government, the Spanish Republic was in a fight for its life. Depicted—despite Franco's use of more than 100,000 Moroccan Muslim troops—as a Christian crusade against godless communism, the Spanish Civil War polarized American opinion. Most of the US press supported the Falange—as the Spanish fascists called themselves; the handful of newspapers sympathetic to the Loyalists, such as the *New York Post* and *The Philadelphia Record* or the *St. Louis Post-Dispatch*, found themselves denounced from pulpits every Sunday, with the archbishops of Philadelphia and Brooklyn calling on parishioners to boycott the offending titles. To Kirchwey the stakes couldn't be clearer. As I.F. Stone, an editorial writer at the *Post* who was fired after refusing to tone down his support for the Spanish Republic put it, if fascism wasn't stopped now, in Spain, the same methods would be "applied tomorrow in Czechoslovakia, the next day in France."[29] Stone soon joined *The Nation*, adding his voice to the chorus calling for "collective security" against the fascists. "1937," Stone insisted,[30] "is not 1914."

Most Americans, however, remained indifferent to Spain's torment, supporting the 1935 Neutrality Act, which barred the export of arms and ammunition to countries at war, and the 1937 act, which extended that ban to include civil wars. President Roosevelt's policy of allowing American oil companies to sell aviation fuel to Franco but blocking any assistance to the Republic—and threatening American volunteers with arrest—may have been shortsighted and hypocritical, but it was not unpopular. For the minority of Americans who did care about Spain, *The Nation* was an essential source of information—and an ideological battlefield. As the only European power willing to aid the Spanish Loyalists, the Soviet Union garnered prestige—and forbearance, even from Louis Fischer, now *The Nation*'s chief correspondent in Spain. Though Fischer had become bitterly critical of Soviet domestic policy, he couldn't help contrast Russian support "with the stupid, scandalous pro-Franco behavior of the democracies."[31] As Franco's troops closed in on Madrid and Barcelona, the behind-the-lines agitation of the dissident Communists in the Partido Obrero de Unificación Marxista—whose ranks included George Orwell—

began to seem like a luxury anti-fascists could no longer afford.

To Kirchwey the American volunteers in the Abraham Lincoln Battalion were heroes, not dupes. Perhaps that's why she dismissed[32] longtime *Nation* contributor Sidney Hook's manifesto[33] calling for a Committee for Cultural Freedom in America in the summer of 1939. The American Communist Party, Kirchwey agreed, "is a nuisance or a menace to all its opponents. Whatever its line may be, its tactics are invariably provocative and often destructive." Yet she felt the impulse "to create a clear division on the left" was dangerous and should be resisted. "The Spanish struggle," she wrote,[34] "taught many lessons, of which perhaps the most important was this one: It is not necessary for liberal lambs and Communist lions to lie down together. Enough if they will move ahead toward their common objectives without wasting time and strength in an attempt to exterminate each other along the way."

This didn't mean the Soviet Union got a free pass. When yet another purge ended with the execution of Nikolai Bukharin, Kirchwey wrote[35] that the grotesque show trial "has broken about the ears of the world like the detonation of a bomb. One can hear the cracking of liberal hopes; of the dream of anti-fascist unity... wherever democracy is threatened, the significance of the trial will be weighed." Still, knowing that anti-fascist unity remained a dream didn't prevent her from working to make it happen. "In spite of the trials," she wrote privately, "I still believe Russia is dependable; that it wants peace, and will join in any effort to check Hitler and Mussolini, and also will fight if necessary."[36]

Eventually her confidence would be vindicated by events. Once he actually joined the fight against Hitler, Stalin would indeed prove a reliable ally; the Red Army's sacrifices made victory in Europe possible. Only by then the Popular Front was dead—murdered by Stalin himself on August 23, 1939, when Vyacheslav Molotov, the Soviet foreign minister, signed a nonaggression pact with his Nazi counterpart, Joachim von Ribbentrop.

§

Like a flash of lighting the Nazi-Soviet Pact illuminated a political landscape of shattered illusions, blasting Louis Fischer, Granville Hicks and his *New Masses* colleague Richard Rovere clear out of communism's orbit. For intellectuals like Hicks, who had joined the party to fight fascism, the pact was a devastating betrayal. For those who, like I.F. Stone, joined not the party but the Popular Front, it wasn't so much the treaty as Russia's casual abandonment of "collective security" principles and "the ease with which [American] party members flip-flop on instruction and are all against Nazism one day and British Imperialism the next" that brought their fellow-traveling years to an abrupt end. Only a month earlier, Stone and *Nation* editor Maxwell Stewart had put their names to the Popular Front riposte[37] to Hook's manifesto, declaring "the Soviet Union continues to be a bulwark* against war and aggression."

Though Stone told Kirchwey he'd signed "because I wanted to see Russia in alliance with the West against Hitler," he had his name removed.[38] Furious[39] both with "the Moscow Machia-

---

* A word redolent of the 1930s, when no self-respecting ideological castle in the air was complete without its bulwark. Other signers included *The New Republic*'s Malcolm Cowley, Dashiell Hammett, Lillian Hellman, Granville Hicks, Dorothy Parker, and the poet William Carlos Williams, who in a triumph of negative capability managed to also sign the Hook manifesto.

velli who suddenly found peace as divisible as the Polish plains" and his "apologists-after-the-fact" at CP headquarters on Union Square, Stone assured[40] *Nation* readers "it is still a war against fascism, despite Mr. Chamberlain, and anti-fascists should urge the repeal of the embargo" to allow arms sales to Britain. Meanwhile Dwight Macdonald, a frequent *Nation* contributor, called for "revolutionary action against the warmakers"; Farrell and Clement Greenberg, the magazine's future art critic, echoed Macdonald's insurrectionary rhetoric, arguing that establishing socialism, rather than defeating fascism, was the first priority.[41] The American Civil Liberties Union suddenly decided that Elizabeth Gurley Flynn, an open Communist who had been one of the organization's founders—and had been re-elected to the board only a few months before—should now be expelled.

For Freda Kirchwey though, the pact, while "a solid and menacing fact that cannot be ignored," changed neither her belief that *The Nation*'s role "is to be analytical and critical and free to present varying views" nor her confidence[42] that "the long-range ambitions of Stalin and Hitler are bound to clash." Spain remained her touchstone, proof that isolationism only handed victory to the fascists, and that division on the left was equally fatal. Eventually America would have to fight, and when it did, she wrote, "I should hate to see *The Nation* left out of this particular international brigade."[43] Given the rampant confusion of the time, it is worth noting that Kirchwey's ability to maintain her own, and *The Nation*'s, ideological balance amid the grinding politics of the 1930s was a feat equaled by none of her peers. Little appreciated at the time, it would eventually became a source of resentment as the grudges and defections and mean compromises of the 1930s laid the course for the future of American politics over the next two decades.

Traumatic as it was, the brutal *Realpolitik* of the pact was also a liberation of sorts. When the Soviet Union invaded Finland in December 1939, Kirchwey responded[44] in terms that must have shocked many *Nation* readers: "The horrors that fascism wreaked in Spain are being repeated, in the name of peace and socialism, in Finland." While Lillian Hellman refused to allow Finnish War Relief to stage a benefit performance of *The Little Foxes*, I.F. Stone followed Kirchwey in reaching for the most crushing comparison, describing Russian conduct in Finland as "strikingly parallel" to the "attack on the Spanish Republic." In Finland, Stone told[45] *Nation* readers, "the Red Army is an aggressor; morale is on the Finnish side."

Which didn't mean that Hitler's invasion of the Soviet Union in June 1941 wasn't a huge relief. Much as *The Nation* seemed to be enjoying its newfound freedom not only to criticize Russia but to lampoon the same Soviet initiatives it once celebrated—"All Southeastern Europe," wrote[46] Robert Bendiner, the magazine's new managing editor, "cringes before the Russian olive branch"— the war in Europe had been going too badly for too long not to welcome even a belated recruit to the anti-fascist ranks. "By his attack on the Soviet Union," I.F. Stone pointed out,[47] Hitler "has 'landed' a huge anti-Nazi army on the Continent."

While Greenberg and Macdonald complained that "the involvement of Russia does not change the issues," no one apart from Trotskyists and American Communists—who suddenly changed their tune from "The Yanks Aren't Coming" to "The Sinking of the Reuben James"[48]—claimed it had. *The Nation* had been consistently—and vocally—pro-war since the fall of France. Fearing that pacifists like Oswald Garrison Villard were living in a "dream world," Kirchwey welcomed Roosevelt's call for universal military training—a position that Villard found "intolerable." In his last column for *The Nation*, Villard wondered[49] how "Freda Kirchwey, a pacifist in the last war...had now struck hands with all the forces of reaction." Privately he was even more caustic, accusing her of having "prostituted *The Nation*," which he hoped "would die very soon." In her belief that pacifism had become appeasement, Kirchwey was supported by *Nation* contributing editor Reinhold Niebuhr, who insisted[50] that "the civilization which we are called upon to defend is full of capitalistic and imperialistic injustice. But it is still a civilization." The title of Niebuhr's article? "An End to Illusions."

It was Villard who, in company with John T. Flynn, a columnist at *The New Republic*, Gen. Robert Wood, president of the National Association of Manufacturers, and William Regnery, an anti-union publisher, formed the isolationist America First Committee, ending up as an apologist for Charles Lindbergh's anti-Semitism.[51] For Kirchwey, who saw *The Nation* as "a weapon—not a pair of scales" in the fight against fascism, the war had taken on personal as well as political significance. Her only son, Michael Clark, dropped out of Harvard to enlist in the British-American ambulance corps. In April 1941, while en route to join the Free French Forces in Eritrea, Clark's ship, the Egyptian passenger liner *Zam Zam*, was torpedoed in the South Atlantic. It was nearly a month before Kirchwey learned that Michael was alive, and another month before he was released.

On December 7, 1941, I.F. Stone, whom Kirchwey had just hired as *The Nation*'s Washington editor, was on his way to his office at the National Press Building when he was stopped by the elevator man. For Stone, as for Kirchwey, the news that America was at war at last brought "relief that a long expected storm had finally broken.... This is really world war," Stone told[52] *Nation* readers, "and in my humble opinion it was unavoidable and is better fought now when we still have allies left."

Though Villard's departure cost the magazine thousands of readers, Pearl Harbor put the seal on something *The Nation* hadn't had in a long time: respectability. A request for a message from the president on the magazine's seventy-fifth anniversary in February 1940 brought a "100 %" endorsement from FDR—and a plug in Eleanor Roosevelt's syndicated newspaper column: "I have always had a great respect for anyone good enough to write for *The Nation*." America's entry into the war solidified such sentiments. In Washington, Stone and other *Nation* editors suddenly found a much warmer welcome at the new wartime agencies; even Harold Ickes, the notoriously touchy interior secretary, now took to the magazine's pages, not just to complain about alleged inaccuracies but to explain[53] the conduct of the war. In New York, Kirchwey, who had long viewed the conflict as a political as much as a military battle, assembled a war cabinet of contributing editors that included Niebuhr, Fischer, British Labour activist Norman Angell, North Carolina newspaperman Jonathan Daniels (the son of Wilson's secretary of the navy, the one who had told Villard that locking him up would be "very popular") and, as the resident expert on European affairs, J. Alvarez Del Vayo, the former foreign minister of the Spanish Republic.

§

With America finally in the fight, *The Nation* carried on as the voice of the "all-outers." Alexander Werth, the magazine's longtime Paris correspondent, became the BBC's man in Moscow, reporting[54] in *The Nation* on life behind the Eastern front. On the home front, Stone highlighted delays in war production caused by corporate America's devotion to "business as usual"—and a reluctance to ramp up production now at the risk of creating a postwar surplus detrimental to future profits. Yet it wasn't only corporate Americans who were expected to put winning the war ahead of any other consideration. *The Nation* had long supported Indian self-determination. But when Mohandas Gandhi launched the "Quit India" campaign in 1942, *The Nation*, arguing that "victory over the Axis" took precedence "above all other considerations," thought the civil disobedience effort was ill timed. "Our sympathy does not blind us," wrote[55] Kirchwey, "as their bitterness blinds them, to the cold fact that an Axis victory would not only end India's chances for independence but destroy the freedom of the rest of the world."

Precisely because she also saw the struggle in political terms, Kirchwey and *The Nation* were early and unwavering backers of Charles De Gaulle and the Free French,* warning that any accommodation with Vichy would undercut America's war effort. A similar mix of pragmatism and attention to the war's political dimension lay behind *The Nation*'s exposé of the "Washington Gestapo"[56]—the FBI's clumsy attempt at politically vetting gov-

---

* In September 1946 Kirchwey was made a Chevalier of the Legion of Honor in recognition of her contribution to the French cause.

ernment employees. By asking questions such as "Does he think the colored races are as good as the white?" or "Does he have too many Jewish friends?" the investigations risked "undermining Washington's...will to fight"—and, not incidentally, were "being used as a club to beat liberals out of town." Published under the byline "XXX," the series guaranteed Kirchwey and I.F. Stone, who vouched for the anonymous author,* a lifetime of unwelcome attention from J. Edgar Hoover.

Maintaining America's will to fight was so important to Kirchwey, she was even prepared to sacrifice civil liberties. Having led the opposition to Texas Congressman Martin Dies and his House Committee on Un-American Activities, Kirchwey now demanded the Justice Department "Curb the Fascist Press,"[57] which she labeled "a menace to freedom and an obstacle to winning the war." Arguing that America could not risk giving the "treason press" a chance to broadcast defeatism, she urged that "they should be exterminated as if they were enemy machine-gun nests in the Bataan jungle." Even the Supreme Court's decision upholding the internment of Japanese-Americans drew only a mild demurral[58] from *The Nation*.

The sole exception—though Kirchwey would not have seen it that way—to *The Nation*'s battlefield conversion to expediency was its stubborn, lonely and outspoken advocacy on behalf of Europe's refugees, especially its Jews. Even before the slaughter

---

* Though J. Edgar Hoover was never able to establish XXX's identity, while researching *American Radical*, my biography of Stone, I discovered a handwritten note among Kirchwey's papers suggesting XXX was Edward F. Pritchard, an official in the Office of Economic Stabilization who had been Felix Frankfurter's first clerk on the Supreme Court. (For details see *American Radical*, pp. 189-190.)

got under way, Kirchwey saw the issue as a personal—as well as political and moral—crusade. "Aliens. Refugees. Exiles. These are America," she wrote[59] in 1939. "Let in the Refugees,"[60] the magazine demanded. "Bring Them Out!"[61] In January 1943, with the Holocaust in high gear, *The Nation* began a series on "The Jews of Europe"[62] in order to "impress on the conscience of free men the vastness and ghastliness of the Jewish tragedy." That March, Kirchwey underlined[63] the cost of American inaction: "If we had behaved like humane and generous people instead of complacent, cowardly ones, the two million Jews lying today in the earth of Poland and Hitler's other crowded graveyards would be alive and safe." We now know her numbers were understated, but even today it is hard to argue with her moral accounting.

§

Though it came too late for European Jewry, the dawn of 1945 seemed filled with hope—for the world, the country and *The Nation*. The success of the Normandy invasion, and the failure of the German counteroffensive in the Battle of the Bulge meant that victory in Europe was finally in sight. The Yalta Conference in February 1945, during which FDR secured Stalin's promise to participate a postwar United Nations organization, seemed a harbinger of durable cooperation among the three Allied powers. And on Vesey Street *The Nation*, which had struggled for survival throughout the Depression, was finally on stable financial ground. Two years before Kirchwey had reorganized the magazine's finances, turning ownership over to a new entity, Nation Associates, which asked subscribers for contributions ranging from $10 to $100. By May 1943 the appeal—which included a $50 donation from novelist Thomas Mann—had generated $36,000, allowing Kirchwey to finally repay the loan from Maurice Wertheim. A dinner celebrating Kirchwey's quarter-century at the magazine in February 1944, featuring a booklet introduced by a tribute from President Roosevelt and a list of 1,400 other sponsors, including Albert Einstein, Justice Hugo Black, John Dewey and Walter Lippmann, raised a further $25,000. The booklet also reproduced a letter from the *Nation* staff praising Kirchwey as a boss whose "liberalism begins at home" and who had "the courage to establish a genuine working democracy" in the office.

In January 1945 the Nation Associates filled Madison Square Garden with a demonstration demanding America sever diplomatic relations with Spain. Backed by Niebuhr, Thomas Mann, California Congresswoman Helen Gahagan Douglas as well as the Congress of Industrial Organizations and the Abraham Lincoln Brigade, Kirchwey pressed FDR to make good his promise that "this war was not being fought to keep fascists or near-fascists in power." Roosevelt wrote to Kirchwey afterward that mere "maintenance of diplomatic relations" did not imply approval of a regime, and then, two weeks later, wrote again to concede that America could have closer relations with governments "based on democratic principals."[64] Though she probably wasn't persuaded by the president's arguments, Kirchwey must have been gratified by the attention. When he died three months later, it was, she recognized, the "End of an Era."

"I do not imply," she wrote,[65] that "Harry S. Truman will move to wipe out the social gains of the past twelve years." Nonetheless, "to millions of Americans" Franklin Roosevelt "*was the New Deal*." A "basic change" had occurred "and it would be dishonest to deny it. The balance of political forces had shifted to the right."

How far to the right was not immediately evident. The news from Hiroshima and Nagasaki was welcomed by *The Nation*. The $2 billion cost of the atom bomb, wrote[66] Kirchwey "was never better spent. The suffering, the wholesale slaughter it entailed, have been outweighed by its spectacular success" in bringing the war to a speedy end. Yet she also recognized "the danger" that the bomb's efficacy "will encourage those in power to assume that, once accepted as valid, the argument can be applied equally well in the future." The bomb, wrote[67] *Nation* managing editor J. King Gordon, needed to become "a world affair" rather than an American monopoly.

Such sentiments were commonplace at the United Nations, where the Canadian-born Gordon would soon move to serve as the secretariat's human rights officer. The United States, however, was heading in a different direction. An early sign of the new political climate came before the war ended, in June 1945, when six people connected with the journal *Amerasia* were arrested in New York and charged under the Espionage Act. One was John Stewart Service, a State Department China hand. Another was Andrew Roth, a young naval lieutenant who was also *The Nation*'s Far East expert. Though *Amerasia*'s publisher, Philip Jaffe, apparently did have Walter Mitty-esque fantasies of becoming a Soviet agent, the other defendants were just playing the traditional Washington game of leaking material to bolster their side in the capital's endless bureaucratic trench warfare.

The charges against Roth were quietly dropped in February. But Service, though never indicted, and cleared by the State Department, would spend the next five years in a vain attempt to clear his name. In March 1951 a special Senate subcommittee on the Investigation of Loyalty of State Department Employees again cleared Service. But when a member of that committee's Republican minority repeated the accusation that Service was a Communist sympathizer, he was forced out of the Foreign Service. The senator's name was Joseph McCarthy.

At first *The Nation* carried on as it always had, with wartime pleas about the importance of maintaining good relations with our Soviet allies giving way to peacetime arguments about the imperative to prevent war in the Atomic Age. In November 1946 the magazine even ran an emollient commentary[68] by Walter Duranty, the *New York Times* correspondent infamous for his blinkered reporting of the Ukrainian famine, on Stalin's postwar purges. But if Kirchwey had not changed her view of the Soviet Union, others had. In June 1945 Louis Fischer resigned, charging[69] *The Nation* with operating "like a party organ," its views determined by "loyalties to organized groups...rather than principles." Kirchwey, who had defended Fischer from the same accusation for years, responded robustly: "We suppose he is charging us with ignoring...the bad behavior of the Soviet Union.... We can only answer quite flatly that he is wrong." The magazine's readers overwhelmingly supported Kirchwey; so did contributing editor Reinhold Niebuhr—for the moment.

By March 1947, however, any pretense of continuity between Truman and his predecessor had been abandoned. In Greece, where the Communist-led Popular Front *Ethniko Apeleftherotiko Metopo* (EAM) or National Liberation Front, which had borne the brunt of resisting Nazi occupation, now faced the British army, Kirchwey felt the British were guilty of treachery equal to Soviet conduct in Poland. Yet the new Truman Doctrine committed the United States to taking over from the British in Greece. On March 22, just ten days after that proclamation, the president signed Executive Order 9835 instituting the Federal Employees Loyalty and Security Program. Within two months the FBI had begun name checks on 2 million federal workers—the match that lit the fires of the witch hunts. Though I.F. Stone condemned the measure as "an experiment in American fascism" he did so in the pages of the newspaper *PM* rather than *The Nation*—Kirchwey had fired him the previous year. (When he left the United States on the trip that became his book *Underground to Palestine*,[70] Stone had kept *The Nation* in the dark while informing Ralph Ingersoll, his editor at *PM*.) Yet when it came to the danger of an American inquisition, Kirchwey agreed[71] with her former employee: "The threat of Communism in this country is insignificant; while the threat of reaction is explicit in the Washington red-hunt and implicit in Mr. Truman's new foreign policy."

§

Though it cost *The Nation* one of its ablest writers, the birth of the Jewish state was one of the few bright spots on the magazine's horizon. Kirchwey made an overground trip to Palestine in May 1946, meeting with her old friend Chaim Weitzmann and with the head of the Histadrut labor federation's political department, Goldie Meyerson (who, as Golda Meir, would later serve as prime minister), as well as Hussein Khalidi, the former mayor of Jerusalem. On a visit to Ein Hashofed, a kibbutz founded by Americans in the north of the country, she was particularly gratified to discover "40 *Nation* readers!"[72] Returning to America, Kirchwey threw herself—and *The Nation*—into the fight for a Jewish state, writing fierce editorials condemning any evidence of wavering by the Truman administration, making speeches for the Jewish National Fund, and publicizing a series of reports by the Nation Associates documenting[73] the wartime collaboration between the Nazis and Muhammed Amin Al-Husayni, the mufti of Jerusalem. She also lobbied Eleanor Roosevelt, Felix Frankfurter and Bernard Baruch on behalf of the Jewish state, whose first foreign minister, Moshe Sharett, she advised on drafting his speeches.

Israeli independence in May 1948 was a rare victory for a magazine that had become increasingly embattled. The following month saw *The Nation* banned from New York City public schools following a series by Paul Blanshard criticizing[74] the influence of theology on medical practice in Catholic hospitals and attacking[75] the church's attempts to censor the curriculum in public schools. Though Eleanor Roosevelt, historian Henry Steele Commager, Max Lerner, Reinhold Niebuhr and Rabbi Stephen S. Wise signed a statement opposing the ban, which *The Nation* challenged in court, it would not be lifted until January 1963. Ruth Brown, a librarian in Bartlesville, Oklahoma, lost her job in 1950 partly for giving shelf space to *The Nation*.[76]

Even more damaging was the self-inflicted wound when, after *The New Leader* published former *Nation* art critic Clement Greenberg's letter[77] in March 1951 accusing J. Alvarez Del Vayo of using his column to transmit "in a more plausible form" the arguments of the Stalin regime, Kirchwey insisted[78] on suing Greenberg and *The New Leader* for libel. Kirchwey felt her integrity, and that of *The Nation*, was at stake. She also feared that Del Vayo, a political refugee, might be deported. "A time is upon us," she wrote,[79] "when frightened men turn with venom to crush those whose views they hate."

She was wrong about the suit. But she was right about the time. And about the stakes. In February 1952 Del Vayo and his wife, returning from a trip to Europe, were detained at Ellis Island under the McCarran Act and held for several days. They were released only after Kirchwey's frantic campaign of phone calls and telegrams resulted in direct intervention by the White House. Kirchwey also advised Andrew Roth, whom she'd sent on a long reporting trip to Asia and the Middle East, against returning to the States. (Ironically Roth's absence may have made life more difficult for another McCarthy target—and *Nation* contributor. One reason for J. Edgar Hoover's fury against Owen Lattimore was the FBI director's suspicion that the Asia scholar was "Pacificus," a pseudonymous expert who'd written a number of wartime articles in *The Nation* criticizing State Department policy in the Far East. But as Roth freely admitted[*] decades later, "Pacificus" was Roth himself, not Lattimore.)[80]

The suit against *The New Leader* was the final straw for Reinhold Niebuhr and Robert Bendiner. By now McCarthy was in full cry in the Senate and on television; among the intelligentsia Arthur Schlesinger Jr. piled on, accusing *The Nation* of "betraying its finest traditions" by printing "week after week, *these wretched apologies for Soviet despotism*."[81] The accusation, as Schlesinger, a frequent *Nation* contributor, must have known, was untrue and unfair. Yet nothing,

---

[*]   In 2004 Roth told me "it should have been obvious" especially since he'd used a lot of the "Pacificus" material in his 1945 book *Dilemma in Japan*.

not *The Nation*'s support for the Korean War, not even *The Nation*'s vigorous protest of the "Great Zionist Conspiracy" show trial of Czech Communist leader Rudolph Slansky in Prague—"for such tactics we have only contempt"—turned the tide of fear and denunciation. When Yale Law School professor Thomas Emerson and Stringfellow Barr, the president of St. John's College in Annapolis, signed an open letter complaining of the difficulty McCarthy's victims often found in obtaining legal representation, Schlesinger used his *New York Post* column to smear them: "None of these gentlemen is a Communist, but none objects very much to Communism. They are the Typhoid Marys of the left, bearing the germs of infection even if not obviously suffering from the disease."[82]

As Carey McWilliams, *The Nation*'s California contributing editor soon retorted, "this was the language of McCarthyism even if spoken with a Harvard accent." The son of Colorado cattle ranchers, McWilliams had been a reformer since the 1920s, when as a newly qualified lawyer in Los Angeles he'd defended striking Mexican farmworkers. His first book, a biography of writer Ambrose Bierce, was lauded by H.L. Mencken; his second, *Factories in the Field* (1939), a portrait of California agriculture, was praised[83] in *The Nation* by I.F. Stone, who wrote "Steinbeck's *Grapes of Wrath* here finds its sequel." Tough enough to face down Imperial Valley landowners' gun-toting vigilantes, McWilliams came to the aid of Chicano youths during the Zoot Suit riots, saw his book *Prejudice: Japanese-Americans: Symbol of Race Hatred* (1944) cited by Justice Frank Murphy in his dissent to the Supreme Court's 1944 decision upholding the internment of Japanese-Americans and, with First Amendment scholar Alexander Meiklejohn, drafted an *amic-*

us brief to the Supreme Court on behalf of screenwriters Dalton Trumbo and John Howard Lawson, two of the Hollywood Ten. In 1950 he'd published *Witch Hunt: The Revival of Heresy*.[84]

Who better, then, to edit a *Nation* special issue on civil liberties? With a cover[85] donated by artist Ben Shahn and articles by Vern Countryman, who would soon be denied tenure at Yale Law School; Zechariah Chafee, a professor at Harvard Law School, Arthur Miller and Matthew Josephson, who wrote about the chilling effect on book publishing, the issue quoted Eleanor Roosevelt's remark "I am tired of being afraid." America's great fear had wounded *The Nation*. In February 1953, faced with a $90,000 deficit, Kirchwey cut the book section back to a single long review and fired Margaret Marshall. For every Richard Hofstadter, who noisily vowed, "I won't write for *The Nation* under the new dispensation—ever," there were many more, such as Irving Howe, who only recently had reviewed Whittaker Chambers's *Witness* for *The Nation*, or the historian H. Stuart Hughes, who just quietly drifted away. The special issue was a gesture against the tide of the times—proof that however diminished its voice, *The Nation* lived to fight on. ✳

Carey McWilliams

CHAPTER SIX

How Free Is Free?

I n the summer of 1955 two men sat talking in *The Nation*'s office, completely misunderstanding each other. Dan Wakefield, a 23-year-old Columbia graduate, struck his interviewer as "a rather shy young man." There had been a murder in Mississippi. A 14-year-old black teenager from Chicago named Emmett Till had been visiting relatives in the Delta where, after being accused of whistling at a white woman, he was dragged out of his uncle's house by a group of white men. Three days later Till's beaten, mutilated corpse was found in the Tallahatchie River. If *The Nation* would stake him to a round-trip bus ticket, said Wakefield, he would go down to Mississippi to cover the trial.

Wakefield, though indeed young, was not at all shy. By the time he presented himself at *The Nation* he'd already talked his way into a job as research assistant to C. Wright Mills, his former

Columbia professor, whose books *Men of Power*, a group portrait of American labor leaders, and *White Collar*, an anatomy of the middle class, both blending journalistic description with sociological theory to potent effect, prepared the way for *The Power Elite*, his devastating critique of the American ruling class. A brief stint at the weekly *Princeton Packet* served to introduce Wakefield to his next mentor, *New York Post* columnist Murray Kempton, who recommended him to *The Nation*.

To Wakefield, a young writer on the make who burned with literary ambition, sexual ardor and the deep shame of having come to New York from Indianapolis, "Carey McWilliams, with his space shoes, buttoned-up cardigan, and thinning black hair slicked straight back from his forehead, seemed like the safe, predictable liberal."[1] He couldn't have been more wrong. His politics may have been consistently, predictably left of center, but there was nothing dogmatic, or safe, about Carey McWilliams.

At 50 *The Nation*'s new editor dressed his age. As a young "expatriate" in Los Angeles in the 1920s, however, after the end of the wartime embargo on Argentine beef brought on the collapse of the domestic cattle market, and with it his family's fortunes in Colorado,[*] McWilliams led a bohemian life equal to anything on offer in Greenwich Village. Putting himself though law school while working at the *Los Angeles Times*, he fell in with a crowd of writers, poets, painters and architects with very little interest in politics (the reformer Upton Sinclair was an exception) and (with

---

[*] Mount Werner, the 10,000-foot skiers' paradise in Steamboat Springs, was just part of the McWilliams family's vast Mesa Ranch.

Sinclair, a devout teetotaler, again the exception) a great enthusiasm for drinking and carousing. Practicing law during the early years of the Depression brought him into contact with victims of California's Criminal Syndicalism Act, which was being used to suppress a huge wave of strikes by farmworkers in the Imperial and San Joaquin valleys.

Politics in California during the 1930s was played by different rules, and on a different scale, than back East. Los Angeles was an "open shop" town; outside the cities landowners hired private armies to keep union organizers off the land. Yet in the summer of 1934 a walkout by longshoremen and sailors in San Francisco sparked a four-day general strike that ended with the union gaining control over hiring at every port on the West Coast. That fall Sinclair, running on a platform promising to end poverty in California, won the Democratic nomination for governor. Though Sinclair lost, four years later the Democrats, who hadn't elected a governor in the state in forty years, sent Culbert Olson to Sacramento. A strong New Dealer, Olson appointed McWilliams—who'd gained a reputation representing a range of unions, from walnut pickers in the United Cannery, Agricultural, Packing and Allied Workers to the Newspaper Guild—head of the state's Division of Immigration and Housing.

During this period McWilliams tried—and failed—to prevent the internment of Japanese-Americans. (Of his involvement in administering the program, McWilliams writes: "It was not a matter of choice: I was co-opted.")[2] The election of Republican Earl Warren, who made a campaign promise to fire McWilliams, prompted him to return to his law practice, where he organized the successful appeal in the "Sleepy Lagoon" murder trial, freeing twenty-four Mexican-American defendants who had been rail-roaded by an all-white jury and a biased judge. He also published *Ill Fares the Land* (1942), a study of migrant labor that followed his bestselling *Factories in the* Field, and *Brothers Under the Skin* (1943), a history of race prejudice in America.

In 1945 McWilliams became *The Nation*'s West Coast contributing editor—a bold move for a magazine that had long viewed the Hudson, rather than the Atlantic Ocean, as an impassable barrier. It was also shrewd. As he soon demonstrated in the pages of his next book, *Southern California Country: An Island on the Land* (1946), McWilliams knew nearly everyone in Southern California—and everything worth knowing about his adopted state. (Nearly thirty years later, McWilliams's account of the diversion of water from the Owens Valley to Los Angeles would give screenwriter Robert Towne the historical background for *Chinatown*.) From the Hollywood stagehands whose union he'd helped to get out from under the grip of mobster Willie Bioff, to the writers he'd met organizing the West Coast Writers Congress, to the farm workers he'd represented, to the Hollywood Ten, to politicians from Attorney General Robert Kenny and his successor (and future governor) Edmund G. "Pat" Brown, to Warren and Richard Nixon, McWilliams knew them all.

He'd known Jack Tenney, the Golden State inquisitor in chief whose California Committee on Un-American Activities anticipated McCarthy by nearly a decade, since the Republican legislator had been a New Deal Democrat whose sole claim to fame was as the composer of the song "Mexicali Rose."[3] Which made it hard for McWilliams to take the politician seriously, even in 1943 when Tenney's committee grilled him over his views on interracial marriage.[3]

Yet nothing had prepared McWilliams for the response to his *Nation* appointment. "The politics of the country, including the politics of the West, had been in a state of freeze, you might say, during the war years," McWilliams recalled.[4] "The politics of the whole West was beginning to bubble. When they announced that I was their West Coast editor…I got all kinds of people sending in materials and letters, wanting me to investigate this, or write about this, that, and the other; and it took a great deal more time than I had any notion of. And I was getting some ridiculous stipend for this. It was not well paying at all. But it got me involved in politics, western politics, in a way I'd never been involved."

In 1946 McWilliams persuaded *The Nation* to organize a conference on the prospects for liberal politics in the West at the Ambassador Hotel in Los Angeles. Lillie Shultz, the talented fundraiser in charge of Nation Associates, worked with McWilliams to produce a two-day program of daytime sessions and evening banquets that raised the magazine's profile—and considerable funds. "They were turning people away from the sessions," said McWilliams. "One of the speakers at those sessions was a gentleman by the name of Ronald Reagan,* who was then a liberal, you know." Four years later the memory of that success prompted Freda Kirchwey to turn to McWilliams for help.

"As a personal favor, she asked if I would come east for a time." McWilliams reluctantly agreed. "I was thoroughly convinced the

---

* In 1946 Reagan was third vice president of the Screen Actors Guild. He became president of the union the following year—roughly the same time he began serving as confidential informant "T-10" for the FBI.

domestic witch-hunt would get much worse, and soon.... In fact I had been urging *The Nation* to take the offensive by bringing out a special civil-liberties issue."[5] McWilliams planned to stay for a month.

But just organizing the special issue took the better part of a year. "When I got there I saw what dire straits the magazine was in," said McWilliams. "And I kept thinking that, well, after six months or a year the situation would change. But it didn't change...."

§

One reason it didn't change is that *The Nation*'s persistent refusal to sign up to the certainties of the Cold War made it perhaps the most despised publication in the country. Though the magazine had been under fire from the right since the Villard years, there were two new elements to the latest attack. One was venomous hostility from Cold War liberals, many of them, like Theodore Draper or Granville Hicks, former Communists themselves or, like Leslie Fiedler, Sidney Hook and Irving Kristol, former Trotskyists. That Kirchwey, who'd never subscribed to either dogma, now had the temerity to disagree with their insistence on the primary importance of their disillusionment, and to argue that finding a means of peaceful co-existence (or what Richard Nixon would, twenty years later, dignify with the French label "détente") still mattered more than "clear divisions on the left" made her a particular target.[6]

In April 1951 Hicks (the same man who in the thirties had damned *The Nation* as an unreliable ally of the CP) opened the attack in *Commentary* with an article[7] on "The Liberals Who Haven't Learned"—backstopped by Irving Kristol, whose dismissive review[8] of McWilliams's book on witch hunts in the same issue was titled "Flying Off the Broomstick." *The New Leader*, founded by

Norman Thomas as a Socialist Party publication but which, under the Menshevik émigré Sol Levitas soon became the voice of fearless anti-Stalinist factionalism, joined the pile-up with managing editor Daniel James accusing *The Nation* of pro-Soviet bias.[9] At a time when the mere suggestion of leftist sympathy was enough to place a person's livelihood in jeopardy, these were dangerous allegations.

But what made life—and fundraising—still more difficult for Kirchwey and *The Nation* was the active hostility of that segment of the American left that had backed the 1948 Progressive Party presidential campaign of Henry Wallace. Like most fervent New Dealers, Kirchwey and McWilliams viewed the former vice president as the authentic heir to Franklin Roosevelt; both were enthusiastic supporters of the movement to encourage Wallace to challenge Harry Truman for the Democratic nomination. In the division between the anti-communist Americans for Democratic Action and the open-to-anyone Progressive Citizens of America, McWilliams, true to his Popular Front principles, had sided with the PCA. But when the PCA persuaded Wallace to run as a third-party candidate McWilliams, who "wanted a serious effort made to carry the fight to the Democratic convention," resigned.

The Nation was even more vocal. Wallace's decision to run as a Progressive "seriously altered the political landscape of the country—and not for the better" the magazine editorialized.[10] *The Nation* also criticized candidate Wallace's opposition to the Marshall Plan, arguing,[11] "The Marshall Plan, if successful, will in the long run make Western Europe less dependent on American industry than it is today." Managing editor Robert Bendiner stated[12] "The Case Against Wallace." As for Freda Kirchwey, she proclaimed[13] her intention to join the "many millions of progressives" who on Election Day would decide "not to 'stand up and be counted' for Henry Wallace." Worrying that the Progressive Party was too reliant on Communist support, and that the CP in turn was "controlled by interests unrelated to the needs and desires of Henry Wallace's 'common man'," Kirchwey urged[14] Wallace to withdraw. Though he ended up with fewer votes than Dixiecrat candidate Strom Thurmond, Wallace still polled over a million votes—and for the considerable portion of those who regarded his candidacy as a crusade, rather than a campaign, *The Nation* was guilty of treason to the cause.

Which meant that from the moment McWilliams arrived in New York in the spring of 1951 "I was in effect the editor," as Kirchwey struggled to keep the magazine afloat. His education in the folkways of eastern intellectuals began with another *Nation* conference, this one on the theme of "Arab-Israel Peace: The Key to Stability in the Middle East" to be held at the Waldorf Astoria in May 1952. Accused of trying to "revive the united front" by *Counterattack*, the blacklister's bible, *The Nation* found its speakers and sponsors melting away under pressure from the *New York World-Telegram & Sun*. Among those who suddenly had pressing engagements elsewhere were Senator Jacob Javits and William Green, president of the American Federation of Labor, who had agreed to co-chair the event. Nor did *The Nation*'s record as the most consistently outspoken American supporter of Israel count with the editors of *The New Leader*, who, noting the presence of some "dubious liberals...wedged in among many respectable sponsors of this affair," wondered how they had been persuaded to lend their names "to such a questionable cause." The attendance of Eleanor Roosevelt, who came in response to a personal appeal from Kirchwey, saved the day—but Nation Associates held no more fundraisers for a long time. [15]

Nothing *The Nation* could do would satisfy its critics. Not Mark Gayn's reminder[16] that while show trials and purges "are part of the Communist system" there was still something extraordinary—and malevolent—in the anti-Semitic persecution of Slansky in Czechoslovakia, Anna Pauker in Hungary and the "Zionist doctors" in Moscow. "If a thieving factory manager gets seven years in prison, a 'bourgeois nationalist' is lucky to escape with his life." Not even Kirchwey's impassioned denunciation[17] of "Communist-inspired anti-Semitism" in which, recalling "with horror how the world refused to believe the first reports of Hitler's extermination program," she called on "the civilized world" to act to "prevent a new possibility of genocide while there is still time."

Irving Kristol had made the rules clear the previous year: "If a liberal wishes to defend the civil liberties of Communists or… fellow travelers," wrote[18] Kristol, "he must show that he knows the existence of an organized subversive movement such as Communism is a threat to the consensus on which…civil liberties are based." To even gain a hearing a liberal "must speak as one of *us*, defending *their* liberties." So when "How Free Is Free?"[19]— McWilliams's special issue on civil liberties—appeared three months after Kristol's catechism, it couldn't have been much of a surprise to read former *Nation* staffer Richard Rovere taking to *The New Leader* to claim the issue "would provoke cheers in the Kremlin"—or to see Rovere's sneers repeated in *Time*.[20]

§

Kirchwey's original plan had been to find a replacement publisher. *The Nation*'s parlous finances were an emotional as well as economic burden for her and her husband. She even considered—more than once—a merger with *The New Republic**. Unlike *The New Republic*, or James Reston and Max Ascoli's *The Reporter*, *The Nation* had no "angel" to pay its bills (Marion Rosenwald Ascoli was the daughter of the chairman of Sears, Roebuck). As *PM* and its successors went under, and the *National Guardian* saw editor Cedric Belfrage imprisoned and then deported, *The Nation* hung on—barely. "On Monday mornings the first order of business was usually a hurried conference on how to meet that week's payroll

---

*   Though the merger fell through over such trivialities as which title would survive, and whether *The Nation* would move down to Washington or *The New Republic* to New York, each magazine faced a unique set of perils. Despite the family's great wealth, Michael Straight's siblings were unhappy subsidizing a magazine whose liberal world-view they disagreed with. Straight, who had recruited Henry Wallace to edit his magazine, also had to cope with the fallout from Wallace's presidential bid, which began by boosting *TNR*'s circulation, and ended with the magazine endorsing Truman! But perhaps the most significant factor in Straight's discomfort—and *The New Republic*'s odd political mood swings—was his fear of being exposed as the Soviet agent he'd become as a student at Cambridge in the 1930s. Though he would later claim to have broken with the Russians before his return to the United States, in the early 1950s Straight would occasionally run into his old friend—and comrade—Guy Burgess, who worked at the British Embassy in Washington. This was of course before Burgess and Donald McLean, another member of their Cambridge cell, fled to Moscow, but at roughly the same time as Straight, who was in the process of remaking himself into a liberal anti-Communist, was advising *New Republic* readers on "The Right Way to Beat Communism" (*The New Republic*, May 1, 1950). For some reason the Red-baiters never bore the same animus toward *The New Republic* as they did *The Nation*—perhaps thanks in part to the March 1951 series by TRB columnist Richard Strout raking over Kingsley Martin and *The New Statesman* for their supposed pro-Soviet bias.

and the printing bill," McWilliams recalled. By 1954 circulation, which had been above 40,000 during the war, had slumped to 28-29,000.[21] A desperate McWilliams arranged for *The Nation* to be printed at the Alabama plant belonging to Aubrey Williams, former head of the National Youth Administration in the New Deal and now publisher of *Southern Farmer*.

"We installed a Teletype system over which copy, corrections, editorials, etc. were transmitted from New York," said McWilliams. "Somehow we managed to make this highly improbable arrangement work, after a fashion, for nearly a year."[22] At the end of that year Kirchwey, too burnt out to carry on, offered McWilliams a sixty-day option to raise $80,000, which would pay off the magazine's debts and allow it to continue for at least another few years. McWilliams—whose salary of $13,000 was his only source of income—managed to find backers who would put up about two-thirds of what he needed, but was about to give up when he heard that George Kirstein, a very casual acquaintance who had recently retired from his job as an executive of the Health Insurance Plan (HIP) of Greater New York, might be interested. Kirstein's father had been president of Filene's department store and a donor to the Sacco-Vanzetti appeal; his brother, Lincoln, had been one of the Monuments Men during World War II and, with George Balanchine, founded the New York City Ballet. Their older sister, Mina Curtiss, edited the English edition of Proust's letters and had written biographies of Degas and Bizet. George Kirstein, who had served on the War Labor Board and as a navy lieutenant in the South Pacific, but had yet to make his mark, soon agreed to take over.

In retrospect, 1955 marks a turning point in the life of *The Nation*—and not just because Carey McWilliams was the first editor of the magazine to come, as he put it, from "west of the Bronx." Or because he'd made it a condition of the transfer that the magazine settle the libel suit against Greenberg and *The New Leader*. (Neither side made any admissions or retractions, and each agreed to cover its own costs.) The suit against the New York City Board of Education was also quietly abandoned.

Though it went on publishing book reviews and poetry—some of it extremely good poetry, especially during Randall Jarrell's brief stint as literary editor just after the war—and music and art criticism, for the past twenty years *The Nation* had chiefly seen itself as a weapon in the anti-fascist struggle. Indeed, for the two years following Margaret Marshall's departure *The Nation* had functioned without a literary editor. Carey McWilliams's politics were every bit as radical as Freda Kirchwey's—on some issues, more radical. But his priorities were different. Where her gaze was usually eastward, across the Atlantic to Europe, or Israel, he looked west—not just back to the house he and his wife Iris still owned on Alvarado Street in Echo Park (which they kept until the 1970s), but to the whole country in the middle.

Listing his interests[23] after ten years as editor—"organized labor and civil liberties, migratory farm labor, race relations, demagogic mass movements and, of course, all things relating to California"—not one of them dealt with foreign policy or international relations. But with the cease-fire in Korea holding, America's only overseas involvements were covert: the August 1953 the ouster of Mohammad Mosaddegh in Iran and the 1954 coup in Guatemala to depose President Jacobo Arbenz Guzmàn.

Andrew Roth's blow-by-blow account[24] of events in Tehran highlighted the Nazi sympathies of army chief Gen. Fazlollah Zahedi, but never even hinted at the central role of the CIA and Britain's MI6. Interestingly, neither did J. Alvarez Del Vayo's commentary on Guatemala, which now reads like just one more denunciation[25] of an "unwarranted attack on a small country." Del Vayo may have been naïve, but at least he avoided the fate of Max Lerner, whose *New York Post* column implicating the CIA's "Kubark" counterintelligence manual worried[26] the agency, but who, returning from a trip to Guatemala in June 1954 decided the coup was justified, since Arbenz had "deliberately and with open eyes accepted Communist aid."[27] Or *The New Leader*, whose editors allowed Edward Bernays, the United Fruit Company's public relations man, to buy up public service ads for the Red Cross at $1,000 a page—far above the magazine's standard rate. *The New Leader*'s Latin America correspondent, Daniel James, obligingly produced *Red Design for the Americas*, a book-length rationale for the coup published by Stein and Day (Richard Day was a key cultural conduit for the CIA). United Fruit then bought it by the hundreds, distributing it to reporters, editors and "opinion makers" like so many poisoned bananas.[28]

It would be over a decade before Americans would learn just how carefully "dissent" was managed during the 1950s. In 1967 Christopher Lasch, using material patiently compiled by McWilliams, would begin to show[29] at what cost America's intellectuals enjoyed "both autonomy and affluence, as the social value of their services became apparent to the government, to corporations and to the foundations." At the same time, evidence emerged that Sidney Hook's American Committee for Cultural Freedom and its European parent, the Congress for Cultural Freedom (and its journal, *Encounter*), all of whom made a habit of targeting *The Nation*, had been heavily subsidized by the CIA. Lasch quoted Andrew Kopkind, who would join *The Nation* himself many years later: "The illusion of dissent was maintained. The CIA supported socialist cold warriors, fascist cold warriors, black and white cold warriors.... But it was a sham pluralism and it was utterly corrupting."

"Twenty years worth of Americans," wrote Kopkind, [30] "were taught that to lie was the highest morality." Carey McWilliams wasn't perfect, but his mistakes were his own. As for his, and *The Nation*'s, many successes, these were typically the result of long patience—and a keen eye for an opening. Unlike Freda Kirchwey, who believed they risked boring and alienating regular readers, McWilliams was a great believer in the "special issue." In the fall of 1952, shortly after he'd finished "How Free Is Free?" McWilliams put together "The Southern Negro." [31] Based on the optimistic—but erroneous—theory that black voters would "hold the balance of power between the Dixiecrats and the New Deal Democrats" in the coming election, the issue, as McWilliams later admitted, was premature.[32] Two years later, in *Brown* v. *Board of Education*, the Supreme Court (led by McWilliams's old nemesis, Earl Warren) put civil rights back on the national agenda.

The Nation had been agitating for such a moment since the early Villard era, publishing W.E.B. Du Bois[33] on the plight of black workers, William Pickens[34] on "Jim Crow in Texas," Walter White[35] on segregation's spread north, E. Franklin Frazier[36] on social discrimination, and Loren Miller[37] on the end of whites-only "covenants"* in real estate. In 1943 the magazine's Washington correspondent, I.F. Stone, resigned[38] from the National Press Club after his lunch guest, Judge William H. Hastie, the dean of Howard University Law School, was refused service. During the Harlem Renaissance, Sterling Brown, Countee Cullen, Langston Hughes and Claude McKay all had poems in *The Nation*, which also published Hughes's epochal 1926 manifesto[39] "The Negro Artist and the Racial Mountain." In 1947 it had printed a review[40] of Maxim Gorky's short stories—the first piece in a national magazine by the young James Baldwin.

Though conspicuous today for the absence of women—a tendency that, sadly, would only get worse under McWilliams—the list is also testimony to *The Nation*'s importance as a talent spotter and outlet for African-American writers, and its longstanding commitment to racial justice. So when Dan Wakefield walked into *The Nation* looking for a ticket to Mississippi—and wider fame—it is fair to say that Carey McWilliams was waiting for him.

§

Wakefield's reports on the Till trial[41] and the rise of the White Citizens Councils[42] launched his career; *The Nation* sent him to

---

* Miller, a California friend and mentor to McWilliams, had argued the landmark *Shelley v. Kraemer* case, which held that racial covenants were illegal and unenforceable, before the Supreme Court with his partner, Thurgood Marshall.

Israel* the following year to cover the Suez conflict and then made him its first staff writer. In return *The Nation* got something far more valuable: an introduction to the nascent Southern civil rights movement, and through Wakefield and Clifford Durr—an old friend of McWilliams who'd written a critique[43] of the Truman Loyalty Boards and was now practicing law in his hometown of Montgomery, Alabama—an introduction to Martin Luther King Jr. In Dr. King, McWilliams, who hailed the bus boycott as a "Miracle in Alabama,"[44] recognized that the Southern movement had finally found its leader and prophet.

"Through Dan and through the contacts that he had and others—a whole list of people that wrote for us about aspects of what was going on in the South—we had sort of an inside track to the thing. And through this I got in touch with King and suggested that we would like to have these annual reports," McWilliams recalled.[45] Starting in 1961 and for the next five years, King contributed a yearly essay to *The Nation* on the state of the civil rights movement. "He was very glad to do them, and we let him reprint them. They used them on money-raising campaigns; they were very useful," said McWilliams. In February 1967—a month before leading his first march against the Vietnam War, and two months before his celebrated speech at Riverside Church in New York—King delivered his first unequivocal public condemnation of the war at a *Nation* conference in Los Angeles on "Reordering National Priorities."

It was also during the 1950s that McWilliams, who'd known

---

*   Where I.F. Stone, running into him on the street, "looked at my ragged appearance and skinny frame and said 'Could I loan you a hundred dollars?'" Wakefield gratefully accepted.

Lincoln Steffens and Upton Sinclair back in California, decided that muckraking was due for a revival. In 1953 Alton Ochsner, a professor at Tulane University medical school, sent in his research[46] on the links between tobacco and lung cancer. Although George Seldes had published a similar study in his newsletter *In Fact* during the war, the national press, heavily dependant on cigarette advertising, suppressed the story.[47] Ochsner, who faced similar obstacles—appearing on *Meet the Press* in the wake of his *Nation* exposé he was told he wouldn't be allowed to mention any causal relationship between smoking and lung cancer on the air—was more persistent, and within less than a decade the Surgeon General had endorsed his findings.[48]

Ralph Nader was another walk-in. In 1959 Nader, who had published an article on automobile safety in the *Harvard Law Record*, a student-run newspaper at Harvard Law School, sent McWilliams "The Safe Car You Can't Buy"[49]—and launched the consumer revolution. Six years later Nader's campaign* against the Corvair[50] began in *The Nation*, which has since published dozens of articles by him. McWilliams knew, though, that he couldn't expect that kind of investigative reporting to just show up in the office. Also, "*The Nation* lacked the resources to indulge in investigative reporting, which tends to be expensive. Nor did it have the space; exposé articles are often lengthy."[51]

Instead of funding original reporting *The Nation* couldn't afford, McWilliams would collect a massive dossier of documents—news clippings, reports, court records, etc.—which he

---

* In the 2000 presidential election *The Nation* split its endorsement between Nader and Democrat Al Gore.

would turn over to a writer, who would then produce an intelligible digest as a "special issue." Bernard Nossiter, a friend and *Nation* contributor, suggested Fred Cook, a colleague on the *World-Telegram & Sun* who was becoming known as a brilliant "re-write" man. After a shorter trial run on capital punishment,[52] Cook was given his first real assignment: to take a fresh look at the case of Alger Hiss, the former State Department official whose conviction on perjury charges in 1950 made him a talisman for both McCarthy and his critics.

Like most Americans, Cook believed Hiss guilty, but as he sifted through the trial transcript and other records he became convinced of his innocence, producing an issue[53] that became a popular success—and igniting a cause that would link McWilliams with both his predecessor and his successor. The following year Cook took aim at an even bigger target: the FBI. Published in book form as *The FBI Nobody Knows*, his *Nation* special issue[54] was the first critical look at J. Edgar Hoover and his men since Max Lowenthal's 1950 study, whose suppression was the subject of Matthew Josephson's contribution to "How Free Is Free?" But whereas Lowenthal's book had been buried, and Lowenthal, though a close friend of President Truman, had been refused a passport, Cook's special issue won a Page One award from the Newspaper Guild; his book became a bestseller. A change was in the air.

Cook and his *World-Telegram* partner, Gene Gleason, who had been among the first reporters to question the press's adulation of New York City's powerful planning czar Robert Moses, went on to produce a special issue on urban corruption[55] and, in 1961, again using one of McWilliams's voluminous dossiers, Cook turned his muck-rake on that most sacrosanct of sacred cow pastures, the CIA.[56] Meanwhile Matthew Josephson uncovered the international arms trade[57] as Richard Cloward and Frances Piven began their inquest[58] into the welfare system. In 1964 Patrick J. Buchanan, a young editorial writer at the *St. Louis Globe-Democrat*, published a searing exposé[59] of conditions at the Missouri state penitentiary, ushering another gifted polemicist onto the national stage.

Eventually *The Nation*'s success with muckraking inspired imitation by better-funded organizations such as *Newsday*, the Associated Press and, eventually, *60 Minutes*. "We could not compete once muckraking had become the new radical chic in American journalism," wrote McWilliams, "nor was there any reason why we should."[60] At the same time the magazine's reputation attracted whistleblowers* such as former FBI agents Arthur Murtagh and William W. Turner,[61] and former CIA agent Victor Marchetti.[62] In October 1962 *The Nation* made a splash when former agent Jack Levine revealed that in the FBI's view the Communist Party, far from representing the clear and present danger of J. Edgar Hoover's rhetoric, had become "a paper tiger" whose members were actually regarded as "a manageable bunch of harmless crackpots." It made an even bigger splash when Levine's lampoon—which also noted that roughly 1,500 of the party's 8,500 members were FBI informants whose dues, dutifully entered on Bureau expense accounts, were paid by the hapless taxpayer—was picked up by Art Buchwald and eventually became a "bit" for Jack Paar on *The Tonight Show*.

---

* In November 2014 editor Katrina vanden Heuvel and contributing editor Stephen F. Cohen traveled to Moscow to interview NSA whistleblower Edward Snowden.

§

From the beginning, McWilliams and Kirstein took a conscious decision to stop chasing new subscribers. "You can go out and double your circulation very easily if you have lots of money to spend," said McWilliams. "But of course it doesn't do you much good because you can't hold them." Nor could they count on "events" and conferences to raise money, since in the political climate of the 1950s even some *Nation* readers didn't want to be publicly associated with the magazine. "The two of us decided just to stop the direct mail activity entirely to see what would happen," said McWilliams. "And the circulation declined. We lost about 2,000 subscribers...and then it began to come back. We took the position that those people were just waiting for that special offer. When they discovered that no special offer was going to be made to them, they subscribed. And actually we were much better off financially, in terms of not spending large sums of money and big mass mailings and advertising campaigns."[63]

In comparison with his predecessor's exuberant anti-fascist evangelism, *The Nation* under McWilliams can seem quieter, more inward looking, more comfortable simply preaching to the converted. Yet McWilliams was also more adventurous as an editor, less inclined to rely on staff writers. "People in certain subject areas would be constantly writing for the magazine.... You know what they're going to do, what kind of manuscript it's going to be; they understand you," McWilliams said. "But then that, too, has its counterproductive side, because if they are writing regularly for the magazine, some of them tend to be a little nonchalant about what they write." McWilliams recruited mathematician Jacob Bronowski;[64] literary critic Raymond Williams,[65] who became *The Nation*'s London correspondent; and historians Barton Bernstein,[66] Eric Hobsbawm,[67] William Appleman Williams,[68] Howard Zinn[69] and Bruce Catton,[70] who was the magazine's Washington correspondent.

Robert Sherrill, who took over the capital bureau in 1965, came to *The Nation* after *Harper's* editor Willie Morris wanted to cut to ribbons an interview he'd done with Texas oil tycoon H.L. Hunt[71] out of fear of a libel suit. Sherrill sent the piece to McWilliams, who printed it intact. (Several years earlier Morris had made his own debut[72] in *The Nation* when McWilliams printed "Mississippi Rebel; On a Texas Campus"—an account of his tribulations as editor of *The Daily Texan*.)

Perhaps the best example of McWilliams's resourcefulness as an editor, though, was his pursuit of a burned-out correspondent for the *National Observer*, a Dow Jones weekly, named Hunter Thompson. In the spring of 1965 Thompson received a package in the mail from McWilliams, an acquaintance, containing a California attorney general's office report on motorcycle gangs and an offer of $100 to write an article on the subject for *The Nation*. "I had known Hunter before he went to live in San Francisco and felt sure the subject would intrigue him," recalled McWilliams.[73] The resulting article, "Losers and Outsiders,"[74] did not please its subjects, who beat the author to a pulp. Expanded into the book *Hell's Angels*, it also made the gang, and the author, into legends—catapulting Thompson far beyond of *The Nation*'s price range.

McWilliams was equally intrepid—or equally lucky—in his dealings with Henrique Galvão. Though forgotten today, in the winter of 1961 Galvão made front pages across the world as the leader of a group that hijacked the Portuguese luxury liner *Santa Maria* as a protest against the Salazar dictatorship. Realizing that this same Galvão, a former Portuguese army officer, was the author of a *Nation* piece on Salazar, McWilliams radioed him aboard the ship, which was wandering around the South Atlantic followed by a British cruiser and two US navy destroyers, and was rewarded with a *Nation* exclusive, "How I Seized the *Santa Maria*."[75] In Luanda the news of Galvão's stunt triggered an attack on the prison—the first action by the People's Movement for the Liberation of Angola (MPLA), which eventually liberated the African colony from Portuguese rule.

In 1959 Carleton Beals, who'd been cabled a $100 advance from Villard to find Sandino in the twenties, and who reported on the advent of Cuban dictator Fulgencio Batista[76] for *The Nation* in the 1930s, wrote to McWilliams asking for a similar sum to report[77] on the young revolutionaries who overthrew his regime. "Not since Sandino resisted the American Marines for six years in the mountains of Nicaragua has any Latin American figure so caught the imagination of the world as Fidel Castro," wrote Beals.

For a brief moment, the enthusiasm was general. A few months after Beals's report the dean of Harvard, McGeorge Bundy, hosted a dinner for Castro at the Faculty Club in Cambridge and then escorted him to Soldiers' Field, where the crowd of 10,000 students rapturously applauded the Cuban leader's invitation to come visit the revolution. Among those who accepted were poet—and *Nation* contributor—Lawrence Ferlinghetti and C. Wright Mills, whose travelogue of the revolution, *Listen, Yankee*, sold 400,000 copies in a matter of months. But you didn't have to be an intellectual, or a beatnik, to love Fidel Castro. In advertise-

ments designed to promote black tourism, boxer Joe Louis point-
edly asked, "Where else can an American Negro go for a winter
vacation?"[78] Even John Kennedy, positioning himself as a liberal
alternative to Adlai Stevenson in his 1960 book *The Strategy of
Peace*, proclaimed: "Fidel Castro is part of the legacy of Bolivar."[79]

Of course it didn't last. Once he'd won the nomination, Kennedy tacked hard to starboard, calling the island "a chink in our
defensive armor" and charging Nixon and Eisenhower with "the
loss of Cuba." *The Nation*'s warnings before the Bay of Pigs would
be ignored, as would the magazine's equally prophetic reporting
from Vietnam. Starting with Andrew Roth's October 1945 des-
patch from Saigon revealing the economic and political bases for
the Vietnamese revolt, *The Nation* published hundreds of articles on
Vietnam—many of them, like Eqbal Ahmad's "How to Tell When
the Rebels Have Won," an acute diagnosis[80] of American myths and
colonial reality, transferable to subsequent conflicts in Asia, Latin
America and the Middle East. But no *Nation* piece would be as trag-
ically prophetic, no writer as important to understanding the nature
of the quagmire, as Bernard Fall's 1954 "Solution in Indo-China."[81]

Fall, an Austrian Jew whose parents were murdered by the
Nazis, and who had fought with the French resistance and then
served as an officer in the French army, was, in McWilliams's
words "a scholar, not a partisan." Yet nearly every word of his
advice—written two months before the French defeat at Dien
Bien Phu—on how France might extricate itself from the war
would be applicable, two decades later, to the United States.
Appearing in *The Nation* gave Fall, an academic at Syracuse and
later at Howard University, greater visibility; in the 1960s his

mere presence in the magazine lent *The Nation* credibility and in turn attracted some of the brightest reporters in the region, who sent McWilliams the pieces their own editors wouldn't publish. Or, in the case of television journalists like Ted Koppel[82] or Mike Wallace,[83] reports too complex, too controversial or just too downbeat for broadcast.

§

In July 1965 *The Nation* turned 100. Kirstein decided it was time for him to move on. "When Kirstein left," said McWilliams, *The Nation* "was relatively free of debt—oh, less than it had at any time in the past—and circulation was up, and it had miraculously survived a decade of McCarthyism."[84] That September the magazine published a 335-page special issue that began with a memorial to David Boroff, an NYU English professor and sometime journalist who had spent two years putting the issue together, then died just before it went to press.* Next came a word from the new publisher, James J. Storrow Jr. Like his Harvard '40 classmate, John F. Kennedy, and his *Nation* predecessor, Storrow had served in the South Pacific during World War II. But unlike the parvenu Kennedy, Storrow, a descendant of Thomas Jefferson, was the fifth consecutive generation of his family to graduate from Harvard. Storrow Drive in Boston was named after his father, James J. Storrow II, an investment banker who helped found General Motors.

Storrow Jr., who came to *The Nation* after running a microfilm business and the Henry Thayer Drug company—purveyors

---

*   Having just spent the past year on a similar project, I type these words with some trepidation.

of Thayer's Slippery Elm Lozenges—outlined his vision for the magazine: "*The Nation*," wrote Storrow, "is neither liberal nor conservative nor radical, nor does it habitually reflect the views of *any* group, political or otherwise." In 1965, with Lyndon Johnson just beginning his second term, and (as of the end of 1964) fewer than 24,000 troops in Vietnam, it might have just been possible to imagine such Olympian detachment. But even a year later, with the American "presence" at 184,000—and rising sharply every month—Storrow's hopes were irrelevant. By November 1966 Carey McWilliams was suggesting that Johnson might not even run for re-election if he wasn't certain of winning. [85]

The following year, in Los Angeles, at the same *Nation* conference on Reordering National Priorities at which Martin Luther King first spoke out unequivocally against the war, McWilliams found himself on the speaker's platform next to Senator Eugene McCarthy. "You know," said McWilliams, "I get a definite feeling here that if someone were to make an issue of this in the '68 primaries, particularly a senator who is not up for re-election...the results might be astonishing." According to McWilliams, McCarthy replied, "Well, I'm inclined to agree with you. I'm inclined to agree with you."[86]

Vietnam and opposition to the war dominated McWilliams's final decade as editor. Throughout the turmoil of the late 1960s and into the Nixon era *The Nation*'s role was never less than honorable. But as a new generation, "bred in at least modest comfort, housed now in universities, looking uncomfortably at the world we inherit,"—the quote is from *The Port Huron Statement*, the 1962 manifesto of Students for a Democratic Society (SDS)—began to cast off the shibboleths of the Cold War, they turned increasingly for guidance to publications like the British *New Left Review* or even *I.F. Stone's Weekly* rather than to *The Nation*. It was in *New Left Review* that C. Wright Mills published his seminal "Letter to the New Left."

Tom Hayden, who drafted *The Port Huron Statement*, didn't write for *The Nation* until 1981. In the 1960s and '70s if you wanted to read Hayden you had to buy *The New York Review of Books*, an upstart literary journal that also soon lured the radical journalist Andrew Kopkind, a refugee from *Time* who had been covering the radical student beat for Gilbert Harrison, who had bought *The New Republic* from Michael Straight.

McWilliams tried his best, commissioning Peter de Lissovoy, a fieldworker in Albany, Georgia, for the Student Non-Violent Coordinating Committee (SNCC), to report[87] on C.B. King's campaign for Congress. (King was the leader of the Albany Movement; de Lissovoy was assistant to Randy Battle, King's advance man.) Jack Newfield, a young staffer at *The Village Voice*, explained "The Student Left"[88] to *Nation* readers. But Newfield, though a supporter of SDS, wrote with a detachment that, as the war dragged on and society became increasingly polarized, only served to emphasize *The Nation's* distance from the young activists. An October 1966 article offering "A White Look at Black Power" was symptomatic of the magazine's limitations.

In time *The Nation* would welcome women's liberation and gay liberation, and rediscover its role as an outspoken critic of American militarism at home and abroad. In the 1950s—in Latin America, Southeast Asia, in Detroit, Los Angeles and Mississippi—America had sown the wind; in the 1960s it inherited the whirlwind. For helping *The Nation* to survive that storm, Kirstein and Storrow are owed a great debt. As for McWilliams, once again the magazine had been fortunate to find the right editor for the times. If his very unflappability rendered him increasingly out of temper with the frenzy of the 1970s, it is also true that no other editor has better expressed what the magazine means. "It is impossible," he wrote,[89] to own *The Nation*, "or possess it or bequeath it or sell it or mortgage it. If it ever ceased to be what it has always been, it would simply not exist—regardless of who 'owned' it…. It is an idea, a spirit, a name without an address; it is fragile, without physical assets, but it is free and so it lives." Thanks in large measure to Carey McWilliams, it still is, and still does. ✷

Victor Navasky

CHAPTER SEVEN

The Importance of Not Being Ernest

C arey McWilliams needed a rest. By 1975 *The Nation*, too, seemed to be on its last legs. The war in Vietnam was finally winding down—and with it the antiwar movement—removing one of the magazine's principal preoccupations. In Spain, Francisco Franco's death in November brought an end to another of *The Nation*'s cherished causes—and furnished a punch line for the satirical news bulletin on a new television program, *Saturday Night Live*, that premiered on NBC that fall[1]. *Esquire* magazine, struggling to make ends meet, agreed to let the Xerox corporation sponsor an article by Harrison Salisbury—a step the writer E.B. White conceded might not be "in itself evil," but which he was nonetheless certain was "the beginning of evil, and…an invitation to evil." *The Nation*, sympathetic to the vicissitudes of magazine publishing, and sufficiently admiring of Salisbury to have printed his work on a number of occasions, also found[2] the advent of sponsored journalism cause for alarm.

Yet James Storrow had become increasingly resentful of *The Nation*'s continuing inability to support itself. Though he was a wealthy man, the magazine was still a drain on his resources. Ideally he'd have liked to find the right person to take it off his hands, but covering the deficit on a loss-making journal, even one as venerable as *The Nation*, was not a proposition that appealed to everyone. And Storrow, whatever his faults, took his responsibility for *The Nation*'s survival very seriously—as did his wife, Linda Eder, the magazine's associate publisher. So in the same December issue as the editorial looking askance at sponsored content, sandwiched between that and Representative Elizabeth Holtzman's withering review of the Watergate special prosecutor's report, Storrow discreetly announced the appointment of his Harvard classmate, Blair Clark, as *The Nation*'s new editor.

"The last man in the class at Harvard hired the next-to-last man," was McWilliams's verdict on his successor. On paper, Clark's credentials were formidable. An heir to the Clark's thread fortune, he'd been elected president and editor of the Harvard *Crimson*, working after graduation at the *St. Louis Post-Dispatch* until his wartime service in the army. In 1946 he'd started a successful Sunday newspaper in New Hampshire, hiring his prep school and college buddy Ben Bradlee as the paper's star reporter. A job with CBS news in Paris began a rise up the network ladder, first in radio and then in television, where he worked with Edward R. Murrow and as general manager of CBS News; his hires there included Walter Cronkite, Dan Rather, Morley Safer and Mike Wallace. Clark had also been associate publisher of the *New York Post* and one of the early backers of *The New York Review of Books*. In 1968 he'd managed Eugene McCarthy's presidential campaign. He was a close friend of poet Robert Lowell. And somewhere between Paris and New York he'd briefly collaborated with the CIA.[3]

"Blair knew everybody," said Victor Navasky, who'd come to know Clark while writing about the McCarthy campaign for *The New York Times Magazine*. "He knew everybody in the financial world who was interested in liberal politics."[4] Perhaps that was the problem: by 1975 the term "liberal" had acquired all sorts of baggage, from Hubert Humphrey's timorous silence over the Vietnam War, to the ineffectual remedies for inner-city poverty proposed by various Democratic mayors, to the liberal Republican Nelson Rockefeller's brutal response to a revolt by inmates at Attica State Penitentiary. For the generation that came of age in the 1960s, "liberal" just didn't cut it. Nor was this simply a question of age—or fashion. At a time when even the resolutely un-hip *I.F. Stone's Weekly*—printed on newsprint and written by a man old enough to have ghosted speeches for Norman Thomas in 1928—saw its circulation swell to 60,000 and more, *The Nation* struggled to attract 25,000 subscribers.

A younger, more energetic publisher might have taken the rising tide of discontent as a cue for expansion—the explosion of "underground" and "alternative" newspapers during the 1960s suggesting a readership hungry for coverage that went beyond the cautious, noncommittal certainties of what had not yet been labeled the mainstream media. James Storrow was not that man. Refusing to spend money either to promote the magazine or to expand its editorial ambit, he installed Clark, who in turn, either awed by *The Nation*'s legacy or inhibited by Storrow's budgets, made few changes to the magazine he'd inherited. Less than a year into Clark's editorship, with little to show beyond a continuing decline in circulation and with his own health deteriorating, Storrow put *The Nation* up for sale.

The chief requirements seemed to be a broad affinity with the magazine's politics and a willingness to continue financing its chronic deficit, and when *The New York Times* ran a story on November 28, 1976, saying that *The Nation* had been sold to Thomas Morgan, who had agreed to spend between $100,000 and $150,000 a year, the matter appeared settled. A former press secretary to New York mayor John Lindsay, Morgan had until recently edited *The Village Voice*. He was also married to Mary Rockefeller, the daughter of Nelson Rockefeller and great-granddaughter of the founder of Standard Oil.

Only it turned out the deal wasn't done. Among *The Nation*'s two-dozen other suitors was Alan Baron, who had been presidential candidate George McGovern's press secretary. Storrow reportedly felt Baron's clear political commitment might compromise *The Nation*'s founding pledge not to serve as "the organ of any party, movement or sect." Whether owing to that fastidiousness or some more obscure motive, when Storrow found out that Morgan had offered Baron a job as *The Nation*'s Washington correspondent—without consulting him— he was furious. Clark, who by this point was also eager to move on, picked up the phone and called Victor Navasky.

§

Though the byline said "G. Mennen Williams" and the article, "'Pros' and Progressives," was illustrated with a caricature of the Michigan governor in one of his trademark bow ties, this[5] July 9, 1960, defense of the Democratic Party's liberal potential was actually Victor Navasky's first contribution to *The Nation*. A newly minted graduate of the Yale Law School, Navasky had taken a day job as Mennen's speechwriter to finance his real passion: editing a satirical magazine.

Now it would be unfair—and perhaps even untrue—to say that in its first eleven decades *The Nation* had been entirely devoid of humor. During the 1930s Heywood Broun fought heroic struggles to get a little bit of facetiousness into the magazine, and Wade Thompson's 1959 article "My Crusade Against Football," which now reads as more strenuous than satirical, was widely anthologized. Throughout the lonely decades when McWilliams defied the witch-hunters *The Nation* was brave, often prescient, even eloquent. Above all, though, it was earnest.

Navasky was not earnest. A product of the Rudolph Steiner School, Manhattan's Little Red Schoolhouse and the famously left-wing Elisabeth Irwin High School, Navasky had been sent as a child to Pioneer Youth Camp, where he served as postmaster and learned songs from the Spanish Civil War. But his father, a successful clothing manufacturer who "sold his share of the family business, at least partly, I always assumed, so I would never have to go into it," was no admirer of labor unions. At Swarthmore he'd gotten into trouble for mocking the college president, and the newly liberalized parietal rules, in the student paper. More wry than funny himself, Navasky functioned as a near occasion of humor in others.

Monocle, the magazine he started in law school, took aim at everything from race relations—comedian Godfrey Cambridge turned Norman Podhoretz's neoconservative *cri de coeur* "My Negro Problem, and Ours" into "My Taxi Problem and Ours," while Robert Grossman chronicled the adventures of the superhero Captain Melanin—to the Cold War. A "leisurely quarterly" (which meant it came out twice a year), *Monocle*'s writers included C.D.B. Bryan, Nora Ephron, Richard Lingeman, Neil Postman, Calvin Trillin and Dan Wakefield. But its look—a mélange of vintage typefaces and cartoons ten years ahead of Monty Python—and pool of illustrators may have been even more influential. Marshall Arisman, Seymour Chwast, Paul Davis, Milton Glaser, Grossman, Ed Koren, David Levine, Ed Sorel and Tomi Ungerer were among those who contributed drawings, covers or cartoons. In 1964 *Monocle* ran managing editor Marvin Kitman, the only staffer over 35 years old, for president—as a "Lincoln Republican" challenger to Barry Goldwater.

Monocle never made any money, but it saved Navasky from having to practice law, and after a few years circulation had grown enough that the distributor ordered triple the usual print run for a much-ballyhooed special issue on the CIA. The issue was scheduled to appear on November 19, 1963, but owing to events in Dallas later that week most of the copies remained in the warehouse, putting an end to Navasky's first experiment in publishing.

There were, however, two codas that would each have long-lasting consequences. In 1966 a brief news report about a "peace scare" sending stock prices tumbling prompted the *Monocle* men to muse about what might happen if the government appointed a blue-ribbon panel to study the impact of conversion from a permanent war economy and concluded that the country simply couldn't afford it. And what if, they mused further, this imaginary top-secret panel's imaginary top-secret study somehow leaked out? The result was *Report From Iron Mountain*—a satire of think-tank jargon and national security rationalization so close to the bone it was confirmed as real by a breathless *U.S. News & World Report* story, which claimed that President Johnson "hit the roof" and ordered it suppressed.[6] Published as nonfiction by Dial Press, whose editor in chief, E.L. Doctorow, was in on the hoax, the book became a bestseller—thanks in part to a review in *The Washington Post* by the eminent psychometrist "Herschel McLandress," the fictional alter-ego of economist John Kenneth Galbraith, another co-conspirator.[7] Though the *Report From Iron Mountain*'s author, Leonard Lewin, confessed all in the *New York Times Book Review* in 1972, that hasn't stopped the far right from embracing *Iron Mountain* with a fervor normally reserved for *The Turner Diaries* or *The Protocols of the Elders of Zion*—two other works of fiction.[8]

Navasky's reluctance to let *Monocle* die sent him down some strange paths, including a brief alliance with comedian Peter Cook, godfather to the British satirical weekly *Private Eye*. Convinced that stable capitalization was the key, Navasky, who had taken the Radcliffe Publishing Procedures course right after law school, set about writing a prospectus to woo investors. He also studied the arcane science of direct-mail solicitation under magazine guru James Kobak.[*] Though his education in how to test and

---

[*] Who in 2002 wrote *How To Start a Magazine: And Publish It Profitably*. Navasky may have skimmed the second part.

refine the subscription price, ad copy and target mailing lists didn't save *Monocle*, it would prove remarkably useful later on.

Meanwhile he wrote *Kennedy Justice*, a critical study of Robert F. Kennedy's Justice Department, which *Commentary* lauded as "subtle and intelligent" (but which the *New York Review of Books* found "regrettably" lenient). He also freelanced, most frequently for *The New York Times Magazine*, which eventually hired him as an editor. At the *Times* he learned what was then known as the "Afghanistan Principle": a writer's "ability to tell the truth was inversely proportional to one's distance from Forty-third Street." (Though the principle doubtless survives, the parameters have presumably changed, since the *Times* is no longer on Forty-third Street—and Afghanistan no longer signifies a far away country about which we know very little.) He also commissioned—and shepherded into print—Merle Miller's pioneering 1971 coming-out piece "On Being Different: What it Means to Be Homosexual." He left the *Times* in 1972 to write a book on the Hollywood blacklist. Two years later he managed Ramsey Clark's US Senate campaign (Clark won the Democratic nomination, but was defeated by incumbent Jacob Javits.)[9]

None of which would have put Navasky on James Storrow's radar. Nor, for that matter, would Storrow have been impressed by the fact that Navasky had recently written a couple of book reviews for *The Nation*—this time under his own name. If he had seen them, he might have noticed the contributor's note saying Navasky "writes frequently on politics and publishing"—a dead giveaway that the author lacked a steady job. But in addition to whatever powers of persuasion he'd honed through the years of pitching for *Monocle*, and whatever grandeur attached to a now-tenuous connection with

The New York Times Magazine, where he wrote a monthly "In Cold Print" column about the publishing business, Navasky had a secret weapon. His name was Hamilton Fish—a moniker that would have immediately registered with Storrow.

The first Hamilton Fish had been governor of New York, a US senator and secretary of state in the Grant administration—and probably a reader of Godkin's *Nation*. His father, Nicholas Fish, had been a colonel in the Revolutionary War; his mother, Elizabeth Stuyvesant, was the great-great-granddaughter of the governor of New Amsterdam. The latest Hamilton Fish's grandfather—the grandson of Hamilton I—served twenty-five years in the House of Representatives, where his isolationism and bitter opposition to the New Deal was immortalized in FDR's litany during the 1940 campaign of "Barton, Martin and Fish" as emblems of reaction. His father, also named Hamilton Fish and also a Republican (but a liberal), served thirteen terms in the House, where as a ranking member of the Judiciary Committee he voted to impeach President Nixon.

"If you got a call from Hamilton Fish, you took it," said Navasky. At Harvard, Fish had organized a get-out-the-vote campaign in response to the Twenty-sixth Amendment lowering the voting age to 18. After graduation he worked as an investigator for the Moreland Commission investigating nursing homes, before joining the Ramsey Clark for Senate campaign as chief fundraiser—an unusual responsibility for a 22-year-old, made more challenging by Clark's pledge to refuse all donations over $100. Despite his lineage, Fish had little personal fortune. He was, however, absolutely shameless in pursuit of a good cause. Reading a 1975 *New York Times* article[10] saying that Marcel Ophuls, the director of *The Sorrow and the Pity*, had just been fired from his latest film, a documentary about the Nuremberg Trials, Fish contacted Ophuls and asked him whether, if he raised the money to buy the rights and footage from the producers, Ophuls would be willing to complete it. Fish raised the money, Ophuls finished his movie, and the acclaimed documentary *The Memory of Justice* premiered at Cannes in 1976.

So when Navasky asked Fish "Why don't you do for *The Nation* what you did for Marcel Ophuls?" he was intrigued. And when the 24-year-old Fish phoned Storrow, the publisher took the call, and over a three-martini lunch at the Harvard Club confirmed that *The Nation* was indeed for sale. But who was this Navasky character? Only when Doctorow (who had just published *Ragtime*), Ralph Nader, philanthropists W.H. and Carol Ferry, and two partners from the Paul, Weiss law firm agreed to vouch for him did negotiations begin. After nearly a year of courtship, Storrow agreed to guarantee the magazine's losses—roughly $125,000 a year—for another three years. Fish had originally hoped Alan Sagner, a real estate developer who had helped to found the Fair Play for Cuba Committee, would take over as publisher. But when New Jersey governor Brendan Byrne appointed Sagner chairman of the Port Authority (a sign, if ever there was one, that the McCarthy era was over) he bowed to the inevitable, joining the masthead as publisher on January 21, 1978.

There was never any question about who would be editor. "Victor was the reason people put up the money," said Fish.[11] Navasky took over in March; *Naming Names*, which he was supposed to be finishing, had to wait another two years. All that canvassing for *Monocle* now paid off, not only in terms of prospective investors—the Fish-Navasky syndicate raised $650,000, enough, when added to Storrow's contribution, to fund *The Nation* for three years of aggressive promotion (after which, if all went according to plan,[*] the magazine would be self-supporting)—but also in personnel. Navasky's first hire was Calvin Trillin, who agreed to contribute a 1,000-word column every third week for a salary "in the high two figures." The actual sum, Navasky revealed, was $65, adding that when the first installment[12] of what became *Uncivil Liberties* appeared in April 1978—devoted entirely to ridiculing him—Blair Clark, who was still in residence, told him that Trillin clearly didn't belong in *The Nation*. "Blair let me know, in his own genteel way, what a mistake I'd made in hiring Bud, and said that if I wasn't up to the task of letting Bud know, he volunteered."[13]

Trillin stayed, and at last count has written over 1,100 pieces for *The Nation*—more than any other contributor in the magazine's history[†].

§

Though it meant that he would forever be known as "the wily and parsimonious Victor S. Navasky," the presence of unabashed wit in *The Nation*'s pages sent a message. Like every new editor, Navasky wanted to shake things up. Rejecting the advice of friends to shift to a biweekly schedule to cut costs—

---

[*]   As you can probably guess, all did not go according to plan.

[†]   He also holds the record for shortest piece: a poem on the O.J. Simpson trial that read simply "O.J./Oy Vey." As Navasky points out, when Trillin switched from prose humor columnist to "Deadline Poet" his rate, which had crept up over the years to $100, remained unchanged, making him also the highest-paid writer, on a per-word basis, in the magazine—and perhaps in the whole country.

"We boasted of being 'America's oldest weekly magazine.' Why would you give that up?"—he and Fish got graphic legends Milton Glaser and Walter Bernard to redesign the magazine with an all-type cover and a new logo that restored the period at the end of the title. To emphasize their hunger for new business, they stole a trick from A. Whitney Ellsworth, publisher of *The New York Review of Books*, printing subscription forms on the back of their business cards. And when Martin Peretz responded to a story in *The New York Times* reporting that a "feud" had developed between the two liberal journals following *The New Republic*'s shift "to the right" with a letter insisting, "We have no feud with that magazine. Its readership is too tiny, its contents too reflexively *gauchiste* to trouble with," Fish and Navasky took out a tiny classified ad on the bottom of the *Times* front page. It read: "Martin Peretz, please come home. All is forgiven. *The Nation*— still unfashionably liberal after all these years."[14]

Yet Peretz had a point—at least about *The Nation*'s circulation, which upon examination turned out to be considerably below the promised 25,000. "It seemed that 5,000 of our subscribers had expired," Navasky explained. "I told Jack Newfield we had 20,000 subscribers, but 8,000 of those were libraries. And he came back with, 'Oh. 8,000 libraries and 12,000 nursing homes.' As Ham used to say, when our subscribers expire, they really expire!" said Navasky. But was Peretz also right about the magazine's politics?

Navasky, who confirmed his admiration for *The Nation* and what he describes as a "reverence for Carey McWilliams" reading through back issues related to the Hollywood black list, says that when he arrived at his new office at 333 Sixth Avenue, "I did not have an ideological program I intended to enforce. But I did think that debates within *The Nation* would not be between the Democrats and the Republicans, but between the radicals and the liberals."

Navasky's political compass had its fixed points—many of them set out in the letter he'd sent James Storrow the previous year: he confessed to "a simplistic, absolutist view of the First Amendment," was an "integrationist" on race who nonetheless thought *The Nation* "an appropriate forum for black nationalists," remained wary of multinational corporations and had "a profound presumption in favor of disarmament over armament and am paranoid about nuclear weapons." He was, he allowed, soft on "old World Federalists," a privacy fanatic who worried about new technology and believed "all forms of electronic eavesdropping ought to be banned.... I have an enduring sympathy for socialist experiments, preferably decentralized, and keep looking for one that works." While conceding that "on an issue like 'Should There Be a Palestinian State?' there is ample room for a symposium," (not a view you would have seen in *The New Republic* in 1977) Navasky shared Heywood Broun's impatience with *The Nation*'s "policy of fair play, and everybody must be heard whether or not he has anything to say."

Though clearly left of center, the list is as notable for what it does not mention— economic policy, energy policy, women's rights, communism, imperialism, the environment, trade unions, Cuba—as what it does. While he obviously saw *The Nation* as committed, and made no pretense of impartiality or objectivity, Navasky's letter ended on a note of skepticism. What made *The Nation* unique, he said, was its willingness "to question the conventional wisdom, to be suspicious of all orthodoxies, to provide a home for dissent and dissenters."[15]

Determined to shock—or shake—the moribund weekly into life, Navasky told *The Wall Street Journal* his aim was to have "the best writers in the country lined up around the block wanting to write for us." Actually, some of them already were, thanks in part to literary editor Elizabeth Pochoda, a staffer from the Clark era whose replacement Navasky had already recruited. A scholar of medieval literature with a doctorate from the University of Pennsylvania, Pochoda had been recommended by Philip Roth, and quickly re-established the *Nation*'s back of the book as a coveted venue for writers and publishers, thanks to her truly inspired ability to "pair" reviewers and topics.

This was something different from W.P. Garrison's search for expertise. Pochoda's assignments took the goal of intelligent appraisal for granted; while shedding light, they also aimed to throw off sparks. The writer Ishmael Reed, for example, had already made waves—and enemies—with his novels *Mumbo Jumbo* (1972) and *The Last Days of Louisiana Red* (1974). Yet to read Edmund White's brilliant appreciation[16] of *Flight to Canada* (1976)—"a comic exploration of slavery by the best black writer around"—is not only to see White, noting that Reed "both invites and outrages moral interpretation," anticipating the dispiriting trajectory of a critical response that prompted Reed to abandon writing novels for nearly two decades. It also reminds us just how far ahead of his time Reed remains. Quickly recognizing that in Pochoda he'd inherited the perfect provocateur—whose taste for starting fires was at least equal to his own, and whose enthusiasm for popular culture might attract readers not quite so close to their expiration dates—Navasky kept her on, promising to restore the total autonomy enjoyed by Margaret Marshall. The list of writers encouraged and nurtured by Pochoda is too lengthy for this brief summary, though Paul Berman, Arthur Danto, Thomas Disch, Barbara Grizzuti Harrison, Stuart Klawans, Margo Jefferson, Katha Pollitt and Edward Said would be on any short list (as would the writer of this history).

All Navasky asked in return was to be sent advance galleys of a new book that claimed to be the final word on the Alger Hiss case. Not all *Nation* readers—or for that matter *Nation* staffers—shared Navasky's doubt[*] about Hiss's guilt. But his careful forensic examination[17] of Allen Weinstein's scholarship led to a libel suit against the author, a retraction by *The New Republic*, and a reinvigorated debate about a supposedly "settled" question of Cold War history that spilled over into *The New York Times*, *Newsweek* and the *Today* show.

§

Another Clark-era holdover originally marked for replacement was Kai Bird. A Foreign Service brat who'd grown up in Jerusalem, Beirut, Dhahran, Cairo and Mumbai, finishing high school in Tamil Nadu, Bird actually had a master's degree in journalism. He and his wife spent a year freelancing their way through India, Pakistan and Bangladesh before Bird, still in his 20s, came to work part time at *The Nation*. After working with him and getting to know him, Navasky made Bird full time. Among his early responsibilities was another item on the investors' prospectus: an intern program.

---

[*]   It was less a matter of faith in Hiss's innocence, says
Navasky, than "the fact that every time I tried to look closely at
the evidence for his guilt, it seemed to me it wasn't there."

In the decades since Nick Goldberg, Julie Just, Alexander Stille and Amy Wilentz arrived in the summer of 1978, more than 900 other young people have followed in their footsteps; *The Nation*'s intern program has figured in at least three marriages and countless office romances, and has been a crucial first step in the career of such journalists as Jane Spencer (whose reporting from China for *The Wall Street Journal* won a Pulitzer Prize in 2007), The Marshall Project founder Neil Barsky, David Corn, Liza Featherstone, Timothy Noah, Michael Tomasky, Mark Gevisser (of *The Nation*'s Southern Africa bureau), Maria Margaronis (London bureau), columnist JoAnn Wypijewski, associate publisher Peter Rothberg, executive editor Richard Kim and, of course, editor and publisher Katrina vanden Heuvel. Of the many former interns outside journalism, Nick Clegg, from the 1990 cohort, is currently deputy prime minister of the United Kingdom, while Ed Miliband (1989 cohort) is leader of the Labour Party and the current favorite to become the next prime minister.

Not bad for a group whose creation was partly Navasky's way of saving money on messengers (back in the days when *Nation* articles were set in type from copy—sometimes typed, sometimes handwritten—that had to be mailed or messengered to the office), and partly due to a desire "to make contact with the coming generation." Unpaid labor at first, *Nation* interns soon began receiving a small stipend, which, in response to intern agitation and managerial reflection, was in 2013 raised to the minimum wage—a change that coincided with the relaunch of what is now officially named the Victor S. Navasky Internship Program.

Somewhat quicker—if more contentiously negotiated—

results were achieved for *Nation* freelancers after a campaign waged by the National Writers Union, an organization that grew out of the 1981 American Writers Congress, organized by The Nation Institute to protest the Reagan administration's assault on culture. More than 4,000 writers responded to the conference summons[18] citing growing concentration in the publishing industry, reduced government funding for the arts, and a rise in book bannings and other forms of censorship as causes for concern—so many that organizers had to open a second venue to handle the overflow crowd. Deliberately modeled on the Popular Front gatherings of the 1930s—author Meridel Le Sueur, who'd attended the first League of American Writers Congress in 1935 provided a living link—the gathering even generated a modest backlash in the form of a statement by something calling itself The Committee for a Free World complaining that writers were biting the hand that fed them. Keynote speaker Toni Morrison's ringing speech calling for "a heroic writers movement—assertive, militant, pugnacious" drew thunderous applause, and led, some months later, to the founding of the freelancers' union.[19] Which in turn led, a little while later, to the threat of pickets outside the Navasky apartment when negotiations at *The Nation* reached an impasse.

The same law of unintended consequences was at work in February 1982 when *The Nation* sponsored a meeting at Town Hall in solidarity with the Polish union Solidarity. The idea, expressed most eloquently by the Mexican novelist Carlos Fuentes in his message to the gathering, was to overturn the Cold War assumptions by which the Reagan administration, in the process of destroying unions in the United States and funding the murder of labor organizers in Latin America, was trying to claim the mantle of the Polish workers and their union. "Let Poland be Poland," wrote Fuentes, "but let El Salvador be El Salvador."

Though Gore Vidal spoke first, and was followed by E.L. Doctorow, Allen Ginsberg, and Kurt Vonnegut, it was Susan Sontag's indictment[20] of the left that got the most attention. "Imagine, if you will, someone who read only the *Reader's Digest* between 1950 and 1970, and someone who read only *The Nation* or the *New Statesman*," she challenged her audience. "Which reader would have been better informed about the realities of communism? The answer, I think should give us pause. Can it be that our enemies were right?"

Sontag's argument about double standards on the left was worth taking seriously. There is little doubt that many in the Town Hall audience—and in the pages of *The Nation*—were more comfortable protesting America's depredations than Soviet oppression. Yet Sontag's solipsistic leap from her own ignorance and bad faith to that of her audience was as unfair and uninformed as her summary of communism as "successful fascism" was crude and unhistorical. She may have viewed Czeslaw Milosz with suspicion until 1980, but I.F. Stone (whom Navasky would soon woo back to *The Nation*) recommended *The Captive Mind*, which he called "a first rate study of intellectuals under Stalinism," to readers of his *Weekly*—in 1957![21] Two years before that *The Nation's* reviewer[22] said that Milosz's novel, *The Seizure of Power* "is not likely to give comfort to any partisan reader…. Coming at a time when fiction dealing with the 'cold war' is usually propagandistic, *The Seizure of Power* is a memorable work in that it condemns the methods power often uses to perpetuate itself."

It was in that same spirit—as an antidote to the *Reader's Digest* triumphalism that was, even then, becoming the dominant narrative of the end of communism—that the meeting at Town Hall had been called in the first place. Sontag's ad-libbed *peccavimus* stole the show, and may even have been a key move in transforming the failed novelist and radical academic who once wrote "the white race *is* the cancer of human history" into the intellectual celebrity she became. But it is hard to read her self-mythologizing[23] "I think that the problem at Town Hall was simply that I was breaking ranks" as anything but an elementary failure of, precisely, solidarity. Or perhaps, given the echo—by so self-conscious a writer—of Norman Podhoretz's *Breaking Ranks*, she was sending a signal. As she later told *The New York Times*: "Of the writers, I think I was the only person who said anything. I said something I wasn't supposed to say, and I knew what I was doing."

The same could often be said of Norman Mailer, who in 1986, as president of the PEN American center, invited Secretary of State George Shultz to give the welcoming speech to the group's International Congress, on the theme of "The Writer's Imagination and the Imagination of the State," at the New York Public Library. A letter[24] protesting the invitation, and pointing out that Shultz's State Department still routinely excluded foreign writers under the provisions of the McCarthy-era McCarran-Walter act was drafted by Pochoda and assistant literary editor Maria Margaronis and signed by a list of literary luminaries that included International PEN vice president (and future Nobel laureate) Nadine Gordimer, three past presidents of American PEN, and a host of poets, essayists and novelists.

The very first name on the list, however, belonged to the group's current vice president, Susan Sontag.

§

Not everyone in *The Nation*'s orbit disagreed with Sontag's Town Hall remarks. Aryeh Neier, former executive director of the ACLU and a Navasky recruit to *The Nation*'s editorial board, who said he couldn't "recall a time when he had a different view of communism" applauded "Sontag's effort to recapture anti-communism." Warmer still was the welcome from one of the magazine's newest additions. "I was pleased that Susan Sontag invited the left to criticize its own record on Stalinism," wrote[25] Christopher Hitchens. Noting that "Having tried to open a debate on the responsibilities of the left, Sontag has done her best to close it again by ill-tempered and ahistorical remarks about fascism and the record of the *Reader's Digest*," Hitchens turned to attack those "who divert an argument about Polish self-determination into an argument about the hypocrisy of Reagan.... By doing so, they devalue solidarity with Solidarity, and I think Sontag was right to say so."

Hitchens, as it happened, had come to *The Nation* from the self-same *New Statesman*, where he'd taken up residence after Oxford and a brief stop at the *Sunday Times* (and a longer sojourn among the Trotskyites). Admiring his reporting from the Middle East, Navasky invited him to send in the occasional dispatch. Hitchens promptly did so, and in 1981 Navasky wrote to Bruce Page, the editor of the *New Statesman*, suggesting a three-month swap of Hitchens, who was eager to explore New York, for Kai Bird. "I took his job and apartment and he took my job and apartment in Stuyvesant Town," Bird recalled. "He got the better deal in every way. His apartment in Notting Hill Gate was in a slum in those days. It was a dump. The kitchen was non-existent. The hot water was iffy. And of course there was no central heating!"[26]

Though Bird would go on to become a distinguished historian, sharing the Pulitzer Prize for his 2006 biography of J. Robert Oppenheimer, he was not, then, primarily a writer. (Nor were many—or any—other writers able to match Hitchens's already storied ability to follow a morning gossiping on the telephone, a heavy lunch, afternoon debate, cocktails, dinner and drinks by withdrawing to produce, as if by magic, a letter-perfect column in time for the next morning's deadline.) So when Bird eagerly returned to *The Nation*, Hitchens, who quite liked the prospects opening up before him in America, stayed on, at first somewhat footloose in New York but eventually as the magazine's Washington correspondent.

His taste for heterodox opinion—which seemed, at the time, as much an aesthetic as a political preference—suited Navasky. And his views[27] on the Middle East, though very much in sync with Bird's, were a bracing change from the unquestioning support for Israel that still paralyzed liberal discourse on the subject. Long before he started writing for *Vanity Fair*, he was the single member of *The Nation* other staffers were most likely to be asked about. But for all his literary brilliance, powerful reportage and burgeoning fan base, Hitchens, perhaps because he was off in Washington, had surprisingly little influence on the culture of the magazine.

The same cannot be said of Andrew Kopkind, who responded to Sontag's speech with a scornful reminder[28] of the time the two of them "huddled in a Communist/fascist air-raid shelter and waited for Freedom's fighters to pass out of danger overhead.

Actually, they were Freedom's *bombers*—B-52s, or some such U.S. Air Force weapons system" during a visit to Hanoi in 1968. The invocation of history was typical of Kopkind, as was the personal connection from a writer who had taken tea with the Shah of Iran while still an undergraduate at Cornell—where as the editor of the *Daily Sun* he'd also become friendly with his *Yale Daily News* counterpart, Calvin Trillin—studied with Ralph Miliband at the London School of Economics; carried Henry Luce's bags as a correspondent for *Time* magazine; covered the civil rights movement and SDS for *The New Republic*, *Ramparts* and *The New York Review of Books*; and then, with Ralph Nader, Robert Sherrill and James Ridgeway, founded the legendary radical newsletter *Mayday* before dropping out to a commune in Vermont, coming out as a gay man and, with his lover John Scagliotti, hosting "Lavender Hour," the first national gay and lesbian radio program. It was the latter, presumably, along with a recent feature in *The Village Voice*, that prompted Sontag to dismiss[29] him as "the noted disco expert of the 70s" in her response.[30]

Navasky persuaded Kopkind to join *The Nation* shortly after Town Hall. But when he started to talk about the magazine's politics, Kopkind interrupted. "It's not about politics," he said. "It's about watching Dan Rather or Brokaw or Jennings or whoever and thinking, 'That's not the way it is. That's not the way it is at all.' We should say that and say why and say the way it is." Kopkind would write movie criticism, cover presidential politics, and report from South Africa and the soon-to-be-former Soviet Union under his own name, but the greater part of his impact on the magazine went largely unseen.

At *Nation* editorial board meetings, Kopkind, sensitive to slights and prone to a stutter, had the influence of the smartest man in a room full of very well informed (and not always shy) people. Mostly, though, he worked the phones, where on the call to discuss that week's unsigned editorial, which Kopkind usually wrote, he played Navasky like a Stradivarius: "He would call in," said Navasky, "ostensibly to get his assignment…. What, he would ask, was the subject of the week? If I didn't come up with the one he had in mind, he would diplomatically make certain that I thought of his subject before too long. Or, if he suspected I was politically retrograde, which was often the case, he would educate me in advance with an esoteric, very funny, not quite contemptuous story about some third-party jerk who believed exactly as I had not yet told him I did, and then ask me what I thought."[31]

Simply by being there, and being who he was—gay, deeply radical, brilliant, charismatic and incredibly sophisticated politically—Kopkind pulled *The Nation*'s center of gravity further to the left. He also led—and sometimes pushed—a magazine more comfortable with the class-oriented analysis of the white male left to realize, and embrace, the importance of women's liberation, gay liberation and what was sometimes denigrated as "identity politics." This was not always a comfortable process—especially since Kopkind was supposed to be speaking for "The Editors." But as Navasky says, "Andy never wrote anything I didn't want to publish. He was too good a writer…. When he wrote something that went beyond where I thought *The Nation* was ready to go in its unsigned editorials, I would suggest it appear with his byline. That was our compromise."

Navasky's tolerance—and respect—for writers more radical

than he is was perhaps most severely tested by Alexander Cockburn. The son of Claud Cockburn, a celebrated British journalist who'd reported the 1929 Wall Street Crash for *The Times* of London and the Spanish Civil War for the *Daily Worker*, and whose one-man newsletter, *The Week*, had exposed the "Cliveden set" of upper-class advocates for appeasing the Nazis in the 1930s, Alexander Cockburn had been writing the *Press Clips* column in *The Village Voice* since 1972, where his witty blend of scurrilous gossip and Marxist critique quickly became required reading among the Manhattan intelligentsia. Suspended by *The Voice* "for accepting a $10,000 grant from an Arab studies organization," Cockburn arrived at *The Nation* in 1984 unbloodied, unbowed and spoiling for a fight.

A close friend of both Kopkind and Hitchens—who carried on bitter feuds with each man over the years—Cockburn added his considerable intellectual weight to the left side of *The Nation*'s political balance, puncturing the benevolent illusions of American exceptionalism and imperial innocence with a pen as sharp as any in print. Cockburn's obvious disdain for the niceties of liberal argument, especially concerning Israel and the Middle East, provoked many *Nation* readers, sometimes to the point of cancelation. And his penchant for shooting first at other *Nation* writers, from Eric Alterman and George Black to Michael Massing and Katha Pollitt, was almost as trying for Navasky as his periodical attacks on the editor himself for "a position I don't hold, an action I hadn't really taken, or a motive I don't have."

In the long, still-to-be-written history of *Nation* feuds, Cockburn would probably occupy pride of place. (At one point there were so many disputes between *Nation* contributors that the editors created a running headline, "In the Family," to keep them from taking over the letters page.) Yet his work was a constant advertisement for the freedom the magazine offered its writers. That freedom wasn't absolute, said Navasky. "Our deal with the columnists is that we granted them 90 percent freedom. The other 10 percent being not ideological but professional: libel, slander, or writing that would embarrass the magazine."[32] But it was more freedom than almost anywhere else with a comparable audience—and for writers who needed it, worth more than any fee.

§

With Cockburn, Hitchens and Kopkind up front, and Danto, Said, and Pollitt, who started by contributing reviews and poetry—her first collection, *Antarctic Traveller*, won the National Book Critics Circle Award—and replaced Pochoda as literary editor in 1982 in the back, *The Nation* regained a reputation for literary distinction. "The quality of the regular contributors was quite extraordinary," said Navasky, which in turn attracted writers like James Baldwin, E.L Doctorow, Arthur Miller, Alice Walker, Gore Vidal and Kurt Vonnegut. Unsolicited manuscripts also poured in, some of them turned into *Nation* articles through the tender ministrations of Richard Lingeman—another *Monocle* veteran, a biographer of Sinclair Lewis and Theodore Dreiser and author of books ranging from drugs to small-town America—whom Navasky lured from the *Times Book Review* to take over from Robert Hatch as executive editor. Film critic Stuart Klawans originally came in "over the transom," plucked out of *The Nation* slush pile by Margaronis.

Daniel Singer[33] had been writing for *The Nation* since 1970. The son of a *zek*—a prisoner in Stalin's gulag—who narrowly escaped the Holocaust himself, Singer got a job at *The Economist* through his friend Isaac Deutscher, and later wrote for the *New Statesman*. But in 1980, living in Paris, he became *The Nation*'s Europe correspondent, bringing what Gore Vidal described as his "Balzacian eye for human detail" to the slow, stuttering self-emancipation of Eastern Europe. Another writer who shared Singer's pessimism of the intellect and his incorrigible optimism of the will was E.P. Thompson, whose 1981 "Letter to America,"[34] helped launch the nuclear freeze movement. The magazine's increasing identification with a revived American peace movement would be a major theme of the Navasky *Nation*.

Meanwhile, just as projected, circulation rose almost immediately to 32,000 and then steadily to 90,000. Advertising picked up as well, though of course most major corporations were leery of subsidizing a journal that went out of its way to attack their interests. On the other hand, after protests over an ad for Blackglama mink coats (featuring Lillian Hellman) and the National Right to Work Committee, the magazine (helped by Aryeh Neier) developed a policy that said *The Nation* started "with the presumption that we will accept advertising even if the views expressed are repugnant to the editors." With landmark special issues such as Kai Bird's prophetic "Myths About the Middle East,"[35] sustained coverage of the Supreme Court and the law by Herman Schwartz,[36] and Stephen F. Cohen's[37] "Sovieticus" column challenging conventional wisdom about the supposed permanence of the Cold War, everything about *The Nation* was booming—including the operating deficit, which instead of turning the corner to profit had expanded to the point where the magazine was now nearly $2 million in debt.

"We never had more than three months' money in the till," Fish recalled. "And it was all on me to keep raising the money to keep the magazine going." And that was before *Harper & Row v. Nation Enterprises*, a landmark Supreme Court ruling arising from a 1979 scoop. Navasky had obtained a galley of former President Gerald Ford's memoirs and published a story based on Ford's account of his decision to pardon Richard Nixon. Harper & Row, which had sold an excerpt to *Time* for $12,500, sued under copyright law. *The Nation* claimed that the story was a matter of legitimate public interest, and that the 400 words it had quoted from Ford's 500-page book were covered under the "fair use" exemption. *The Nation* lost in federal court, won on appeal (before Irving Kaufman, the judge who had condemned the Rosenbergs to death), and then lost in the Supreme Court in 1985 in a decision written by Sandra Day O'Connor.

It was also in 1985 that Adrian De Wind, the partner at the Paul, Weiss law firm who handled *The Nation*'s affairs, said he had another client who might be interested in buying *The Nation*. Arthur Carter had made a fortune* in investment banking; Carter, Berlind, and Weill, the firm he founded with Roger Berlind and Sanford Weill, became Shearson Loeb Rhoades and was later acquired by American Express. In the 1970s Carter had once suggested to Fish that all the loss-making left-liberal magazines in the country should merge, creating a profitable monopoly. Now, however, Carter, who had founded a small weekly near his country house in Connecticut, wanted to do something larger in journal-

---

* Estimated by *The New York Times* at $200 million.

ism. After months of negotiation he, Navasky, Fish and their law-
yers hammered out a thirty-three-page agreement for a three-year
"trial marriage" in which Carter agreed to "preserve the character
and tradition of *The Nation* magazine," promised to protect the
magazine's absolute editorial independence—and pledged at least
$500,000 a year toward the magazine's running costs.

Navasky tells his side of the relationship in *A Matter of
Opinion*, and perhaps someday Carter will write his own memoirs. Until then, there are really only two salient points. The
first is that despite articles that sometimes criticized his friends,
and political positions he must have often found uncomfortable,
Carter never once interfered with *The Nation*'s editorial decision
making—even after the trial marriage, when he officially became
the magazine's owner. (Navasky and Fish each kept a 10 percent stake.) He did object to an ad for a "penis poster" showing
the comparative endowments (to scale) of the animal kingdom,
on the grounds that he thought it demeaned the magazine—but
after meeting the entire staff for a high-decibel discussion, an
acceptable compromise was found. The other consequence of
Carter's ownership was continued expansion at a time when other left-of-center journals were in retreat; circulation rose above
100,000 for the first time in *The Nation*'s history. (And, of course,
Carter enjoyed the kind of media attention—including a lengthy
profile in *Vanity Fair*—mere millionaires don't usually attract.)

Whether Carter ever wanted to interfere is another question.
"I think Victor turned out to have more resilience than Arthur
could possibly have imagined," said Fish, who sold his stake in
the magazine in 1987, when he waged the first of his three unsuc-

cessful campaigns for the House of Representatives. By 1994 Carter, who in founding the *New York Observer* created a much more responsive vehicle for his views, offered to sell *The Nation* back to Navasky for $1 million. Navasky, who was on sabbatical at the time, didn't have $1 million—and with *The Nation*'s annual losses now running at $500,000, he figured he needed to raise another $2 million to keep the magazine going until the new break-even point, now a mere four years away.

But Carter's terms were generous—no money down, and $100,000 a year at 6 percent. And by reconstituting The Nation Associates—with a big boost from actor Paul Newman, who agreed to put in $500,000 a year—and spending yet another sabbatical fundraising when he was supposed to be writing a book, Navasky managed to close the deal. Meanwhile, who was running *The Nation*? A former student in Blair Clark's "Politics and the Press" course at Princeton, where she'd written her senior thesis on McCarthyism's impact on ordinary Americans, and had spent her *Nation* internship in 1980 organizing Carey McWilliams's papers. Her name: Katrina vanden Heuvel. ✳

Katrina vanden Heuvel

CHAPTER EIGHT

Onward!

P erhaps the most surprising thing about Navasky's decision to turn the *Nation* editor's chair over to 35-year-old Katrina vanden Heuvel was how uncontroversial that choice was in a magazine whose writers often seemed at war with one another—and whose readers, as Milton Glaser once observed, regarded even the introduction of color as "using the tools of the enemy." Though she shared the downtown New Yorker's penchant for dressing in black, there was very little about vanden Heuvel that was not colorful.

Her father, attorney William vanden Heuvel, was the son of immigrants, the Dutch surname inherited not from old New York patroons but from a father who came to the United States in 1923 and worked at the French's Mustard factory in Rochester. His mother, who arrived from Belgium in 1920, kept a boarding house.

A protégé of William J. Donovan, founder of the Office of Strategic Services, the World War II predecessor of the CIA, in 1960 William vanden Heuvel had been the Democratic Party candidate for Congress from the Upper East Side "silk stocking" district—in a race won by the Republican, John V. Lindsay. As a special assistant to Attorney General Robert F. Kennedy, vanden Heuvel supervised the opening of a model integrated public school system in Prince Edward County, Virginia, and in 1979 had been appointed deputy ambassador to the United Nations by President Jimmy Carter. In 1984 he became president of the Franklin and Eleanor Roosevelt Institute; he also founded the Four Freedoms Park Conservancy.

Her mother, the writer Jean Stein, is author of *American Journey: The Times of Robert Kennedy* and *Edie: American Girl*, about the actress and Andy Warhol muse Edie Sedgwick. A prominent supporter of progressive and cultural causes, and editor of the literary and visual arts quarterly Grand Street, Jean Stein was also Hollywood royalty; her father, Jules Stein, had been a founder of the Music Corporation of America (MCA), a booking and talent agency that from its roots in Chicago nightclubs eventually moved to Hollywood, where it became a power in television (producing *Wagon Train*, *Leave It to Beaver* and *Alfred Hitchcock Presents*—Hitchcock, a client, owned shares in MCA), records (initially Decca, then the ABC and Paramount labels) and movies (in addition to acquiring Universal Studios, the agency also represented Fred Astaire, Bette Davis, Henry Fonda, Greta Garbo, Judy Garland, James Stewart and Ronald Reagan).

Her parents divorced when she was 10, and vanden Heuvel grew up in New York City, far from Hollywood. "I will admit to going to a holiday party or two with Ronald Reagan and his kids," she said. "We kids all smoked pot in the basement."[1]

Though not the first *Nation* intern to write for the magazine (a distinction jointly held by Alexander Stille and Amy Wilentz), vanden Heuvel was probably the only intern to have done so after already publishing an op-ed[2] in *The New York Times*. Like her *Times* essay, which called for a $2-a-barrel tax on imported oil to fund international development, vanden Heuvel's *Nation* debut,[3] a report on a pro-détente lobbying group hobbled by "its low-key, elitist" approach and rejection of grassroots campaigning, revealed a mind already reaching beyond the conventional horizon of campus activism. Taking a full year off from Princeton to work at *The Nation* rather than the standard summer internship, vanden Heuvel formed a deep bond with Iris Dornfeld, the widow of Carey McWilliams, and with Navasky.

"Iris was still very raw from Carey's death. I remember she cried in Victor's office when he introduced us. But Victor arranged for me to go there almost every day for half a day to help her with Carey's papers," said vanden Heuvel. "That gave me a real sense of *The Nation*'s history, and its role."

After graduation vanden Heuvel applied to the School of International and Public Affairs at Columbia, but within a few weeks dropped out to work at Close-Up, the documentary division of ABC, where she turned her senior thesis into "American Inquisition," which won the Edward R. Murrow award.

"I was very much influenced by Victor, and *Naming Names*, but at the same time resisted his interest in what you might call the 'stars' of the McCarthy period—the Hisses and the Rosenbergs," she said. Navasky had been a consultant to the documentary, and in the spring of 1984 he asked vanden Heuvel to return to *The Nation* as an assistant editor. For the next four years her apprenticeship included the usual assigning and editing, while also writing her own articles exposing censorship at Radio Liberty[4] and questioning the wisdom of Soviet dissidents receiving US government funds.[5] She also contributed unsigned editorials on topics ranging from West Germany's *Ostpolitik* to South African apartheid, and kept a close eye on the improbable rise of a Soviet functionary named Mikhail Gorbachev.

"Rarely, if ever, have Soviet reformers placed their hopes so squarely on one contender in a succession struggle," wrote Stephen F. Cohen, *The Nation*'s "Sovieticus" columnist in November 1984, introducing readers to the formerly obscure party boss from Stavropol who became, at 49, the youngest full member of the Politburo. In June 1987 vanden Heuvel edited a special issue[6] on the new Soviet leader. Vanden Heuvel and Cohen had met at Princeton. By December 1988, when the two married, *perestroika* was firmly established. One consequence of *glasnost* was that Cohen's biography of the Bolshevik founding father Nikolai Bukharin, killed in Stalin's Great Terror, could be published in Russia; another was that Cohen and vanden Heuvel could visit Moscow.

"Steve and I couldn't get a visa. Steve was refused because he was viewed as too close to dissidents. And when I tried alone, under my own name, I was denied. The week after Gorbachev came to power we got a visa," said vanden Heuvel. The couple began spending a portion of each year in the Soviet Union, where she became an editor "at large and at liberty" for *The Nation* and also helped found *Vyi i Myi*, a Russian-language feminist newsletter. Vanden Heuvel covered the Soviet Union's first genuinely contested elections for the English-language Moscow News as well as filing dispatches for *The Nation*. She and Cohen also co-edited *Voices of Glasnost*, a collection of interviews with Gorbachev's reformers.[7] In 1991 their daughter, Nicola, was born. Meanwhile during one of her returns to New York, Navasky asked vanden Heuvel to edit an anthology, *The Nation: 1865–1990*, in effect making her the custodian of the magazine's history.

"You can dig through this anthology as you would a hope chest," wrote E.L. Doctorow in his introduction. "This is your family's life and you hold it in your hands." Far more ambitious than the 120-page special issue[8] published to mark *The Nation*'s 120th anniversary, vanden Heuvel's 530-page anthology, which opened with Doctorow's magical evocation of the "dark broadcloth days of 1865," came right up to Richard J. Barnet's evisceration of George H.W. "Bush's Splendid Little War" with Panama, and ended with Josephine Jacobsen's poem "Tears"—though Navasky did allow himself, in an "Afterword," the last word—was, as its editor noted, a powerful reminder of the persistence of so many of the magazine's abiding concerns:

"Passionate support for civil rights and civil liberties, opposition to racism in all its guises, and unrelenting struggle against militarism, imperialism, corruption and abuse of power. It is remarkable how many of the controversies that engaged the moral and political concern of *The Nation* twenty-five, fifty or seventy-five years ago still do."[9]

Though both of them assumed it would only be for a year, by the time Navasky asked vanden Heuvel to sit in for him (while he did research on "journals of opinion" at Harvard and Columbia) she had been a presence at the magazine for nearly fifteen years. It was, she wrote, "a kind of political and journalistic boot camp. The office was full of vivid characters, creative dissenters and shoe-leather journalists."[10]

For his part, Navasky had no doubts. "She seemed to me to have the character, values and, not least, the temperament for the job; and to understand that, as Robert Borosage once put it, '*The Nation* walks on two legs—one inside the establishment and one outside.' I knew that unlike anyone else in the office...she would not cause factional grumbling." There was an additional consideration. "Here was an ideal opportunity for an audition—by a woman not yet in her 40s."[11]

§

Vanden Heuvel passed her audition. To understand why, look no further than *The Nation* she oversaw for July 4, 1994.[12] In many ways a typical issue—beginning with an unsigned cover editorial criticizing "the hand-washers and wafflers of the Clinton foreign policy team" for the "paltry U.S. response to the Rwanda holocaust"; an angry letter from peace activist Joanne Landy taking exception to a recent Hitchens column arguing in favor of US intervention in Haiti and Bosnia; another letter complaining about Cockburn's attack on Frank Wells, the recently deceased head of Disney; a signed editorial by Bruce Cumings urging Washington to negotiate with Pyongyang; a fresh Cockburn column comparing the media drumbeat of demands that blacks distance themselves from Louis Farrakhan with the *pianissimo* response to Martin Peretz's recent pronouncement that blacks were "culturally deficient"; and ending with music critic Gene Santoro's fond farewell to sax players Earle Warren and Red Rodney—the cover line "Liberation, Honey!" signaled that this was not your father's *Nation*. Or even your uncle Victor's.

"AIDS in Our Time," David Kirp's unsentimental audit of the plague in its thirteenth year, might have run in any enlightened journal. But "After Stonewall," Kopkind's clarion claim that "the Stonewall Riot must count as a transformative moment of liberation, not only for homosexuals, who were the street fighters, but for the entire sexual culture" was far too radical for buttoned-down gay spokesmen like *New Republic* editor Andrew Sullivan, who only recently had advised gays to limit their efforts to the rights to marry and to serve in the military.[13] Yet it was also too queer for the sectarian left press, who in any case wouldn't have approved of the way Kopkind took the leader of the Bolshevik Revolution's name in vain: "Lenin said somewhere that 'revolutions are festivals of the oppressed,' and although Stonewall wasn't remotely Leninist, it was certainly festive and it definitely was a low-down crowd that poured out of that bar."

The centerpiece of the issue, though, was Tony Kushner's luminous manifesto "A Socialism of the Skin." Kushner, who had won the Pulitzer Prize the previous year for *Angels in America*, argued decorously, almost deferentially, that Sullivan's assimilationist agenda of weddings and weaponry—"an attainable peaceable kingdom, in which gay men and lesbians live free of fear (of homophobia, at least)"—just wasn't good enough. Invoking Oscar Wilde—"A map of the world that does not include Utopia is not worth even glancing at, for it leaves out the one country at which Humanity is always landing"—Kushner demanded "a socialism of the skin."

"Gay rights may be obtainable," wrote Kushner, "but liberation depends on a politics that goes beyond, not an anti-politics. Our unhappiness as scared queer children doesn't only isolate us, it also politicizes us. It inculcates in us a desire for connection that is all the stronger because we have experienced its absence. Our suffering teaches us solidarity; or it should." The demand for solidarity was a radical one, but Kushner's vulnerable, reasonable—but utterly uncompromising—insistence that Utopia remain on the agenda was revolutionary.

It was vanden Heuvel who brought the playwright into the magazine. "I met Tony, who was incensed by Sullivan's argument, so I put him and Andy together," she recalled. "I think Victor saw me as someone who understood the magazine, and who would combine continuity and change. A *Nation* editor needs to be part diplomat, part referee, and part editor—and also I think he saw me as someone who could do that."

When Navasky returned from his sabbatical, which included a detour to the Harvard Business School, he asked vanden Heuvel to stay on as editor in chief while he became publisher and "editorial director." She also joined Paul Newman, Robert Redford, Doctorow and a small group of investors as "limited partners" in *The Nation*; as the sole "general partner," Navasky held the controlling interest. Though none of this had been foreseen a year earlier, the transition to a new ownership structure and new editor "was fairly seamless," according to vanden Heuvel. "Victor and I never had any written agreement. We had our different roles—I was more day-to-day. We never had any political disagreements—except silly ones. I remember I was furious that he invited Ralph Nader to come on the *Nation* cruise soon after the 2000 election, because it seemed to imply an endorsement in what was still a very raw moment."

Yet with every passing week *The Nation* became a little bit more vanden Heuvel's magazine. Some of the changes were the fruition—and continuation—of moves begun under Navasky. Katha Pollitt joined the rotation at the front of the magazine. "Victor's brilliance was in understanding Katha would be a great columnist. We both had the idea of bringing Patricia Williams on," said vanden Heuvel. A professor at Columbia Law School who had written compelling *Nation* cover stories on the fortieth anniversary of *Brown v. Board of Education*[14] and the O.J. Simpson murder trial,[15] Williams began her "Diary of a Mad Law Professor," a unique blend of the personal, the political and the philosophical, in 1997.

But it is hard to imagine the June 3, 1996, special issue[16] on "The National Entertainment State" under any other editor. Building on years of reporting by Ben Bagdikian and Herbert Schiller—*Nation* contributors since the McWilliams era—the issue highlighted a spectrum of opinions, and experience, ranging from Michael Arlen, Walter Cronkite and Lawrence Grossman (the former president of NBC News) to Bill McKibben and Oliver Stone for suggestions on "how to make media goliaths accountable to readers, viewers, listeners." Danny Schecter sounded an early alarm on the steady rightward march of PBS. André Schiffrin, who'd published Studs Terkel and Edward Said at Pantheon Books before he was forced out by a dividend-driven corporate owner, detailed the impact of mergers and marketization on the life of the culture. And Leslie Savan showed how, in the brave new media landscape, corporations even "own their own backlash…. In Disney's sequel to *The Mighty*

Ducks, D2, a kids' hockey team is morally corrupted by corporate sponsorship and endorsement deals—even as Disney marketing partner Coca-Cola gets repeated product placement."

The issue also contained *The Nation*'s first-ever "gatefold," opening to reveal not an unclothed human model but the unsightly forms of the four corporate colossi—General Electric (which owned NBC), Time Warner (which owned HBO and was in the process of digesting CNN), Disney/Capital Cities (which owned ABC) and Westinghouse (CBS)—which together held a monopoly on television news. As Mark Crispin Miller pointed out, the web of conflicts laid bare in the centerfold, while doing much to explain why NBC "might find it difficult to introduce stories critical of nuclear power," also "portend the death of broadcast journalism." And though the World Wide Web was just out of its CERN swaddling clothes, *The Nation*'s focus on the dangers of what vanden Heuvel calls "consolidation, conglomeratization, Murdoch-ization" could hardly have been more prescient.

Equally, if more evidently, prophetic was Jonathan Schell's "The Gift of Time."[17] Though his older brother, the China scholar Orville Schell, had been writing for *The Nation* since the late '60s, Jonathan Schell had long been associated with *The New Yorker*, which serialized his book *The Fate of the Earth* in the 1980s. In the '90s he'd become a columnist for *Newsday*. Bringing Schell to *The Nation* was a coup in any event, but his issue-length debut article, later expanded into a book, had a radical clarity that seemed new. Pointing out that the great nuclear arsenals "were created as instruments of the cold war," Schell challenged readers to think the unthinkable: "Now that the war is over, can't we stand down the arms that were built to fight the war? Over a period of years, the peoples of the Soviet empire dismantled the system of totalitarian terror under which they lived. Can't we and they together now dismantle the system of nuclear terror under which we have all been living? Can't we, at long last, abolish nuclear weapons? This issue of *The Nation* proposes an affirmative answer to that question."

§

A similar line—call it the arc that bends toward justice—can be traced from Alexander Cockburn's early[18] and persistent[19] criticism of the North American Free Trade Agreement and Noam Chomsky's March 1993 cover story,[20] "Notes on NAFTA," to *The Nation*'s coverage of the anti-globalization movement in 1999. Chomsky, as he so often does, unpacked the human cost: "One consequence of the globalization of the economy is the rise of new governing institutions to serve the interests of private transnational economic power. Another is the spread of the Third World social model, with islands of enormous privilege in a sea of misery and despair."

Even before the protests in Seattle in November 1999, *The Nation* predicted[21] "people concerned about human rights, workers' rights and environmental protections will be forced to develop national, state and local challenges to the global corporate economy" that would question both "the authority and legitimacy of the World Trade Organization." Analyses by William Greider[22] and Doug Henwood[23] lent substance to the protesters' critique. But *The Nation* went further, not just explaining or interpreting but taking a stand—and taking sides.

For vanden Heuvel, that ability to extend the arc of engagement with social movements through Occupy Wall Street to protests against the Trans Pacific Partnership, while remaining true to its journalistic skepticism, is what makes *The Nation* unique. "We covered Seattle as journalists," she said, "not as activists. Because we are journalists. But ours is a journalism that takes activists and activism seriously, unlike much of the mainstream media, which generally covers people in power. Our role has always been to report on the dissidents, troublemakers and others who are challenging the status quo. In 1999, we broke with the Washington consensus to say the kids in the street are right, and the think tanks and armchair economists and lobbyists are wrong. So-called free trade, promoted by Clinton and then Bush, was not working, and it wasn't going to work."[24]

Though E.L. Godkin would have been dismayed (and not for the first time) to see just how far the magazine he founded had strayed from his laissez-faire creed, Victor Navasky proved a far more supportive predecessor. Still very much a presence in the *Nation* office (which moved from the cramped warren at 72 Fifth Avenue to light, spacious quarters at 33 Irving Place in 1998), Navasky, perhaps mindful of James Storrow's litany of complaint when Victor first took over, remained a resource rather than a source of reproach.

"Victor was more of a philosopher/publisher, more Talmudic," said vanden Heuvel. "Maybe because one of his mentors was the philosopher Sidney Morgenbessor, who when asked if he disagreed with Chairman Mao's saying that a proposition can be both true and false at the same time, famously replied, 'I do and I don't.' Whereas I'm more linear. But he was always there to think things through. Like how to deal with the columnists. 'Can't you all just get along?' was our mantra."

Over the years, she said, "I've kept a small file of my correspondence with Victor. There are e-mails, scrawled handwritten notes on yellow legal pads, even sketches and notes on napkins. One of the e-mails goes like this: 'Katrina—Don't despair. No advice—

think what you are doing is exactly right.'[25] Victor was very involved in strategizing about how to cover the Clinton impeachment"—a spectacle that alternately delighted (Christopher Hitchens) and dismayed[26] (the rest of the staff) *The Nation*. Even Gore Vidal, who had never displayed much public affection for Clinton, was sufficiently outraged to suggest[27] Kenneth Starr be charged with treason, on the grounds that the special prosecutor's "attempt to overthrow the presidential elections of 1992 and 1996 constitutes a bold, massive blow at the American people themselves."

So far as overturning elections went, it seemed the Clinton Calvary was merely a dress rehearsal. When the Republicans got away with it on their second attempt, in November 2000, *The Nation* asked the author of a recent book on *Why O.J. Simpson Got Away With Murder* for his view of *Bush v. Gore*.[28] Vincent Bugliosi, the former Los Angeles County district attorney, did not mince words: "When Justice Thomas was asked by a skeptical high school student the day after the Court's ruling whether the Court's decision had anything to do with politics, he answered, 'Zero.' And when a reporter thereafter asked Rehnquist whether he agreed with Thomas, he said, 'Absolutely, absolutely.' Well, at least we know they can lie as well as they can steal."

§

Nation issues used to close on Wednesdays. September 11, 2001, was a Tuesday. From Fifteenth Street and Irving Place to the World Trade Center was a little over two miles—forty blocks. "Like everyone else in America we watched television— horrified, saddened, angry. People wept, and at the same time took notes and got on the phones," vanden Heuvel recalled.[29]

But the *Nation* phone lines ran under 7 World Trade Center, which caught fire when the twin towers collapsed, and then itself collapsed just after 5:00 that evening. It is a measure of how little was known, amid the smoke, the dust, and the fear rising in the back of the throat, that the lead editorial of the issue[30] that vanden Heuvel, managing editor Karen Rothmyer and the rest of the *Nation* staff somehow managed to see to press over the next thirty-six hours still held out hope for survivors: "We have taken a great wound, we Americans, and our first task is to rescue survivors if that is still possible, to grieve and to remain alert until we better understand what happened to us."

One of those trying hardest to understand was Jonathan Schell: "On Tuesday morning, a piece was torn out of our world. A patch of blue sky that should not have been there opened up in the New York skyline. In my neighborhood—I live eight blocks from the World Trade Center—the heavens were raining human beings. Our city was changed forever. Our country was changed forever. Our world was changed forever." In the weeks to come, as the debate inside the magazine raged between those who agreed with Christopher Hitchens's column[31] on "fascism with an Islamic face," castigating leftists who drew a causal relationship between US foreign policy and the attacks, and those, like Robert Fisk, who while the rubble still smoldered pointed[32] to "the historical wrongs and the injustices that lie behind the firestorms," Schell's sober, stunned, heartbreakingly rational "Letter From Ground Zero" columns came to represent the voice of the magazine—or at least the voice of sanity.

"Should the terrorists who carried out Tuesday's attacks be brought to justice and punished as the President wants to do?",

Schell asked. "Of course. Who should be punished if not people who would hurl a cargo of innocent human beings against a fixed target of other innocent human beings?" But with the attackers already dead, the next steps were fraught with danger.

"The United States can unquestionably defeat the Taliban in a ground war and occupy Afghanistan," Schell warned in November 2001. "But politics will not disappear because it has been ignored. The state that is already missing in Afghanistan will still be missing. The Taliban and Al Qaeda will certainly remain as an underground force, exacting a steady price from the occupying armies.... Meanwhile, occupation of a Muslim country by US forces would be an outrage to Muslim opinion and a recruiting poster for terrorist organizations throughout the Middle East, which would almost certainly gain in strength. The United States can win the war in Afghanistan, but only at the cost of losing its war on terrorism."*

The aftermath of the attacks on September 11, 2001, was a testing time for the country's leaders—and for *The Nation*'s. "One of my roles as editor has been to figure out the bridge from personal to political," wrote vanden Heuvel. "How do you balance individual grief and anger at the attacks with proportionality, justice and wisdom in response?" Those questions, which divided *The Nation*—and the left—dominated "A Just Response," a special

---

* It is, frankly, hard to read these words in 2015 without weeping—for the terrible waste, the thousands of dead and the maimed Americans, Afghans and Pakistanis, and not least for Schell himself, who died in March 2014 having lived long enough to see the execution of Osama bin Laden but not the end of the Afghan war, let alone the "war on terror."

issue[33] whose lead essay, by Richard Falk, tried to grapple with what justice might now mean in a world "on the brink of a global, intercivilizational war without battlefields and borders." Amid the news of FBI round-ups of Arab-Americans and calls for the CIA— as spectacularly ineffective as ever in thwarting the attacks—to be "unleashed," Eric Foner reminded readers that civil rights and civil liberties "are not gifts from the state that can be rescinded when it desires." Invoking *The Nation*'s—and the country's—proud tradition of dissent and debate, Foner wrote "at times of crisis the most patriotic act of all is the unyielding defense of civil liberties, the right to dissent and equality before the law for all."

Expanded into a book, the issue revealed deep disagreements, with contributions from Edward Said, who demolished Samuel Huntington's much-invoked "Clash of Civilizations" thesis, novelist John Le Carre, who responded to George W. Bush and Silvio Berlusconi's call for a "crusade" against terrorism by wondering "am I out of order in recalling that we actually lost the Crusades?", Michael Massing, who flayed a supine press for aiding and abetting the Bush administration's rush to judgment, and Ellen Willis, who worried that the current mood of national unity, though welcome, would "reinforce the denial of our deeper social problems. In emergencies—and war is the ultimate emergency—such long-range concerns are suspended. This may be unavoidable, but it is never desirable, except to tyrants. I'm not a pacifist—I believe that war is sometimes necessary—but I agree with pacifists that there's nothing ennobling about it." Inside the magazine any unity was short-lived, with Hitchens's eagerness to join the coming battle against "Islamofascism" bumping up against Katha Pollitt's refusal[34] to let her daughter fly an American flag from the living-room window.

Though sprouting from Brooklyn brownstones, Malibu lawns, Vermont commune barns, New York "taxicabs driven by Indians and Pakistanis," and construction sites across the country, the flag remained for Pollitt an emblem of "jingoism and vengeance and war." Like the bruising exchange[35] between Hitchens and Chomsky on *The Nation*'s website, Pollitt's provocative rhetoric obscured her subtler point: "there are no symbolic representations right now for the things the world really needs—equality and justice and humanity and solidarity and intelligence." Yet it would be vanden Heuvel's task as editor— and *The Nation*'s triumph—to resist the siren song of consensus, either for or against the war, and the stampede to join the Bush administration's bandwagon.

"The speedy passage of the repressive PATRIOT act, with scarcely a murmur of dissent in Congress, the secret detentions of more than 1,000 people, and the establishment of military tribunals were troubling signs that a wartime crackdown was under way," wrote vanden Heuvel. The risks were as clear in 2001 as they had been in 1918. "Criticizing government policy in wartime is not a path to popularity," she wrote. "Our independent stand on the war and criticism of what we called 'policy profiteering' by conservative Republicans in Congress (who sought to use the war as a pretext to push through their agenda) drew virulent attacks by the pundits and publications of the right, who questioned our patriotism and trotted out the old chestnut of the left's 'anti-Americanism.' Such attacks are nothing new."[36]

§

This time, though, the mud didn't stick. Some of the credit belongs to Eric Alterman, who in 1992 poked a sharp stick in the eye of the mainstream media in the form of his first book *Sound and Fury: The Making of the Punditocracy*. Hired as a pundit himself* by MSNBC in 1996, where he became a pioneer blogger, and made a *Nation* columnist[37] two years later, Alterman's attentions may have prompted a greater effort at "balance." So did the proliferation of "talking heads" programs on cable television. Having a poised, articulate, attractive young female editor probably didn't hurt either. Whatever the reason, even as the country skewed to the right in the wake of 9/11, with *The Nation* coming under the usual attacks, the magazine always remained part of the national conversation. Vanden Heuvel became a familiar presence on programs such as *Larry King Live* and *Reliable Sources* on CNN, *Hardball with Chris Matthews* on MSNBC, *Bill Moyers Journal* on PBS, *This Week* on ABC, and even *The O'Reilly Factor* on Fox, where Michelle Malkin once called[38] her a "smear merchant."

In her wake Christopher Hayes,[39] who succeeded David Corn[40] as *The Nation*'s Washington editor, soon became a regular on the Sunday morning panels, also filling in for Rachel Maddow on her daily MSNBC show. Starting with *Up With Chris Hayes* on weekend mornings in 2011, since 2013 Hayes has anchored the daily *All In With Chris Hayes*, making him the youngest host in prime-time national television. In 2012 *Nation* columnist Melissa

---

* Twenty years earlier Cockburn had used much the same strategy via his "Press Clips" column in *The Village Voice*. Naturally, the two men loathed each other.

Harris-Perry[41] joined MSNBC as the host of her own weekend program. *Nation* writers often feature on both shows, as does the editor in chief, who for the past five years has also written a weekly column[42] for *The Washington Post*.

The Nation's new visibility, and the magazine's role as the principal venue for those opposed to the policies of George W. Bush—leaving aside the question of relative quality, *The Nation*'s greater frequency gave it an influence that likeminded journals such as *Mother Jones* and *The American Prospect* probably lacked—sent circulation to unimagined heights. The magazine's finances began to enjoy a new vigor. "We were losing a significant amount of money—about $2 million a year," said Teresa Stack, who joined the magazine as circulation director in 1993 and became president in 1998. "And then Bush was elected. We sent out 500,000 pieces of direct mail, and instead of a 4 percent response we'd get 6 percent. We doubled our circulation, doubled our revenue, and cut the deficit in half—and then in half again."

The Nation's new confidence, and higher profile, was more than just good for business. It helped turn a haven for dissent into a campaigning organ. In September 2002, as the drumbeats for invading Iraq grew louder and louder, liberals were still fighting the last war. In "The Left and 9/11"[43] Adam Shatz toured the front line of the debate, from Tariq Ali and Chomsky on one side of the barricades to Hitchens and *Dissent* editor Michael Walzer on the other. Shatz, who would soon become *The Nation*'s literary editor, had a keen eye for cant, deftly filleting Paul Berman's "flair for wishful theorizing" in a 1996 review[44] of the newly minted "terrorism" expert (and former *Nation* drama critic)'s book on the generation of 1968. But here he put his own ambivalence front and center: having seen the Twin Towers on fire from his Brooklyn apartment, Shatz admitted "despite my fear that the response would be disproportionate, I wasn't going to be attending any peace rallies, at least not yet." The difficulty, said Shatz, was knowing "where to draw the line between self-defense and imperial aggrandizement."

Yet less than a month later *The Nation* did draw that line, in "An Open Letter to the Members of Congress"[45] urging them to vote against Bush's war in Iraq. Unlike earlier interventions in Bosnia and Haiti, where the magazine, like the left, had been divided, or the first Gulf War or even the war in Afghanistan, where there had been an attempt to maintain a kind of balance, this time *The Nation* spoke out without equivocation.

"A time comes when silence is betrayal," said the editorial, quoting Martin Luther King Jr.'s comment on the Vietnam War. Addressing the failure of nerve on the part of Congressional Democrats—"You are the opposition party, but you do not oppose,"—it continued: "The case against the war is simple, clear and strong." There was no connection between Iraq and the September 11 attacks, and no compelling evidence that Saddam Hussein possessed weapons of mass destruction. Even if he did, "a policy of deterrence would appear perfectly adequate to stop him, just as it was adequate a half-century ago to stop a much more fearsome dictator, Joseph Stalin."

Instead the administration policy "trades deterrence for pre-emption—in plain English, aggression. It accords the United States the right to overthrow any regime—like the one in Iraq—it decides should be overthrown." This would not make the world a safer place. And its effect on America would be catastrophic. In an echo of *Nation* editorials dating back to the annexation of Hawaii and the conquest of the Philippines, it warned that today Americans are "threatened by a monster of unbalanced and unaccountable power—a new Leviathan—that is taking shape among us in the executive branch of the government. This Leviathan—concealed in an ever-deepening, self-created secrecy and fed by streams of money from corporations that, as scandal after scandal has shown, have themselves broken free of elementary accountability—menaces civil liberties even as it threatens endless, unprovoked war."

This was too much for Hitchens, whose final "Minority Report,"[46] attesting "not the least doubt that [Saddam Hussein] has acquired some of the means of genocide and hopes to collect some more," ran two weeks later, under the headline "Taking Sides." Hitchens would write one more piece for *The Nation*, in November 2004, expressing a slight preference for Bush's re-election and declaring, of his own political transformation, "once you have done it, there's no going back…. The relief is unbelievable."

"Perhaps my most important time as editor," said vanden Heuvel, "was leading the magazine in opposition to the Iraq War, when few media outlets opposed the debacle and far too many liberals succumbed. As I like to say, *The Nation* never lost its head while too many were giving head. (Thank you Lou Reed!) Part of that opposition was also an effort to trigger a debate in this country about what a sane foreign/national security policy would look like. And though we didn't succeed in preventing the war, that work remains, and is something I care deeply about, especially as we sink into a new Cold War."[47]

In February, just before the invasion began, Jonathan Schell, reviewing the charade of UN Resolutions and dodgy dossiers, quoted Robert Lowell's lines from the poem "Fall 1961": *we have talked our extinction to death*. "Has any war," Schell wondered,[48] "been so lengthily premeditated before it was launched?" Yet "while we were all talking and the danger was growing...the war was being lost.... The novelty this time is that the defeat has preceded the inauguration of hostilities."

Millions had come out into the streets to voice their opposition to the war—only to be ignored by the officials they had elected. Schell, typically, counseled against despair: "The movement *against* the war in Iraq should also become a movement *for* something, and that something should be a return to the long-neglected path to abolition of all weapons of mass destruction."[49]

§

In 2005 vanden Heuvel became publisher as well as editor, buying out Navasky's controlling stake for $250,000—a little less, after inflation, than Freda Kirchwey had paid some seventy years before. *The Nation* had always been a for-profit corporation; while nonprofit status would have allowed investors a charitable deduction for their losses, and saved the magazine money on postage, it also might have left it reliant on those savings—and thus more vulnerable to government pressure. (Which is exactly what happened to *Mother Jones* during the Reagan administration, when an IRS decision to revoke its tax-exempt status nearly put that magazine out of business. *Mother Jones* successfully challenged the ruling, but the legal fees would have funded a lot of reporting.) Actually making money, however, was something new.

Under vanden Heuvel's editorship, subscriptions had already risen to 185,000, and would briefly approach the 200,000 mark before Bush left office. Now for the first time in its history the magazine not only broke even—as it had done briefly during the 1920s—it made an operating profit. Navasky, who stayed on the masthead as "publisher emeritus," blamed George Bush for this embarrassing turn of events. "If it's bad for the country it's good for *The Nation*," he quipped. *Nation* cruises—inspired by a similar venture run by *National Review*—brought in hundreds of thousands of dollars a year. The magazine also started licensing its archives. There was even a *Nation* credit card, which, according to Teresa Stack, brought in $100,000 a year.

As each month turned President Bush's boast of "Mission Accomplished" into grotesque self-parody, *The Nation* continued to press the case against the war. Reporting is expensive; investigative reporting is even more expensive. The magazine's healthy finances—and The Nation Institute, where Hamilton Fish returned to fundraising—made it possible to send Jeremy Scahill to report[50] from Baghdad, where "Blood Is Thicker Than Blackwater,"[51] his exposé of misconduct by the private contractor, won the 2008 George Polk Award. He was soon joined by Christian Parenti, who also chronicled[52] the effect of the Iraq campaign on the war in Afghanistan. Naomi Klein, who had been covering the anti-globalization movement for *The Nation* since Seattle, examined the Iraq War's political economy, exposing Paul Bremer's mismanagement[53] of the occupation, Halliburton's profiteering,[54] and the continuing toll[55] of the war on Iraqi society.

But "telling people the truth" was no longer enough. In November 2005, *The Nation* declared that the war had become "the single greatest threat to our national security. Its human and economic costs are running out of control, with no end in sight." It pledged:[56] "We will not support any candidate for national office who does not make a speedy end to the war in Iraq a major issue of his or her campaign. We firmly believe that antiwar candidates, with the other requisite credentials, can win the 2006 Congressional elections, the 2008 Democratic presidential primaries and the subsequent national election. But this fight, and our stand, must begin now."

§

The Nation's "if we build it they will come" approach to electoral politics may not have put Barack Obama in the White House (though there is little doubt Hillary Clinton's vote in favor of the Iraq War was a crucial factor in her defeat). But anyone who doubts the magazine's influence in New York City will have to argue with Mayor Bill de Blasio, whose come-from-nowhere victory in the crucial Democratic primary got an unlikely assist: "Well, you know, I didn't get the endorsement of the *New York Post*, or the *Daily News*, or even *The New York Times*. The one magazine I did get endorsed by was *The Nation*, so you could say that the road to City Hall goes through *The Nation* magazine," said de Blasio. The magazine has also been a longstanding supporter of the Working Families Party—an attempt to break out of the two-party deadlock—which was started in New York in 1998 and now has branches in eight states.

But electoral politics has never been *The Nation*'s main priority. When Hurricane Katrina battered New Orleans *The Nation* sent Parenti[57] to investigate, Klein to illuminate[58] the workings of "disaster capitalism" on the home front, and asked Adolph Reed Jr., who had left town just ahead of the storm surge, to cover the class angle.[59]

But as the country moved on, *The Nation* maintained its focus, with two lengthy reports by Mike Davis,[60] a cover story by Rebecca Solnit[61] and, nearly four years after the levees broke, another cover story by A.C. Thompson on "Katrina's Hidden Race War,"[62] which won a Lovejoy Award for its investigation of police shootings.

That kind of sustained coverage isn't about winning prizes (though over the years *The Nation* has won five National Magazine Awards—and been a finalist twenty-one times). Contributing writer Scott Sherman's 2011 investigation[63] into the New York Public Library's plans to gut the stacks beneath its Forty-second Street flagship caused far too much annoyance to the city's cultural establishment to win any prizes. But it did get results; in May 2014, after numerous follow-up stories by Sherman, campaigning by citizen groups and a promise to oppose the plan by mayoral candidate de Blasio, the library gave up.[64]

Not every *Nation* story has a happy ending. Cohen's "Soveticus" columns prodding the West to take Gorbachev's reforms seriously were eventually viewed as prophetic; however his—and *The Nation's*—more recent warnings[65] against the danger of reigniting the Cold War in Ukraine challenged the mainstream narrative but have not, so far, been embraced by the political or media establishment. In 2008 the magazine joined the American Civil Liberties Union to file suit against the government to end warrantless wiretapping of American citizens under the Foreign Intelligence Surveillance Act (FISA). In February 2013 the Supreme Court dismissed the suit. "There are no lost causes. There are just causes waiting to be won," says vanden Heuvel, adding that in light of revelations by whistleblower Edward Snowden, the magazine has returned to court.

Nor is the payoff always evident. It was also in 2008 that *The Nation* devoted a special issue to "The New Inequality."[66] In the middle of an election campaign in which the widening gap between rich and poor never got much attention—this was four years before Mitt Romney's slip about the "47 percent"—articles by Doug Henwood and Barbara Ehrenreich fleshed out the facts behind, as the issue's centerfold put it, America's "Plutocracy Reborn." Though this issue did win a prize,* the real dividend on the magazine's investment came three years later, in Zuccotti Park, when Occupy Wall Street put inequality on the world's agenda.

§

As the magazine enters its 150th year—and vanden Heuvel her third decade as editor—the state of *The Nation* is robust. Though the Obama presidency had a predictable downward effect on print circulation—currently about 130,000—2015 is also the twentieth anniversary of TheNation.com. Besides bringing more than 40,000 new print subscribers to *The Nation*, the number of paid "digital-only subscribers" has been growing steadily, thanks partly to an early decision to buck the Internet trend and retain the pay wall. "I'm really glad we held that line," says Stack. "The theory of 'free content' is you attract advertisers who pay for eyeballs. But our kind of content isn't ever going to be paid for by advertising," she says, adding that unlike conventional media, *The Nation* has a "double bottom line: we want to get our content in front of as many people as possible. But that content has to be paid for."

---

* From the Sidney Hillman Foundation, for "journalists, writers and public figures who pursue social justice and public policy for the common good." This was *The Nation*'s fifth Hillman prize.

Since Freda Kirchwey's day *The Nation* has relied on subscriber support to pay its bills—a necessity Fish and Navasky made into a virtue, creating a "Circle of 100" donors who in return for a certain level of annual support were given equity in the magazine. Though the corporate structure has recently changed to a limited liability corporation—partly, says Stack, so that new partners can be clear about their degree of exposure—the principle remains the same. While *The Nation* has been fortunate in attracting a few large donors, a group that over time has included Paul Newman, Robert Redford, Norton Utilities founder Peter Norton, Alan Sagner, publisher William Randolph Hearst III and investor Scott Roth, it has always been the smaller donors who have had the biggest impact on the magazine's bottom line. A fifth of *Nation* subscribers make an additional contribution to the magazine. "I've never seen anything like the passion the readers have for this place," Stack says.

That passion, says vanden Heuvel, is not just for the magazine but for "what *The Nation* has stood for: a belief that there are always alternatives—in history, politics, in life—that would make our country and the world a more humane, just and secure place."

If *The Nation* is to continue to thrive, the magazine will have to find a way to keep those conversations—and those vital connections—with readers, activists and social movements, despite all the digital distractions clamoring for attention. "Taking *The Nation* into the digital age will be tough," admits vanden Heuvel, who has been fortunate in being able to rely on executive editor Richard Kim and managing editor Roane Carey to help navigate this new territory. But while her course is set firmly toward the future, for vanden Heuvel *The Nation*'s rich past is a gift, not a burden. "After all, there aren't many publications that can boast they were around from the telegraph age to the debut of Twitter," she says.

In considering *The Nation*'s future, vanden Heuvel is confident. Embracing the digital future has considerably extended the magazine's reach, with half a million visitors accessing *The Nation* every week via twelve digital platforms. And with a major new investment in TheNation.com planned for the 150th anniversary of the first issue in July, vanden Heuvel believes the magazine can continue to grow both of its double bottom lines.

"I've made *The Nation* a forum for ideas about our political future," she says, "in the belief that while we do critique pretty well, and must continue to challenge orthodoxy and consensus, it is also important not only to expose, but to propose. To lay out the road ahead, a society that people would want to be part of. Because if they don't know alternatives exist, that they are *real*, will people take the leap?"

The point is not to interpret the world, a wise man once wrote—a mere twenty years before the first issue of *The Nation*—"The point is to change it." ✳

Afterword

As you will have noticed, the story you are reading is unfinished. Today *The Nation* is, as reported in the last chapter, very much alive and kicking. That happy circumstance makes things awkward for the biographer, who has to deal not merely with the relics and remains of a life completed—a past, as it were, safely in the past—but with the shifting priorities and reversals of fortune that attend any ongoing enterprise. My distinguished predecessor in the London bureau, Henry James, once put it this way: "Really, universally, relations stop nowhere." The writer's job, he said, is to draw the "circle within which they shall happily *appear* to do so. He is in the perpetual predicament that the continuity of things is the whole matter, for him, of comedy and tragedy; that this continuity is never, by the space of an instant or an inch, broken, and that, to do anything at all, he has at once intensely to consult and intensely to ignore it."[1]

I hope that the preceding chapters have conveyed something of both the comedy and the tragedy in *The Nation*'s first 150 years. And while I have tried to draw my circle in a way that doesn't do too much violence, or leave out too many significant actors or events, I'm acutely aware of what is missing. To take just one example, and despite the impression that may have been fostered in the preceding pages, no editor puts out a magazine single-handed. A full-dress history of *The Nation* would—and should—render due acknowledgment to all of the men and women without whose labor, etc.... Also, though I have tried to give some sense of the magazine's material basis, and the means of its continuing production, those who hunger for a full accounting of *The Nation*'s accounting will find scant satisfaction here.

Those gaps are one reason this book calls itself a biography rather than a history. Another is my own affinity for stories, which are sometimes tolerated by historians but prized by biographers. And while dates offer necessary anchor points, it's the details—of character, connection and context—that I really wanted to get across.

If I've paid particular attention to political disputes it's because for a magazine like *The Nation*, controversy is life. Not only, or even primarily, in the sense of a record of positions taken, but in the heat of argument, the clash of opinions and the long chain of consequences that connect words to actions. "*The Nation* was forged in the crucible of emancipation," Katrina vanden Heuvel recently observed.[2] The magazine's birth came at the resolution of this nation's greatest trial. Yet the end of the Civil War, that bloody contest over whether a government half free and half slave could endure, also marked the beginning of a furious argument among abolitionists—former allies—on the way forward.

That passion, and also that optimistic certainty that there is a way forward, are the clearest signs of our inheritance from *The Nation*'s founders. And so I invite you to consider this book as both a record of that passion and optimism—which is, after all, the best of what we mean by a life—and a bet on *The Nation*'s continuing ability to find a new way through the challenges ahead. Or perhaps that should read, "to find new *ways*"?

Because as you may not have noticed, this particular bet is hedged. Like its subject and namesake, this biography is an amphibious creature, living partly in the world of paper and print and partly in the multiverse of pixels and platforms. Except where *The Nation* magazine remains, at least for the moment, firmly rooted in the periodical culture whose origins go back to the coffeehouses of eighteenth-century London, this biography was conceived and written as an e-book. Reading the links on the preceding pages is relatively easy. *The Nation*'s history is rich, and strange, and thanks to my collaborators on this project, much, *much* more accessible.

I still love the tactile pleasure of turning pages, and the smell of fresh ink. So I am glad this biography exists in print as well as electronically. As for the magazine's future, my optimistic certainty is that print and web versions will continue to evolve, if not always in the same direction, then in ways that feed each other, extend the magazine's reach and enable its dual bottom lines to

grow. That brave new *Nation* will likely be a very different creature from the amphibian you can read today on your pad or your
phone or your laptop—or on the Broadway local or in the bath.

In looking through our back pages, I have repeatedly been
struck by what a poor guide to the future the past often turns out
to be. Yet it is the only guide we have. So what can we learn from
The Nation's past?

That conventional wisdom is often wrong—and unconven-
tional wisdom no route to popularity. That radicals and liberals
need each other—and a venue to continue their endless, important
argument. That equality and justice and civil liberties are not gifts
of the state. That America can never be wholly free while the great
work of Reconstruction remains unfinished. And that if you tell
the people the truth, sometimes they can change the world.

As for *The Nation*'s future, that, dear reader, is up to you. ✻

Acknowledgments

I n the spring of 1979 I sent dozens of letters to various publications whose addresses I'd obtained from *The Writer's Market* in my college library asking for a summer job. I got two semi-encouraging responses. One was from the *Daily Nation* in Nairobi, saying that if I had the means to get to Kenya they would probably find something for me to do. The second was from Kai Bird, at the other *Nation*, regretfully informing me that the magazine did not have summer jobs. There was, however, an intern program, and while my letter had arrived after the deadline, it just happened that someone had dropped out, so if I was prepared to work without pay, they would be willing to have me.

I did not have the means to get to Kenya. I did not even have the means to live in New York. But encouraged by a friend with more worldly knowledge I accepted, supporting myself by driving a cab on the weekends and freelancing for the *Soho News*—which at least in my own eyes made me a hard-boiled newshound. Kai was kind, and Victor, perhaps because he could see I was keen—or maybe just to keep me out of his hair—set me to reading through the magazine's long-defunct International Relations section and asked me to write him a memo on how *The Nation* could improve its foreign coverage. At the end of the summer Betsy Pochoda handed me a small pile of books to review, for which I was paid $50.

It's hard to say when I began to think of *The Nation* as my journalistic home, but without Kai and Victor and Betsy I'd never have made it through the door. Once I did, Katha Pollitt, Adam Shatz and John Palattella in the back of the book, and Karen Rothmyer, Roane Carey and Richard Kim in the front, have always made me welcome, challenged me to think harder and improved my writing. And for the past twenty years I've been very fortunate in having Katrina, whom I'd known even before our intern days, as both friend and boss.

Yet despite my abiding sense of indebtedness to *The Nation*, and deep emotional investment in the magazine's continued flourishing, when Katrina called and asked if I might consider writing a history to mark its 150th anniversary I resisted. I'd recently spent twenty years writing the life of I.F. Stone—and he was just one *Nation* correspondent! An account of the magazine on a similar scale might take, well, a lot more time than the year-and-a-bit I'd have. But as anyone who has ever dealt with her can attest, Katrina's combination of velvet and steel is very persuasive. First she told me

Eric Foner had nominated me for the job—a naked appeal to my vanity by invoking one of my intellectual heroes. Then she made me an offer I simply couldn't refuse: rather than a scholarly tome, I would be writing an e-book which could focus on whatever aspects of *The Nation*'s past I found most interesting. I'd have a free hand, and would be given whatever research assistance I needed.

The other thing I've learned about Katrina is that she always delivers. She and Victor were both generous with their time and, given the chance to review the relevant chapters, patient in pointing out errors of fact or interpretation. But no one ever leaned on me to change a single word. I am grateful for their forbearance and candor, and for the education in *The Nation*'s finances I received from Ham Fish and Teresa Stack.

I'm especially grateful to Katrina for more than keeping her promise regarding research assistance. Richard Kreitner is a talented writer and a phenomenally energetic researcher with a brilliant future ahead of him. Without his help—and his tireless willingness to chase up obscure records or long-lost contributors—this book would simply not have been possible. His splendid memorandums summarizing the magazine's coverage of various issues were models of scholarly concision and always a pleasure to read. He's also the man who made sure the links actually work. Most of my many other research debts are acknowledged in the endnotes, but I'm particularly obliged to longtime *Nation* reader Edward Feinglass, whose splendid monograph on "*The Nation* and the era of Reconstruction" was an invaluable guide to that complex and difficult period in the magazine's life.

Judith Long, *The Nation*'s legendary former copy chief, kindly agreed to edit the pages you are reading. Only she knows how much I owe her boundless erudition, fastidious sensibility and eagle eye. Omar Rubio was responsible for turning my chapters into the book on your device. Art Stupar has been remarkably tolerant of my taking every possible day—and then a little bit more—to finish. And if you are reading this on paper, then you share my debt to him and to Peter Rothberg for pushing for a print edition and to Robert Best for making it beautiful to behold.

Eric Foner got me into this, and I am grateful to him for suggesting me, and even more grateful for his guidance in helping me to think about *The Nation*'s difficult passage through the Gilded Age. He and Katrina and Ricky Kreitner read every chapter, and each made suggestions that improved the book and saved me from error. For the errors that remain I alone am responsible. ✳

Endnotes

To access the following endnotes, including hyperlinks to articles from *The Nation*'s archives and other supporting materials, please visit http://www.thenation.com/150-endnotes.

CHAPTER ONE

1. "Are We Training Cuban Guerrillas?", November 19, 1960, p. 378

2. http://www.nytimes.com/library/world/ americas/040761cuba-invasion.html (retrieved 11.14.14)

3. "The St. Domingo Row," *The Nation* 11 (Dec 29, 1870), p. 432

4. Karl Marx, "The Excitement in Ireland, *New-York Daily Tribune*, January 11, 1859: http://www.marxists. org/archive/marx/works/1858/12/24.htm (*endnotes marked with an asterisk are purely for reference, and are not meant to be converted to hyperlinks)

5. William L. Armstrong, *E.L. Godkin: A Biography*, SUNY Press, 1978, p. 63

6. Edwin Lawrence Godkin, *The Gilded Age Letters of E.L. Godkin*, edited by William L. Armstrong, SUNY Press, 1974, p. 25

7. http://explorepahistory.com/displayimage.php?imgId=1-2-1E65

8. Armstrong, *E.L. Godkin*, p. 79

9. Godkin to C.E.Norton, April 13, 1865

10. *The Nation* Prospectus

11. "The Essence of The Reconstruction Question," I (July 6, 1865): 4

12. "The Great Festival," I (July 6, 1865): 5

13. Calculations courtesy of http://www.measuringworth.com/

14. http://eh.net/encyclopedia/the-economics-of-the-civil-war/ (retrieved 11.21.14)

15. http://www.independent.co.uk/news/uk/home-news/britains-colonial-shame-slaveowners-given-huge-payouts-after-abolition-8508358.html (retrieved 11.21.14)

16. Christopher Hayes, "The New Abolitionism," (May 12, 2014): 12-18

17. "The Eight-Hour Movement," I (October 26, 1865): 517

18. I.F. Stone, "Free Inquiry and Free Endeavor," February 10, 1940, pp. 158-161.

19. Godkin to Edward Atkinson, July 17, 1865.

20. "The Power of Congress to Enforce Equal Suffrage," II (April 26, 1866), 518-519; "The Disfranchising Power," I (July 13, 1865): 39-40

21. "The Political Sense at the South," VII (September 10, 1868), 205

22. "Southern Policy," I (October 26, 1865), 516

23. "Is the President Mistaken?" I (December 28, 1865), 806 and "Southern Indiscretion" I (November 23, 1865), 647

24. I (August 24, 1865), 229

25. "Andrew Johnson on Civil Rights," II (April 5, 1866) p. 422

26. IV (June 20, 1867), 497

27. II, (February 8, 1866), 166

28. "The Disenfranchising Power," I (July 13, 1865), 39-40

29. Godkin to C.E. Norton, July 18, 1865

30. Godkin, *The Gilded Age Letters*, p. 128; Charles E. Heller, *Portrait of an Abolitionist: A Biography of George Luther Stearns, 1809-1867*, Greenwood: 1996, p. 198

31. Godkin to Norton, December 28, 1865

CHAPTER TWO

1. II (January 4, 1866): 1

2. "Utilization of the Sun's Heat," II (May 29, 1866): 676

3. "Republics and Equality," I (July 27, 1865): 101

4. IV (1867): 394

5. "The National Highways," I (October 5, 1865): 424-425

6. Eric Foner, *The Story of American Freedom*, (New York: Norton, 1998), p.107

7. John G. Sproat, *The Best Men: Liberal Reformers in the Gilded Age*, Oxford University Press, (Oxford: 1968), p. 146

8. "Democratic Nationality," I (July 13, 1865): 39

9. "The Duty of Impeachment," (February 28, 1867): 170-172

10. III (October 18, 1866): 310-311

11. "The Crisis at Washington," VI (February 27, 1868): 164-16

12. The Impeachment Trial," VI (April 16, 1868), 305

13. Fred Kaplan, *Henry James: The Imagination of Genius* (New York: Open Road, 2013), p. 1868

14. William L. Armstrong, *E.L. Godkin: A Biography* (Albany: SUNY Press, 1978), p. 92

15. I (Oct. 26, 1865): 527; "Spendthrifts and Prices," (May 29, 1866): 681

16. "The One Humanity," *The Nation* I (October 26, 1865): 521

17. Nancy Cohen, *The Reconstruction of American Liberalism: 1865-1914* (Chapel Hill: University of North Carolina Press, 2002), p. 12

18. John Richard Dennett, *The South As It Is*, (New York: Viking Press, 1965), p.x

19. VI (May 21, 1868), 406

20. https://archive.org/details/slavesongsunite00garrgoog (retrieved November 26, 2014)

21. VII (October 29, 1868), 344

22. "Women Suffrage in Michigan," XVIII (May 14, 1874), 311-12

23. XII (April 20, 1871): 270-272

24. XVI (May 1, 1873): 296-297

25. Richard C. Sterne, "Political, Social and Literary Criticism in the Nation: 1865-1881, p. 98. PhD Thesis, Harvard University, 1957

26. Ibid., p. 90

27. XVIII (January 29, 1874), 68

28. IV (January 17, 1867): 50

29. VII (August 20, 1868): 144

30. "The Week," X (February 10, 1870): 83

31. "The Week," X (March 31, 1870): 199

32. "The End at Last," X (May 19, 1870): 314

33. "A Republican Form of Government," X (April 28, 1870): 266

34. "The South," XIII (December 7, 1871): 364

35. "The Week," XIII (August 3, 1871): 65-66

36. "The Force Bill," XII (April 20, 1871): 268-270

37. "The Third Term," XIX (October 8, 1874): 230-231

38. "Socialism in South Carolina," XVIII (April 16, 1874): 247-248

39. "Twenty-one Years," XXXXIII (July 8, 1886): 26

40. Sproat, *The Best Men*, pp. 35-36

41. "Who Are the Friends of Negro Suffrage?" XXIV (January 25, 1877): 53-5

42. "Edwin Lawrence Godkin," *Literary Digest* XXIV:22 (May 31, 1902): 730-731

43. "The South and the Election," XIV (November 14, 1872): 308

44. "The Week," V (July 4, 1867): 3

45. Sproat, *The Best Men*, p. 225

46. D.D. Guttenplan, "A Judicious Dose of Hemp: the Long Shadow of the Haymarket Bombing," *History Workshop Journal* LXVII:1 (2009): 252-261

47. Sproat, *The Best Men*, p. 204

48. "Execution of the Anarchists," (November 10, 1887), pp. 366-367

49. "A Word to Social Philosophers," XLV (November 17, 1887): 388

50. "Communistic Morality, XII (June 15, 1871) 413-414

51. XXV (August 2, 1877), 68-69

52. Ibid.

53. E.L. Godkin, *The Gilded Age Letters of E.L. Godkin*, (Albany, SUNY Press: 1974), pp. 139, 141

54. "Chromo-Civilization," XIX (September 24, 1874): 201

55. William L. Armstrong, *E.L. Godkin*, pp. 141-142

56. Godkin, *Letters*, pp. 275-278

57. Armstrong, *E.L. Godkin*, pp. 148-156

CHAPTER THREE

1.   Richard C. Sterne, "Political, Social and Literary Criticism in the Nation: 1865-1881," PhD Thesis, Harvard University, 1957, p. 133

2.   XXIII (July 6, 1876): 4-5

3.   "The Cormorants and the Commune," (September 9, 1880): 181

4.   "Cleveland's Nomination," (July 17, 1884): 46

5.   William L. Armstrong, *E.L. Godkin: A Biography* (Albany: SUNY Press, 1978), p. 156

6.   "The Week," (October 16, 1884): 320

7.   John G. Sproat, *The Best Men: Liberal Reformers in the Gilded Age*, Oxford University Press, (Oxford: 1968), p. 135

8.   Barbara W. Tuchman, "The First Anti-Imperialists," CCI (September 20, 1965): 77-82

9.   "The Week," LXI (December 26, 1895):454-461

10. "The Nation and the New Slavery," LIX (July 12, 1894):22

11. Tuchman, "The First Anti-Imperialists"

12. http://radioopensource.org/james-vs-roosevelt-letters-to-the-crimson/

13. "Protectorates," (January 21, 1869): 44-45

14. "Hail Columbia," LVI (February 23, 1893): 136

15. Armstrong, *E.L. Godkin*, p. 172, citing "Hawaii," *Evening Post*, February 3, 1893

16. "Hawaiian Annexation," LXV (November 27, 1897): 410

17. "Navalism," LIV (Jan. 21, 1892): 44

18. See also "Naval Politics," *Evening Post*, March 7, 1893

19. "Fictitious War," LVIII (Mar. 29, 1894): 225

20. Tuchman, "The First Anti-Imperialists"

21. For a more expansive discussion of this point see Myles Beaupre, "What are the Philippines going to do to Us?" E.L. Godkin on Democracy, Empire and Anti-Imperialism" *Journal of American Studies* 46(3): 711–727

22. (March 3, 1898): 157

23. Armstrong, p. 191, citing "The New Political Force," *Evening Post*, April 30, 1898

24. LXII (July 23, 1896): 62

25. Tom Coffman, *The Island Edge of America: A Political History of Hawai'i* (Honolulu: University of Hawaii Press, 2003), p. 20

26. "Peace and Indemnity," LXVII (July 28, 1898): 64

27. Tuchman, "The First Anti-Imperialists"

28. "What to do with the Philippines," LXVII (Oct. 6, 1898): 254

29. http://www.kiplingsociety.co.uk/poems_burden.htm

30. "The Pesky Anti-Imperialist," LXXIV (May 8, 1902): 360-361

31. "The Week," X (February 10, 1870): 83

32. W.P. Garrison, "Dissolving Punctuation," *Atlantic Monthly*, August 1906

33. W.P. Garrison," "Authority in Language," LXXV (September 4, 1902): 186

34. Richard Clark Sterne, "*The Nation* and its Century," CCI (September 20, 1965): 51

35. Viscount Bryce, "Two Editors," CI (July 8, 1915): 41.

36. Henry Holt, "A Young Man's Oracle," CI (July 8, 1915): 45

37. John Richard Dennett, "Knickerbocker Literature," V (December 5, 1867): 459-461.

38. Arthur C. Danto, introduction to *Brushes With History: Writing on Art from* The Nation, *1865-2001* (New York: Thunder's Mouth Press, 2001), p. xxiii.

39. Alexander Laing, "*The Nation* and Its Poets," CCI (September 20, 1965): 212-218.

40. *Writings of Charles Sanders Peirce*, (Bloomington: Indiana University Press, 2003), VI, p. lxxv.

41. Charles S. Peirce in *Letters and Memorials of Wendell Phillips Garrison*, (Cambridge: Riverside Press, 1908), p. 156

42. *Writings of Charles Sanders Peirce*, IV, p. 88 .

43. http://library.brown.edu/cds/portraits/images/large_bp100.jpg

44. "The Week", LXXXII (June 7, 1906): 460

45. "Graft in Business," LXXXII (May 31, 1906): 440

46. http://www.newrepublic.com/article/104918/ mr-more-and-the-mithraic-bull

47. Brian Domitrovic, "Paul Elmer More: America's Reactionary," *Modern Age*, XLV:4 (Fall 2003).

48. Henry F. Pringle, *Theodore Roosevelt* (New York: Harcourt, Brace, 1931), pp. 542-543

49. Fabian Franklin, "Whither is Roosevelt Drifting?", CXI (September 10, 1910): 233

50. http://www.thenation.com/article/oswald-villard-naacp-and-nation

51. Richard Clark Sterne, "*The Nation* and its Century," CCI (September 20, 1965): 272

CHAPTER FOUR

1. http://credo.library.umass.edu/view/pageturn/mums312-i0418/#page/1/mode/1up

2. Michael Wreszin, *Oswald Garrison Villard: Pacifist at War* (Bloomington: Indiana University Press, 1965), p. 10.

3. Oswald Garrison Villard, *Fighting Years: Memoirs of a Liberal Editor* (New York: Harcourt, Brace, 1939), p. 21

4. "The Cast Notion of Suffrage," LXXVII (September 3, 1903): 182

5. http://teachingamericanhistory.org/library/document/open-letter-to-woodrow-wilson/

6. XCVI (1913): 432.

7. XCVIII (1914): 151

8. Wreszin, *Villard*, p. 27

9.   Eric Foner, *The Story of American Freedom*
     (New York: W.W. Norton, 1998), p. 153

10. Anglo-Saxondom and World Peace," XCVII
     (September 4, 1913): 203-204

11. http://4.bp.blogspot.com/-MBsmwyOnTD0/
     U65wOAJqgrI/AAAAAAAAs2Y/54Vv_EEyvNE/s1600/
     Women%27s+Peace+Parade+in+New+York+City,+1914+
     %281%29.jpg [Fanny Villard is the woman in the white
     dress and black hat holding the banner on the left.]

12. Wreszin, *Villard*, pp. 38-45

13. Ibid., 50-51

14. See Tabe Ritstert Bergman, "Polite Conquest?: 'The New
     York Times' and 'The Nation' on the American Occupation
     of Haiti," *Journal of Haitian Studies*, Vol. 17, No. 2 (Fall
     2011), pp. 33-49, for a full analysis of US press response.

15. Ronald Steele, *Walter Lippmann and the American
     Century*, (Boston: Little, Brown, 1980), pp. 101-115

16. Wreszin, *Villard*, p. 63

17. Richard Clark Sterne, "*The Nation* and its
     Century," CCI (September 20, 1965): 286

18. David Kairys, "Freedom of Speech," in *The Politics of
     Law* (New York: Pantheon, 1982), pp. 140-171

19. http://www.presidency.ucsb.edu/ws/?pid=29556

20. Wreszin, *Villard*, pp. 84-86

21. "The Week," CVII (September 21, 1918): 307

22. "Samuel Gompers," CI (September 23, 1915): 380

23. "The Week" and "The One Thing Needful,"
CVII (September 14, 1918): 279, 283

24. Wreszin, *Villard*, pp. 97-98

25. Freda Kirchwey, "Memoir," CCI (September 20, 1965): 27-35

26. William MacDonald, "The Madness at Versailles,"
CVIII (May 17, 1919): 778-779

27. Floyd Dell, "Can Men and Women Be Friends?"
CXVIII (May 28, 1924): 605-606

28. http://tabletmag.com/jewish-arts-and-
culture/books/979/comeback-kid

29. Wreszin, *Villard*, p. 150

30. James Weldon Johnson, "Self-Determining Haiti,"
CXI (August 28; September 4, 11, and 24, 1920)
pp. 236-238, 265-267, 295-297, 345-347

31. http://www.thenation.com/article/lenin-trotzky-and-gorky

32. Oswald Garrison Villard, "Russia Through a
Car Window: The Spirit of the Government,"
CXXIX (November 20, 1929), 576-578

33. Oswald Garrison Villard, "The Soviets and the
Future," CXXIX (December 11, 1929): 712-714

34. "Massachusetts the Murderer," CXXV
(August 31, 1927): 192-193

35. William MacDonald, "Take Every Empty
House," CXI (August 28, 1920): 231-232

36. Wreszin, *Villard*, p. 235

37. Wreszin, *Villard*, pp. 4, 126, 196, 298 n.14

38. http://www.cooperativeindividualism.org/navasky-victor_oswald-garrison-villard-1990.html

---

CHAPTER FIVE

1. For much of this chapter I am indebted to Sara Alpern, *Freda Kirchwey: A Woman of* The Nation, (Cambridge: Harvard University Press, 1987), pp. 14, 79

2. Alpern, *Kirchwey*, pp. 27, 36-37

3. Norman Thomas, "A Socialist Program For Banking," March 22, 1933: 309

4. Abraham Epstein, "'Social Security' Under the New Deal," CXLI (September 4, 1935): 261-263

5. Paul Ward, "Roosevelt's Hollow Triumph," CXLI (September 11, 1935): 293

6. Michael Wreszin, *Oswald Garrison Villard*, p.268

7. "The New Deal Ends," CXLI (November 27, 1935): 609

8. "Father Coughlin in the Garden," CXL (June 5, 1935): 644

9. Raymond Gram Swing, "The Buildup of Long and Coughlin," CXL (March 20, 1935): 325-326

10. http://www.ushmm.org/wlc/en/article.php?ModuleId=10005201

11. "The Shape of Things," CXLVII (October 22, 1938): 393-394

12. Richard Clark Sterne, "*The Nation* and its Century," CCI (September 20, 1965): 319-320

13. "Moscow Trials," (October 10, 1936): 409

14. Leon Trotsky, "Revolutionary Interlude in France," CXLIII (August 8,1936): 153-155

15. Louis Fischer, "U.S.S.R. in 1936," (October 10, 1936): 412-414

16. http://www.loc.gov/exhibits/archives/ukra.html

17. Paul Y. Anderson, "If the Supreme Court Objects," CXXXVII (July 19, 1933): 64

18. "Purging the Court," February 13, 1937: 173-174

19. Oswald Garrison Villard, "What Is *The Nation* Coming To?" CXLIV (March 27, 1937): 352

20. Maurice Wertheim, "*The Nation* and the Court," CXLIV (April 10, 1937): 399-400

21. Heywood Broun, "Is There a *Nation*?" CXLIV (April 17, 1937): 437

22. http://www.loc.gov/pictures/resource/van.5a52455/

23. Alpern, *Kirchwey*, pp. 109-112

24. "The Press: Angel Steps Out," *Time*, June 14, 1937

25. http://www.unz.org/Pub/NewMasses-1937dec08-00008

26. Edmund Wilson, "Russia: Escape from Propaganda," (November 13, 1939): 531-535

27. Freda Kirchwey, "Russia and the World," CXLV (November 13, 1937): 521

28. "Yankee Communism," (June 4, 1938): 632

29. D.D. Guttenplan, *American Radical: The Life and Times of I.F. Stone* (New York: Farrar, Straus, and Giroux, 2009), p. 111

30. I.F. Stone, "1937 is Not 1914," (November 6, 1937): 495-497

31. Richard Clark Sterne, "*The Nation* and its Century," CCI (September 20, 1965): 318

32. Freda Kirchwey, "Red Totalitarianism," (May 27, 1939): 605-606

33. "Manifesto," (May 27, 1939): 626

34. Freda Kirchwey, "And Rebuttal," (June 17, 1939): 710-711

35. "Russian Tragedy: Act III," CXLVI (March 12, 1938): 288

36. Alpern, *Kirchwey*, p. 123

37. "To All Active Supporters…" Letters to the Editor, (August 26, 1939): 228

38. Guttenplan, *American Radical*, pp. 147-150

39. I.F. Stone, "Chamberlain's Russo-German Pact," (September 23, 1939): 313-316

40. "With Organized Minorities Deluging," (September 30, 1939): 335

41. Christopher Phelps, *Young Sidney Hook: Marxist and Pragmatist* (Ann Arbor: University of Michigan Press, 2005), pp. 203-206

42. Freda Kirchwey, "Moscow-Berlin Axis," CXLIX (October 7, 1939): 365

43. Alpern, *Fred Kirchwey*, p. 127

44. Freda Kirchwey, "By Fire and Sword," (December 9, 1939): 639-640

45. I.F. Stone, "The Finns at Geneva," (December 16, 1939): 667-668

46. Robert Bendiner, "Glossary for 1940," (February 10, 1940): 187

47. I.F. Stone, "F.D.R.'s First Task," (August 23, 1941): 155-156

48.   https://www.youtube.com/watch?v=ICy5P1pKy5A

49. Oswald Garrison Villard, "Valedictory," CL (June 29, 1940): 782

50. Reinhold Niebuhr, "An End to Illusions,"
     (June 29, 1940): 778-779

51. Wreszin, *Oswald Garrison Villard*, pp. 262, 265-268

52. I.F. Stone, "War Comes to Washington," (December 13, 1941)

53. Harold Ickes, "The Battle of Oil," (August 1, 1942): 86-87

54. Alexander Werth, "Russia Behind the
     Lines," (April 18, 1942): 454-457

55. Freda Kirchwey, "The Indian Dilemma," (August 22, 1942): 144

56. XXX, "Washington Gestapo," (July 17,
     1943): 64-66; (July 24, 1943): 92-95

57. Freda Kirchwey, "Curb The Fascist Press!,"
     (March 28, 1942): 357-358

58. I.F. Stone, "The Supreme Court and Racialism,"
     (December 30, 1944): 788-789

59. "Jews and Refugees," (May 20, 1939): 577

60. "Let in the Refugees" (June 1, 1940): 669-670

61. "Bring Them Out," (June 29, 1940): 773

62. Philip S. Bernstein, "The Jews of Europe: The
     Remnants of a People," (January 2, 1943): 8-9

63. Freda Kirchwey, "While the Jews Die,"
     (March 13, 1943): 366-367

64. Alpern, *Freda Kirchwey*, pp. 167-168, 281 n.25

65. Freda Kirchwey, "The End of an Era," (April 24, 1945): 429-430

66. Freda Kirchwey, "One World or None," (August 18, 1945): 150

67. J. King Gordon, "The Bomb is a World Affair," (November 24, 1945): 542

68. Walter Duranty, "The Soviets Clean House," (November 2, 1946): 499-500

69. "Letters to the Editor," (June 2, 1945): 631

70. D.D. Guttenplan, "Introduction" to I.F. Stone, *Underground to Palestine: And Other Writing from Israel and the Middle East*, (New York: Open Road, 2015)

71. Freda Kirchwey, "Liberals Beware," (April 5, 1947): 385

72. Alpern, *Freda Kirchwey*, pp. 195-199

73. http://babel.hathitrust.org/cgi/pt?id=mdp.39015028745217;view=1up;seq=3

74. Paul Blanshard, "The Catholic Church in Medicine," (November 1, 1947): 466

75. Paul Blanshard, "The Catholic Church and Education," (November 15, 1947): 525-528

76. Louise S. Robbins, *The Dismissal of Miss Ruth Brown: Civil Rights, Censorship, and the American Library*, (Norman: University of Oklahoma Press, 2001), p. 55

77. "*The Nation* Censors a Letter," *The New Leader*, XXXIV (March 19, 1951): 17-18

78. "Letters to the Editors," (July 7, 1951): 20

79.   Freda Kirchwey, "Why *The Nation* Sued," (June 2, 1951): 505

80.   Interview with Andrew Roth, London, November 18, 2004
      See also Robert P. Newman, *Owen Lattimore and the "Loss" of
      China*, (Berkeley: University of California Press, 1992). P. 128

81.   Quoted in Peter Viereck, "Sermons of Self-Destruction,"
      Saturday Review of Literature, XXXIV (August 18, 1951): 39-40

82.   Arthur Schlesinger Jr., "History of the Week," *New York
      Post*, September 2, 1951, cited in Victor S. Navasky,
      Naming Names (New York: 1980), pp. 52-53

83.   I.F. Stone, "Class Conflict—Sunkist Style,"
      (August 5, 1939): 150-151

84.   https://archive.org/details/witchhuntrevival00mcwi

85.   *The Nation* (June 28, 1952): 611

CHAPTER SIX

1.   Dan Wakefield, *New York in the 50s*, (New
      York: St. Martins, 1999), pp

2.   For much of the material in this chapter, I am indebted
      to Carey McWilliams, *The Education of Carey
      McWilliams* (New York: Simon and Schuster, 1978)

3.   Peter Richardson, *American Prophet: The Life and
      Work of Carey McWilliams*, (Ann Arbor: University
      of Michigan Press, 2005), pp. 126-127

4.   "Honorable in All Things," Carey McWilliams Oral History,
      UCLA, http://content.cdlib.org/ark:/13030/ft2m3nb08v/

5. *The Education of Carey McWilliams*, p. 145

6. Alan Wald's indispensable *New York Intellectuals* (1987) remains by far the best guide to the political landscape of the 1930s, '40s and '50s

7. https://www.commentarymagazine.com/article/the-liberals-who-havent-learned-why-the-soviet-illusion-still-lingers/

8. https://www.commentarymagazine.com/article/witch-hunt-the-revival-of-heresy-by-carey-mcwilliams/

9. *The New Leader*, August 27, 1951

10. "P.C.A.'s Quixotic Politics," (December 27, 1947): 693

11. "The Shape of Things," (March 6, 1948): 261

12. Robert Bendiner, "The Case Against Wallace," (March 6, 1948): 279-280

13. Freda Kirchwey, "Wallace: Prophet or Politician?," (January 10, 1948): 29

14. Freda Kirchwey, "A Word to Mr. Wallace," (March 13, 1948): 294

15. Sara Alpern, *Freda Kirchwey: A Woman of* The Nation, (Cambridge: Harvard University Press, 1987), pp. 217-219; also McWilliams, *The Education of Carey McWilliams*, p. 153

16. Mark Gayn, "The Purges: Villains and Scapegoats," (February 7, 1953): 117-119

17. Freda Kirchwey, "Why the Jews?" (January 31, 1953): 92-93

18. https://www.commentarymagazine.com/article/%E2%80%9Ccivil-liberties%E2%80%9D-1952%E2%80%94a-study-in-confusiondo-we-defend-our-rights-by-protecting-communists/

19. *The Nation*, (June 28, 1952)

20. Richard Rovere, "How Free is *The Nation*?" *The New Leader* (July 14, 1952), pp. 12-14; *Time* (July 21, 1952)

21. McWilliams Oral History

22. McWilliams, *The Education of...*, p. 150

23. Carey McWilliams, (September 20, 1965): 21-26

24. Andrew Roth, "Iran's New Strong Man," (September 5, 1953): 192-193

25. J. Alvarez Del Vayo, "Aggression is the Word," (June 26, 1954): 537-538

26. http://www.google.com/url?sa=t&rct=j&q=&esrc=s&-source=web&cd=1&ved=0CB0QFjAA&url=http%3A%2F%2F-www.foia.cia.gov%2Fsites%2Fdefault%2Ffiles%2Fdoc-ument_conversions%2F89801%2FDOC_0000921175.pdf&ei=DLavVPuMHczPaJW0gLAG&usg=AFQjCNGwN-bEqpzidJaEGL6PuXKwrERJgCQ&bvm=bv.83339334,d.d2s

27. Hal Draper, "The Imperialist Apologetics of Max Lerner," *Labor Action*, (November 8, 1954), p.6

28. Stephen Schlesinger and Stephen Kinzer, *Bitter Fruit: The Story of an American Coup in Guatemala* (Cambridge: Harvard University Press, 1999), pp. 89-90

29. Christopher Lasch, "The Cultural Cold War," (September 11, 1967): 198-212

30. http://www.nybooks.com/articles/archives/1967/mar/23/the-big-fix/

31. "The Southern Negro," September 27, 1952

32. McWilliams, *The Education...*, p. 205

33. W.E.B. Du Bois, "The Hosts of Black Labor," (May 9, 1923): 539-541

34. William Pickens, "Jim Crow in Texas," (August 15, 1923): 155-156

35. Walter White," "Negro Segregation Comes North," (October 21, 1925): 458-460

36. E. Franklin Frazier, "The Negro and 'His Place'," (April 3, 1943): 496-497

37. Loren Miller, "A Right Secured," (May 29, 1948): 599-600

38. I.F. Stone, "Capital Notes," (April 10, 1943): 511-513

39. Langston Hughes, "The Negro Artist and the Racial Mountain," (June 23, 1926): 692-694

40. James Baldwin, "Maxim Gorki as Artist," (April 12, 1947): 427-428

41. Dan Wakefield, "Justice in Sumner," (October 1, 1955): 284-285

42. Dan Wakefield, "Respectable Racism," (October 22, 1955): 339-341

43. Clifford Durr, "How to Measure Loyalty," (April 23, 1949): 470-472

44. Carey McWilliams, "Miracle in Alabama," (March 3, 1956): 169

45. McWilliams Oral History

46. Alton Ochsner, "Lung Cancer: The Case Against Smoking," (May 23, 1953): 431-432

47. George Seldes, *Facts and Fascism* (New York: In Fact, 1943), pp. 268-273

48. http://www.ncbi.nlm.nih.gov/pmc/articles/PMC3145444/

49. Ralph Nader, "The Safe Car You Can't Buy," (April 11, 1959): 310-313

50. Ralph Nader, "The Corvair Story," (November 1, 1965): 295-301

51. McWilliams, *The Education*..., pp. 213-214

52. Fred J. Cook, "Capital Punishment: Does It Prevent Crime?" (March 10, 1956): 194-198

53. Fred J. Cook, "Hiss: New Perspectives on the Strangest Case of our Time," (September 21, 1957): 142-180

54. Fred J. Cook, "The FBI," (October 18, 1958)

55. Fred J. Cook and Gene Gleason, "The Shame of New York," (October 31, 1959)

56. Fred J. Cook, "The CIA," (June 24, 1961)

57. Matthew Josephson, "The Big Guns," (January 14, 21, and 29, 1956)

58. Richard Cloward and Frances Fox Piven, "A Strategy to End Poverty," (May 2, 1966): 510-517

59. Patrick J. Buchanan, "The Pen That Just Grew," (November 10, 1964): 355-356

60. McWilliams, *The Education of*..., p. 220

61. William W. Turner, "Crime is Too Big for the FBI," (November 8, 1965): 322-328

62. Victor Marchetti, "CIA: The President's Loyal Tool," (April 3, 1972): 430-433

63. McWilliams Oral History

64. Jacob Bronowski, "Science and Human Values" (December 29, 1956): 550-567

65. Raymond Williams, "The Culture of Politics," (January 3, 1959): 10-12

66. Barton Bernstein, "The Limitations of Pluck," (January 8, 1973): 38-41

67. Eric Hobsbawm, "Goliath and the Guerrilla," (July 19, 1965): 33-38

68. William A. Williams, "The Outdoor Mind," (October 30, 1954): 384-385

69. Howard Zinn, "Finishing School for Pickets" (August 6, 1960): 71-73

70. Bruce Catton, "Red Herring—and White: The Great Crusade Picks Up," (November 28, 1953): 445-447

71. Robert Sherrill, "Portrait of a Super Patriot," (February 24, 1964): 182-195

72. William W. Morris, "Mississippi Rebel. On a Texas Campus," (March 24, 1956)

73. McWilliams, *The Education of ...*, pp. 235-236

74. Hunter S. Thompson, "Losers and Outsiders," (May 17, 1965): 522-526

75. Henrique Galvão, (April 15, 1961): 315-332

76. Carleton Beals, "The New Machado in Cuba," (August 7, 1935): 152-154

77. Carleton Beals, "Revolution Without Generals," (January 17, 1959): 43-46

78. For a brilliant, vivid evocation of that whole period see Van Gosse, *Where the Boys Are: Cuba, Cold War America and the Making of a New Left* (New York: Verso, 1993), *passim.*

79. John F. Kennedy, *The Strategy of Peace* (New York: Harper, 1960), pp. 167-168

80. Eqbal Ahmad, "How to Tell When the Rebels Have Won," (August 30, 1965): 95-100

81. Bernard Fall, "Solution in Indo-China: Cease-Fire, Negotiate," (March 6, 1954): 193-195

82. Ted Koppel, "WHAM," (June 26, 1967):812-13

83. Mike Wallace, "The Deserters," (June 26, 1967): 811-812

84. McWilliams Oral History

85. McWilliams, *The Education of ...*, p. 278

86. McWilliams Oral History

87. Peter de Lissovoy, "Gambler's Choice in Georgia," (June 22, 1964): 618-621

88. Jack Newfield, "The Student Left," (May 10, 1965): 491-495

89. Carey McWilliams, "A Personal Note," (September 20, 1965): 21-27

CHAPTER SEVEN

1. https://www.youtube.com/watch?v=butZyxI-PRs

2. "Presented by Xerox," December 27, 1975, pp. 677-678

3. Victor S. Navasky, *A Matter of Opinion*, (New York: Farrar, Straus, and Giroux, 2005), pp. 138-139

4. Interview with Victor Navasky, January 17, 2015

5. "Pros and Progressives," July 9, 1960, pp. 24-26

6. "Hoax of Horror? A Book That Shook White House," *U.S. News & World Report*, November 20, 1967

7. Herschel McLandress, "News of War and Peace You're Not Ready For," *Book World*, November 26, 1967, p. 5

8. http://www.nytimes.com/1996/07/01/business/onetime-political-satire-becomes-a-right-wing-rage-and-a-hot-internet-item.html

9. A much fuller account of all these events—and much else in this chapter—can be found in *A Matter of Opinion*.

10. http://timesmachine.nytimes.com/timesmachine/1975/04/27/issue.html

11. Interview with Hamilton Fish, January 19, 2015

12. Calvin Trillin, "Variations," (April 1, 1978): 354, 358

13. Interview with Victor Navasky

14. Navasky, *A Matter of Opinion*, pp. 179-182

15. Navasky, *A Matter of Opinion*, pp. 141-142

16. Edmund White, "A Fantasia on Black Suffering," (September 18, 1976): 247-249

17. Victor Navasky, "The Case Not Proved Against Alger Hiss," (April 8, 1978): 393-401

18. https://books.google.co.uk/books?id=aeYDAAAAM-BAJ&lpg=PA9&ots=qgie4zbN1S&dq=%22Writ-ers%20Congress%22%20%22The%20Na-tion%22&pg=PA9#v=onepage&q=%22Writers%20Congress%22%20%22The%20Nation%22&f=false

19. http://www.nytimes.com/1981/10/10/arts/writers-congress-opens-with-calls-for-solidarity.html

20. Susan Sontag, "Communism and the Left," (February 27, 1982): 229-231

21. I.F. Stone, "The Polish Election and Ibn Saud's Tender Feelings," *I.F. Stone's Weekly*, January 28, 1957, p.4. Can be downloaded athttp://www.ifstone.org/weekly_searchable.php

22. Stanley Cooperman, "Of War and Man," (July 23, 1955): 80

23. http://www.nytimes.com/1982/10/24/books/susan-sontag-past-present-and-future.html

24. Maria Margaronis and Elizabeth Pochoda, "Bad Manners and Bad Faith," (February 1, 1986): 116-119

25. Neier and Hitchens, "Comment" (February 27, 1982): 236-237

26. https://corbinhiar.wordpress.com/2009/04/24/kai-bird-the-nations-foreign-editor/

27. Christopher Hitchens, "Israel and the American Left," (December 5, 1981): 605-611.

28. Kopkind, "Comment" (February 27, 1982): 234-235

29. Sontag, "Reply" (February 27, 1982): 237

30. Andrew Kopkind, "The Dialectic of Disco: Gay Music Goes Straight," *The Village Voice*, February 12, 1978, p.1

31. Navasky, *A Matter of Opinion*, p. 193

32. Interview with Victor Navasky

33. http://www.thenation.com/authors/daniel-singer

34. E.P. Thompson, "A Letter to America," January 24, 1981

35. Kai Bird, "Myths About the Middle East," December 5, 1981

36. http://www.thenation.com/authors/herman-schwartz

37. http://www.thenation.com/authors/stephen-f-cohen

CHAPTER EIGHT

1. Interview with Katrina vanden Heuvel, February 2, 2015

2. Katrina vanden Heuvel, "A Global Challenge," *New York Times*, June 7, 1980, p.19

3. Katrina vanden Heuvel, "The Non-Selling of Détente," (September 26, 1981): 272-274

4. Katrina vanden Heuvel, "No Free Speech at Radio Liberty," (December 7, 1985): 612-614

5. Kevin Coogan and Katrina vanden Heuvel, "U.S. Funds for Soviet Dissidents," (March 7, 1987): 273-277

6. "Gorbachev's Soviet Union," (June 13, 1987), entire issue

7.   Stephen F. Cohen and Katrina vanden Heuvel, *Voices of Glasnost*, (New York: W.W. Norton, 1991).

8.   "Looking Ahead at the United States," (March 22, 1986)

9.   "Editor's Note," in Katrina vanden Heuvel, ed., *The Nation: 1865-1990* (New York: Thunder's Mouth)

10. Katrina vanden Heuvel, "Introduction," *The Change I Believe In* (New York: Nation Books, 2011), p. xiii

11. Victor S. Navasky, *A Matter of Opinion*, (New York: Farrar, Straus, and Giroux, 2005), p. 331

12. *The Nation*, (July 4, 1994): entire issue

13. Andrew Sullivan, "The Politics of Homosexuality," *The New Republic*, May 10, 1993

14. Patricia J. Williams, "Among Moses's Bridge-Builders," (May 23, 1994): 694-698

15. Patricia J. Williams, "America and the Simpson Trial," (March 13, 1995): 337-340

16. "The National Entertainment State" (June 3, 1996): entire issue

17. Jonathan Schell, "The Gift of Time," (February 2, 1998): 9-60

18. Alexander Cockburn, "Beat the Devil," (November 9, 1992): 530-531

19. Alexander Cockburn, "Beat the Devil," (March 22, 1993): 366-367

20. Noam Chomsky, "Notes of NAFTA: The Masters of Mankind," (March 29, 1993): 412-416

21. "The People vs. The WTO," (December 6, 1999): 3-4

22.   William Greider, "Global Agenda," (January 31, 2000): 11-16

23.   Doug Henwood, "Whose Trade?," (December 6, 1999): 11-17

24.   Interview with Katrina vanden Heuvel

25.   E. Ethelbert Miller, "The One Question Interview With Katrina vanden Heuvel,"http://eethelbertmiller1.blogspot. co.uk/2015_02_01_archive.html#4422520552920156633

26.   "Impeachment Juggernaut," (October 26, 1998): 3

27.   Gore Vidal, "Coup de Starr," (October 26, 1998): 6

28.   Vincent Bugliosi, "None Dare Call It Treason," (February 5, 2001):11-19

29.   Katrina vanden Heuvel, "Foreword," *A Just Response: The Nation on Terrorism, Democracy and September 11, 2001* (New York: Nation Books, 2002), p. xi

30.   *The Nation* (October 1, 2001): entire issue

31.   Hitchens, "Minority Report" (October 8, 2001): 8

32.   Robert Fisk, "Terror in America," (October 8, 2001): 7

33.   "A Just Response," (October 8, 2001): entire issue

34.   http://www.thenation.com/article/put-out-no-flags

35.   http://www.thenation.com/article/reply-hitchens

36.   Katrina vanden Heuvel, "Foreword," *A Just Response*, p. xiii

37.   Eric Alterman, "Republic Opinion," (June 29, 1998):10

38.   http://dev.thenation.com.569eldb01.blackmesh. com/blog/talk-about-smear-merchant

39. http://www.thenation.com/authors/chris-hayes

40. http://www.thenation.com/authors/david-corn

41. http://www.thenation.com/authors/melissa-harris-perry

42. http://www.washingtonpost.com/katrina-vanden-heuvel/2011/02/24/ABMj4XN_page.html

43. Adam Shatz, "The Left and 9/11," (September 23, 2002): 26-32

44. Adam Shatz, "A Friendly Nod to B-52s," (July 29/August 5, 1996): 25-28

45. "An Open Letter to the Members of Congress," (October 14, 2002), pp. 3-5

46. Christopher Hitchens, "Taking Sides," (October 14, 2002)

47. Interview with Katrina vanden Heuvel

48. Jonathan Schell, "The Case Against the War," (February 13, 2003): 11-23

49. Katrina vanden Heuvel, "Foreword," *A Just Response*, p. xiii

50. Jeremy Scahill, "Inside Baghdad," (April 7, 2003): 11-13

51. http://www.thenation.com/article/blood-thicker-blackwater

52. Christian Parenti, "Afghanistan: The Other War," (March 27, 2006): 11-18

53. Naomi Klein, "Shameless in Iraq," (July 12, 2004): 14

54. Naomi Klein, "Bring Halliburton Home," (November 24, 2003): 10

55. Naomi Klein, "You Break It, You Pay For It," (January 10, 2005): 12

56. http://www.thenation.com/article/democrats-and-war

57. Christian Parenti, "The Big Easy Dies
    Hard," (September 26, 2005): 6-30

58. Naomi Klein, "Needed: A People's
    Reconstruction," (September 26, 2005): 12

59. Adolph Reed Jr., "Class-ifying the Hurricane," (October 3, 2005)

60. Mike Davis, "Who Is Killing New
    Orleans?" (April 10, 2006): 11-20

61. Rebecca Solnit, "The Lower Ninth Battles
    Back," (September 10, 2007): 13-17

62. A.C. Thompson, "Katrina's Hidden Race
    War," (January 5, 2009): 11-18

63. http://www.thenation.com/article/164881/
    upheaval-new-york-public-library

64. http://www.thenation.com/article/179742/
    nypl-shelves-plan-gut-central-library

65. http://www.thenation.com/article/181399/
    patriotic-heresy-vs-new-cold-war

66. "The New Inequality," (June 30, 2008): entire issue

AFTERWORD

1. Henry James, *Roderick Hudson*, "Preface to
   Volume One of the New York Edition"

2. http://new.livestream.com/schomburgcenter/
   thirdreconstruction/videos/73874844